32 Problems in World History

SOURCE READINGS AND INTERPRETATIONS

For Oscar Handlin, Charles R. Keller, Robert Walcott, and Paul L. Ward

designer, Thomas J. Gorman
globe model, George Sawa
globe puzzle, Thomas J. Buehler

32 PROBLEMS IN WORLD HISTORY

SOURCE READINGS AND INTERPRETATIONS

EDWIN FENTON, *Carnegie-Mellon University, Pittsburgh*

with the assistance of SHERRILL ABERG, *formerly Bethel Park High School, Bethel Park, Pa.*

critic reader, DANIEL POWELL, *Northwestern University and Nicholas Senn High School, Chicag*

SCOTT, FORESMAN AND COMPANY

Copyright © 1964, 1969 by Scott, Foresman and Company, Glenview, Illinois 60025.
All Rights Reserved. Printed in the United States of America.
Regional offices of Scott, Foresman and Company are located in
Atlanta, Dallas, Glenview, Palo Alto, and Oakland, N.J.
Library of Congress catalog card No. 68-24607

4

Table of Contents

Chart
of
Skills
and
Issues

The chart presents important elements brought out in each of the Problems in this book. The second column lists historical skills and tools—the means by which evidence may be organized, examined, and evaluated. The third column relates the specific subjects under discussion to basic ideas debated by historians over the centuries. It should be noted that the entries in these two columns are not necessarily the only relevant skills or issues, but those selected as the most practical for classroom use.

SKILL OR TOOL	ISSUE
Using artifacts as evidence	Technology and cultural change
Drawing conclusions from source materials	Relationship of a legal system to society
Defining terms historically	Development of political institutions
Detecting bias	Nature of a social system
Drawing conclusions from source materials	Relationship of a legal system to society
Using fiction as evidence	Nature of a social system
Using artifacts as evidence	Role of religion in a society
Judging an interpretation	Role of the individual in history
Using fiction as evidence	Role of religion in a society
Drawing conclusions from source materials	Relationship of morality to government
Using artifacts as evidence	Cultural diffusion
Drawing conclusions from source materials	Development of political institutions
Drawing conclusions from source materials	Relationship of morality to government
Asking analytical questions	Nature of causation
Drawing conclusions from source and secondary materials	Multiple causation
Weighing different interpretations	Role of the individual in history
Judging documents in their cultural setting	Theoretical basis of government
Weighing different interpretations	Relationship of historical movements
Establishing criteria for historical judgment	Significance of a peace settlement
Defining terms historically	Theoretical basis of government
Using economic analysis	Technology and cultural change
Judging documents in their cultural setting	Nature of an economic system
Judging a personalized account	Technology and cultural change
Defining terms historically	Multiple causation
Using new evidence in historical interpretation	Immediate vs. long-range causes
Drawing conclusions from source materials	Nature of an international agreement
Establishing criteria for historical judgment	Nature of an international agreement
Reinterpreting historical movements	Role of the individual in history
Defining terms historically	Relationship of political institutions to society
Asking analytical questions	Significance of a peace settlement
Analyzing a contemporary problem	Relationship of historical movements
Judging an interpretation	Cultural lag

How to Use This Book

A GUIDE FOR TEACHERS AND STUDENTS

This book is different. It is not a textbook. It is not a record of one segment of world history such as the French Revolution. Neither is it the story of one major historical figure like Adolf Hitler. It is a collection of readings drawn from the accumulated literature of the world. Some selections were written during the period in question, and are called primary sources; others are a step or more removed in time from the events concerned, and are known as secondary sources.

These selections, fifty-one in all, have been assembled in thirty-two Problems designed to stimulate and enliven high school scholarship in world history. Although the arrangement of Problems exactly parallels the chapter organization of *Living World History*, by T. Walter Wallbank and Arnold Schrier (Scott, Foresman and Company, third edition, 1969), the volume may be adapted as a supplement to any of the better textbooks in the field. A teacher or student need only examine its contents briefly to determine how *32 Problems* will best fit in with his text.

One of the important aims of this volume is to acquaint high school students with the nature of history as an academic discipline and with the writing of history as an art. The Chart of Skills and Issues on pages 6 and 7 indicates the relevant historian's skill or tool brought out in each selection and the historical issue concerned. Although not every historical skill or issue can be covered here, these readings illuminate some of the most interesting and vital problems in world history.

The Problems can be used in several ways. They can be most appropriately employed as a basis for class discussion. As you will note, each Problem is preceded by an introduction and a number of study questions. The introductions provide background and a point of departure for the reading or readings. The study questions are designed to stimulate thinking, and can be used by the teacher to organize and direct class discussion.

A student should not read a selection merely to find answers to the study questions, nor should he be encouraged to write out the answers. Instead, after reading the introduction and study questions, he should take time to review what he already knows about the subject. He should try to recall what he has learned from his textbook and other sources. This process should bring to the forefront of his mind the most vital issues likely to come up in the reading, and thus prepare him to read more intelligently and effectively. He should then read the entire Problem and take notes. After he has done this, he will be ready to think anew about the study questions as he prepares for class discussion.

The teacher, using the volume in exactly the same way, may wish to organize class discussion around the study questions or to pose other issues raised by the reading. What seems most appropriate for discussion will depend in part upon the textbook used in the course. It will also be affected by the teacher's own approach to instruction techniques and by his particular subject competence. Although suggested procedures for each Problem are provided in the book of Lesson Plans, a teacher should feel free to structure his own lesson in order to emphasize what he thinks most important. By treating a limited number of points that seem vital, the instructor can confine discussion of a Problem to a single class period. Use of the Chart of Skills and Issues will help remind students and teachers of the topics already investigated and those to be considered later.

Several other approaches to *32 Problems* may be suggested. Some of the readings can serve as subjects for individual reports by students to the class. Among others, the selections from Gimpel (Problem 7) and Gladwin (Problem 11) are particularly well-suited to this purpose. Several of the Problems which include a number of selections can be used as references for short papers on topics such as "Motives for Colonization" (Problem 15) or "19th-Century Imperialism" (Problem 24). Finally, the Problems may be assigned simply as supplementary reading.

Many of the introductions call attention to Problems appearing elsewhere in the book. For example, the introduction to Sidney Hook's essay on Lenin (Problem 28) mentions earlier readings about Peter the Great (Problem 16). Through this method of cross reference, students will be able to review their notes and possibly discover some familiarity with the new Problem. Teachers may further amplify and strengthen preparation by holding a brief discussion based on review of former assignments. Students may be asked to give short review reports on topics mentioned in the introductions to help provide a sound setting for discussion.

Although these readings are adaptable to a variety of uses, they should not replace other important academic activities. Teachers should continue to assign reports, papers, and library work, and to take advantage of audio-visual presentations. There is no single magic road to historical knowledge and understanding. This book tries to blaze only one new trail.

Note: Within the readings, bracketed words in roman type were supplied by the original editors or publishers of the material; italic words in brackets have been added by Edwin Fenton or Scott, Foresman and Company.

What Is History?

People often use words imprecisely. For example, students, parents, politicians, and teachers sometimes refer to a measure as "socialistic" without stating exactly what they mean by socialism. The word *history* is open to similar abuse. "History tells us . . . ." you will often hear people say. But what do they mean when they use the word *history* in this fashion? Do they mean that the events of the past speak for themselves? Do they mean that some historian has interpreted these events and drawn a moral from his interpretation? Do they mean that we can know the "truth" about the past?

Every student beginning a course in history ought to decide just what he is studying—that is, what the word *history* means. Although the task seems easy, it is really quite difficult. Even historians disagree among themselves about the nature of their discipline. Because of this disagreement, each student must work out his own definition of history as he studies his assignments. The Problems in this book are specifically designed to raise questions that will help him do this. This first essay gives the point of view of the author.

As you read, keep the following questions in mind:

1 What are the chief steps leading to the definition of history given in the paragraph beginning "This line of reasoning . . . ." Why not just look up a definition in a dictionary?

2 In addition to looking for the possible bias of an author, can you think of any other techniques a historian uses when he reads or writes history?

3 If history is only interpretation, what should be the focus of work in a history course?

HISTORY AS INTERPRETATION / by Edwin Fenton

History is often taught as most high school students think of it: as a record of the past or as an account of what happened in earlier times. Teachers assign a number of pages to students, tell them to learn the facts they find, and ask them to repeat these facts in class the next day. But is history really this simple?

Our knowledge of the past is incomplete. Let us imagine that we are studying the 1st century A.D. in the Western world. Many of the developments we would most like to know about can never be known. Men left records of only a tiny proportion of all the events that took place. They recorded the names of famous men and women and something about their lives. Archives tell us a little about Church affairs and some of the more notable political struggles. Literature written during the period and the remains of buildings reveal still further information. But most of what happened was never recorded, and much that was recorded has been lost since the fall of Rome.

Just think of all the things we do not know. We have few accurate statistics on population or trade or government income. We know next to nothing about the lives of the poor. We are not sure what motivated most of the individuals who adopted or rejected Christianity. One of the major reasons historians disagree so much about the history of Rome is that their data are so fragmentary. We probably know only a fraction of 1 per cent of what has happened in the past. So history cannot be a complete record of what happened; at best it can be a record only of those events that were recorded in a form that has come down to us.

This conclusion is particularly significant. It implies that the historian must be able to judge whether or not the documents he finds contain information accurately representative of the events that took place. Because most documents were written by men who were better educated and more intelligent than the average, is it not likely that the records we have reflect disproportionally the point of view of the educated upper classes? How much must we question these accounts because of this possible bias? The task of reconstructing exactly what happened is enormous. We can only approximate the "truth" about the past; we can never know it fully.

A historian cannot learn everything about an event or period. Let us suppose that a scholar set out to read in the original languages all remaining source material about the 1st century and to supplement his knowledge by examining buildings and other artifacts from this period. He would have to become an accomplished linguist. Then he would be forced to travel all over the Western world reading manuscripts in a number of languages and looking at ruins in Mediterranean lands and in museums. No one man could read and see everything in one lifetime. Any history he wrote, therefore, could not possibly be a tabulation of everything that had been recorded; it could be a tabulation only of what one scholar had been able to find and investigate.

A historian must select from available material. It would be absurd if he listed in chronological order all the facts he discovered. We would be bored to death if we read such a compilation, and any publisher who printed it would lose money. A historian could not even take down in his notes all the material he researched. He would be forced to select information to note on his cards, just as students doing research in the library note down some things and omit others. But as soon as the historian makes a note of one event and decides not to make a note of another, he interprets. He says, in effect, "This fact is important, and the other one is not." But how does he know what is important, what is worth noting down? He already has in mind an interpretation of history in order to make this decision.

Let us suppose, for example, that a historian is trying to explain the origins of the fall of Rome. In doing research, he makes a note of everything he can find out about the lives of the Roman emperors in the 1st century A.D. At the same time, he decides not to jot down information about economic life during this period. Clearly he believes that the lives of emperors are more important to what he is explaining than is the development of an economic system. He makes an interpretation of history when he acts in this fashion, implying that the activities of political leaders are more important than economic developments to the decay of empires. Now this may be so, but whether the historian is correct is beside the point. What is significant to us is that he has interpreted in the very process of taking notes. He can do nothing else. Either he notes everything, or he selects. If he selects, he does so with some principles in mind. As soon as he establishes principles of what is important, he interprets.

A textbook cannot be a record of what has happened in the past. It can only be an interpretation of what happened by the historian or historians who wrote it. The typical author of a textbook in world history is an expert in one area — for example, the history of France or the development of imperialism. Although he has read extensively about other areas and periods he describes in his textbook, he cannot be expert on every topic. Instead of reading the manuscripts — the original records — of each area, he reads accounts written from these records by other historians. His text is, therefore, at least third hand. A person who witnessed the event wrote the first-hand account; of course, if this record came from the pen of a man who was simply writing down what he had been told by another person, it is second hand. The next account was written by a historian who interpreted the original source according to his own opinions of the nature of history. Finally, the author of the textbook decided which of several historians' interpretations was correct and included it in his book.

A historian interprets not only by selecting certain material, but also by presenting it in a certain way. Suppose that the author of a textbook decided to try not to interpret, but only to list facts and let the reader draw his own conclusion. He is only deceiving himself, and if you believe that he can do this, he is deceiving you too. He must select the facts he includes in his book and eliminate other facts because space is limited. Let us suppose that he decides that students should know something about the causes of the First World War. He might then make a list of "significant" events as follows:

formation of the Triple Alliance, 1882

formation of the Entente Cordiale, 1904

first Moroccan crisis, 1905

Austrian annexation of Bosnia and Herzegovina, 1908

second Moroccan crisis, 1911

First Balkan War, 1912

Second Balkan War, 1913

assassination of Francis Ferdinand, 1914

outbreak of World War I, 1914

By arranging these events in a list and printing them in a book, our historian implies that they are related and important. Otherwise, why list them and why learn them? Students can quickly see that each event concerns either the formation of an alliance or an international crisis and that this list of events ends with the outbreak of World War I. A student might well come to the conclusion that the alliance system led to a number of incidents which eventually touched off war. This is an interpretation of history. Some historians have argued that economic rivalry, or the race to acquire colonies overseas, was largely responsible for the war. By selecting one series of events and omitting others, a historian leads his readers to select one interpretation of history and to reject or disregard a second.

This line of reasoning leads inevitably to the conclusion that all history is interpretation. Sometimes we call it an argument, to emphasize the interplay of evidence and conclusion. What is important about history as a discipline is the set of rules to be followed in making interpretations, rules that we will learn as we use this book. History is really a way of reading and writing about events in the past. Professional historians write about the past according to the rules accepted by their peers. If we are to study history intelligently, we must learn the rules historians follow when they interpret.

Take the matter of the bias of an author, for example. Not all books are equally reliable as sources of information; in fact, some are specifically designed to present one point of view rather than a balanced account of a problem. Even when an author tries carefully to present the "truth" about a matter, unconscious bias may mislead him. A Protestant may approach the history of the Reformation, for example, with a point of view quite different from that of a Roman

Catholic. Despite a conscientious attempt to attain objectivity, his pen may still be guided subtly by an attitude toward religion he has had all his life. Historians should always try to determine the bias of an author they are reading; this is a rule of their craft. We know a number of ways to detect bias, and each student of history should learn to use them.

The readings in this collection have been chosen both to illuminate the past and to introduce beginning students to the historian's craft. Organized around the belief that all history is interpretation, they lead the reader through many of the most significant aspects of this process. A student who learns the rules by which a historian interprets and learns to ask the sort of question that will yield rich insights ought to become a good student of history.

Studying history properly requires an alert, active mind; a student must constantly be aware that he is reading someone's interpretation of the past. So he must search for it, knowing that in books which seem to be primarily collections of facts it is often implied rather than stated in so many words. One way to train oneself to find interpretative statements is to skim quickly over an assignment, reading the first paragraph, the first sentence of every other paragraph, and the conclusion. This preliminary skimming will reveal what the author is discussing and will often disclose the interpretation he presents. Then careful reading will permit the student to find and judge the evidence for the author's argument. This skill—the ability to find an argument and to determine whether or not evidence supports it—is an important historical technique as well as vital preparation for citizenship. It will put the student on guard against accepting everything he reads or hears without applying adequate tests of reliability. Thus he will become an effective member of a democracy.

Some of the world's greatest writings are collected in this book; to read them well, students must develop a variety of skills. Thucydides, Machiavelli, and John Locke are all represented. So are a number of contemporary historians. Famous documents—the Code of Hammurabi, Magna Charta, the Versailles Treaty—add variety and call for the use of different skills. Several problems in which students are required to build an interpretation from pieces of evidence demand still different techniques. But most exciting of all is the opportunity to read and discuss some of the great ideas that have challenged mankind throughout time. To this high calling we invite you, in confidence that you will enjoy a great intellectual adventure.

The Importance of the
Neolithic Revolution

As you can see by looking at the chart at the beginning of this volume, historians use many skills and tools in their art. Often they have only a few scattered documents to help them throw light on some historical question. But think of the more complicated task of archaeologists! Studying about men who lived before the development of writing, archaeologists are forced to reconstruct a society from bones and artifacts (man-made objects) such as tools and pottery. They rely heavily on hypotheses—educated guesses designed to explain tentatively the evidence under examination. For example, if an archaeologist finds useful objects in a grave, he may adopt the hypothesis that the people who buried them there believed in an afterlife where they would be needed. A single new discovery may turn a pet hypothesis topsy-turvy and set off a whole series of new interpretations.

This reading reveals something about the way in which archaeologists work. The careful reader will find throughout the excerpt references to the evidence the author used to support his conclusions. The reader will also observe how the author formed hypotheses.

The subject matter of the reading is the Neolithic Revolution—man's discovery of farming and domestication of animals during the New Stone Age. Agriculture was a technological development, which, like the first use of fire and the invention of the steam engine, changed the very nature of human society. Because this one innovation led to drastic changes in the economy, social organization, the political system, the arts, and religion, it is termed a revolution.

As you read this excerpt, consider the following questions:

1 Upon what evidence does the author base his conclusions about the development of farming? (Examine paragraphs five and six carefully.) Do Howells' conclusions follow from the evidence he presents?

2 How does Howells relate the domestication of animals to farming?

3 How did the Neolithic Revolution affect men's way of life?

4 Is it possible to separate prehistoric periods exactly? historic periods?

BACK OF HISTORY (MAN IN THE BEGINNING) / by William Howells

Copyright 1954 by William Howells. Reprinted by permission of Doubleday & Co., Inc. and G. Bell & Sons, Ltd. Pp. 135-140, 143-145.

With the end of the Ice Age the hunting peoples were pressing into every part of the habitable world, except the outer islands of the Pacific and perhaps such poor places as Greenland and Baffin Land. For a time they even roamed the plain between Britain and Denmark which now lies under the North Sea. Making the most of nature, they discovered every kind of available food, including those which have to be specially treated to be edible, like acorns. And in different places they gave themselves the benefit of many fairly intricate inventions, whether weapons or hunting tricks, even though typically they could carry their entire cultures around as they traveled, in their heads or on top of them.

Then, about 6000 B.C., and somewhere in the Near East (as far as we know), the Neolithic way of life began. It is still called "Neolithic" (New Stone Age, as Mesolithic means Middle, and Paleolithic means Old Stone Age), because the older anthropologists saw everything in the light of stonework, and thought of this "period" as the age of polished stone axes. But it means, rather, a state of culture in which food is planted and bred, not hunted and gathered — in which food is domesticated, not wild. If we had to choose the greatest single change in human history right up to the present, this would be it. I mean, of course, a change by cultural evolution, as distinct from a biological change like standing erect, or gradually becoming able to use culture and language in the first place. And I do not mean that the change was sudden, or dramatic to those who were changing, as though a light were being switched on. It was dramatic, but long after, in its consequences, because everything else we have achieved flowed out of this as a beginning.

By about 4000 B.C. there were farming villages spread widely in the Near East, all the way from the Faiyum Basin in Egypt (just up the Nile from Cairo and the Pyramids), through Palestine and Syria, over to Iraq and Iran. They were not all the same, by any means, but a summary picture of their culture was something like this. The people lived in houses, of mud brick or mud and brush walls. They grew wheat and barley; they cut the grain with straight sickles made by setting flint blades in a row in a piece of wood or bone; they stored it (in some places) in granaries or pits lined with basketry; and they ground it for bread on rotary hand mills of stone, or in some other kind of grindstone or mortar. They raised cattle, sheep, goats and pigs (and dogs, although remember that a dog is a Mesolithic contraption used for hunting, and not a barnyard animal). But they also hunted wild animals, and took birds and fish, especially in the Faiyum, to fill out their diets. They made bowls and jars of pottery. And they wove linen cloth out of flax.

This is a culture which, emphatically, you would not try to carry around on your head, even forgetting the houses and granaries. Its origins have not been pinpointed, but they must have been in this same part of the world, the Near East. There seem to have been Mesolithic hunters in the area down to nearly 6000 B.C., according to radiocarbon dates. And one of the earliest villages of farmers yet discovered must have been founded by 5000 B.C. or earlier; this was already a full-fledged village, so that the formative period must have been some time prior to this. In fact, during such a formative period, it is easy to suppose that farmers might leave their village, which we recognize as "Neolithic," and go off on a hunting expedition during which they left remains in a cave which we would dig up and label "Mesolithic."

This early village, called Jarmo, is in the hill country of Iraq above the Tigris-Euphrates Valley. It was made up of simple houses of packed mud walls, and lasted long enough so that eight levels could be made out by the excavators. Grains of wheat and barley were found, along with the household tools for making flour, especially hand mills. And there were bones of cattle, sheep, pigs and dogs.

Now it might be hard to prove just what was the state of domestication of these animals, but here at any rate was the basic domestic livestock in a group; and all wild animal bones — i.e., those which were clearly products of the hunt — amounted to only five per cent of the total. One feature of the houses was burning basins of clay (hearths?), but aside from the remains of these there were no signs of pottery until the highest levels, at the end of the settlement, when some fragments of poor-grade stuff appear. And there were no signs of weaving at all. So here was a group of very early farmers, lacking even the two typical arts of "Neolithic" peoples, pottery and weaving, but with the domesticated grains and animals well in hand.

Something very similar existed in ancient Jericho, in Palestine. Here the oldest levels are probably as old as Jarmo, and may prove to be directly descended from the Mesolithic inhabitants of the region. Yet this very early Jericho had already assumed the form of a true town. Before they were making any pottery, the people had built a town wall of rough stone. And the wall still stands, not thrown down by the trumpets and the Lord; it has been uncovered well beneath the remains of the later Jericho that Joshua fit the battle of.

None of this tells us how the business of domestication came about, and here we have to fall back on a little imagination. But let it be the right kind of imagination, and not one that sees a Mesolithic genius waking up in a hut, exclaiming, "Why didn't I think of that before?" and smartly laying out a garden and planting it full of good things. On the contrary, rapidly though it happened by Paleolithic standards, the deliberate sowing of grain must have come about by accidental steps, at the hands of gatherers.

There is impressive proof that the Mesolithic hunters had come to know and eat every possible kind of natural food, and in this part of the world they surely made use of edible seeds, as in all other parts. Many such people must have anticipated the ripening of wild crops, and perhaps come early to places where they grew, possibly even to pull up weeds or chase birds away. Here in the Near East, in fact, the Natufian people of Palestine seem to have had a very late Mesolithic culture. Yet they had sickles, which is thought to show that they harvested wild grasses and grains on an important scale. Realize also that these cereals, wheat, barley, the millets (grasslike grains including sorghum, very ancient in use), will keep well if they are stored in a proper cache, and you have something which emphasizes the importance of that crop and exerts a steady pull back to the place where it grows well, or where an otherwise wandering group keeps its stores of the grain. And suppose that little by little the people find other ways of helping the crop, and camp near it, or carry ripe grain home to one of their main camps, and accidentally spill it around so that it grows there. Then the final purposeful growing of this kind of food is probably inevitable. Now the whole process might be very slow, or too difficult entirely, for many wild vegetable types, and it is probable that the particular qualities of these grains, like their yearly growth (as opposed to a treeborne fruit), their high food value, and above all their storability, would have helped the incipient farmers along in their unconscious process of domestication.

You might think that it would be possible to find the home of all this by finding the natural home of the grains themselves. Unfortunately, the grains grow wild in too many parts of the Near East and northern or eastern Africa to make this possible. And the same thing applies to the animals. This last is especially true, because, once the idea of domesticating them had been clearly established and herds had been introduced into new territories, then some of the local wild forms in these new territories may have been brought under domestication, as a way of enlarging the flocks. This seems to have happened with cattle and pigs in Europe, for example. That would tend to make it look as though the original domestication had taken place all over creation, instead of in one principal place. The chances are strong, however, that cattle domestication, like that of wheat and barley and other early plants like flax, happened in the Near East.

It is actually surprising that the main animals — cattle, sheep, goats and pigs — all show up together in the lowest archaeological levels of the oldest village, Jarmo. This is the kind of thing that suggests Neolithic beginnings must have gone back well before Jarmo's founding in about 5000 B.C., and perhaps before 6000 B.C. But in any event it is likely that the grains were domesticated before the animals.

For the essence of village farming life is building a village and farming; that is, staying in one place. And it is plants that stay in one place, and so ask the people to do the same, while the animals may wander. If the people are wandering, and living by hunting, they cannot afford the time to care for livestock. Sometimes hunters bring live animals to camp as a way of having the next day's food at hand. But these animals never survive more than a day or so. And a hunter's real reaction to a food animal is to shoot it; this was the Bushman's approach to Hottentot or Dutch cattle, and the Sioux Indians did the same thing when the Great White Father was trying to make them settle down and gave them some cows.

But domesticating cattle is not simply stockading them, or even taming them; it means rather causing them to breed successfully while they are dependent on human beings. And this means living on something else while waiting for the animals to reproduce and grow and give milk. Now if you are a hunter, not a farmer, it would seem preposterous to be hunting rabbits or gazelles if you have oxen and sheep at hand, all ready to be killed. Of course we do not know what actually happened in 6000 B.C., and there may have been special circumstances. And also there are the reindeer nomads of Siberia, who give the impression that they are in the very act of bringing the reindeer to heel; but the circumstances are peculiar. On the face of it, it would seem that the domestication of wild cattle would be slow enough and hard enough to suggest strongly that it was done by homesteaders, not hunters. . . .

This brings us . . . to the meaning of the so-called Neolithic revolution. If you generalize, and take the typical effects on culture of hunting life on the one hand and of farming life on the other, you can see that something stupendous took place. . . . it was a breaking of one of nature's bonds, the freeing of man from the limits of the natural supply of food.

. . . simple hunter-gatherers . . . . have a few crude ideas about conservation and some, like the Australians and the Magdalenians, exerted themselves in pious rites to make the game more plentiful. But that is wishful thinking; nature is in control, not they. Nature goads them about from spot to spot like howling monkeys, and there is nothing they can do about it. They cannot stockpile their food: when they have eaten, it is high time to start thinking about the next meal. Around any camp there are only so many wild animals and so many edible plants, because of the balance of nature. When these have been hunted or picked beyond a given point, the supply becomes too short and cannot recover, perhaps, for that season. What do the people in the camp do? They pick up and move on, to a place where the game is untouched. So this band must have enough territory to keep rebuilding the supply, it must preserve the supply against poachers, and it must move, move, move.

What about the numbers of people? Since they are actually part of the balance of nature themselves, they will be limited to a number which their territory can support in its worst (not its best) years. So the whole human population must be relatively sparse and spread out.

And the size of the band? Actually the simplest family can carry on this kind of a life, the man to hunt and the woman to collect vegetables, insects, water and firewood and to tend to odd jobs. But this leaves them with no help if they have need of it, while larger groups may not only protect themselves better but hunt more effectively, whether by co-operating in a rabbit drive or by multiplying the chances of finding and killing a large animal on which all can feed. However, the size of the band soon reaches a point at which it presses too hard on the food supply. There will simply not be enough food within their radius of action around the camp, or the band itself will not be able to move fast enough and far enough to tap the resources it needs. Only once in a while can bands come together in tribal meetings, and then perhaps when a natural crop—a cactus pear or a kind of grub—comes into season, and for a while creates plenty for everybody. The rest of the time the bands must keep their distance, and the number of each will be something like fifty souls, more or less.

These laws of nature have teeth in them: many such peoples accept the necessity of killing some of their infants at birth because the mother already has all the young children she can cope with on the march; and most of them ruthlessly abandon the sick or the helplessly old to freeze or starve. If, rarely, they put forth efforts on the aged one's behalf, these efforts are visibly strenuous. Such action is not subhuman callousness. Even though they may appear to take it calmly, the people have no choice at all in what they do, or even the face they put upon it.

We see, in fact, human beings like ourselves trapped, without knowing it, in a life which prevents them from having higher material inventions and social combinations. Small nomadic bands can hardly become civilized if they cannot even set up substantial households. They must find some escape from nomadism first, and from isolation and the limits of small numbers. They must find some escape from the tread-mill of food-getting, which has them almost always either hunting or getting ready to hunt, and so keeps them from having any specialization of their energies, and makes the only division of labor that between the animal-hunting man and the plant-hunting woman. This escape was found with domestication, when the ordinary balance of nature was broken and food was made to grow not by nature but by man. Camps changed to villages, and dozens of people to hundreds.

But the millennium did not arrive with a rush. This was the basic change, ideally, but it was gradual, and there has always been a lot of overlapping. The Siriono Indians, nomadic hunters of eastern Bolivia, are normally so hungry that their conversation is largely about food, or squabbling over food, or begging one another for food (they are perhaps the least honorable of the hunters, and will eat in the middle of the night to avoid sharing). And yet they plant small plots of corn and other vegetables around the house or at some place near which they expect to be hunting; still the corn patch fails to rescue them from their hard lot. Many Neolithic peoples hunt and fish avidly and, as we shall soon see, the more primitive ones cannot even remain long in one place because of the inefficiency of their methods of farming. Even in archaeology we can see the gradual nature of the development.

Law and Life in Two Ancient Societies

This Problem provides an opportunity to study original source materials dealing with life in the ancient Near East. The readings are taken from the literature of the Babylonians and Hebrews, and can provide insights into their social, political, and economic practices, as well as their religious and moral beliefs.

In his opening essay, "What Is History?" the author argued that all history is an interpretation of the past. Historians make their interpretations from remaining records. Since we have little first-hand evidence about either the Babylonians or the Hebrews, we have been forced to rely for information on what we can gather from scattered documents such as those you will read in this assignment.

The Code of Hammurabi was discovered in 1901 by French archaeologists who were excavating the site of the ancient city of Susa in Iran. The code had been compiled by Hammurabi about 1750 B.C. and engraved on a stone pillar in cuneiform writing. A bas-relief at the top of the pillar shows a seated sun god presenting the code to Hammurabi, who stands before him in an attitude of reverent obedience. This version of the code was almost certainly based upon earlier Sumerian codes of law.

The surviving literature of the ancient Hebrews is almost entirely concerned with religion. The selection of laws presented below comes from the books of Exodus, Leviticus, and Deuteronomy, which are parts of the Old Testament. Historians believe that the Old Testament was written down between 900 B.C. and 100 A.D. Although it is a religious work, it contains a wealth of information about the secular lives of the Hebrews.

As you read the selections below, think about the following questions:

1   What are some of the ways in which the Babylonians and Hebrews made a living?

2   What do these laws reveal about the class structure in each society?

3   What do the Babylonian laws about water rights and the Hebrew laws on weights and measures reveal about the extent of governmental control?

4   What similarities do you see between these ancient laws and American laws today? what differences?

I

THE CODE OF HAMMURABI

Babylonian and Assyrian Laws, Contracts and Letters, edited by C.H.W. Johns. New York: Charles Scribner's Sons, 1904.

1.   If a man has accused another of laying a *nêrtu* [death spell?] upon him, but has not proved it, he shall be put to death. . . .

3.   If a man has borne false witness in a trial, or has not established the statement that he has made, if that case be a capital trial,
that man shall be put to death. . . .

6.   If a man has stolen goods from a temple, or house, he shall
be put to death; and he that has received the stolen property from
him shall be put to death. . . .

14.   If a man has stolen a child, he shall be put to death. . . .

21.   If a man has broken into a house he shall be killed before
the breach and buried there.

22.   If a man has committed highway robbery and has been
caught, that man shall be put to death.

23.   If the highwayman has not been caught, the man that has
been robbed shall state on oath what he has lost and the city or district
governor in whose territory or district the robbery took place shall
restore to him what he has lost.

24.   If a life [has been lost], the city or district governor shall
pay one mina of silver to the deceased's relatives. . . .

42.   If a man has hired a field to cultivate and has caused no
grain to grow on the field, he shall be held responsible for not doing
the work on the field and shall pay an average rent. . . .

53.   If a man has neglected to strengthen his dike and has not
kept his dike strong, and a breach has broken out in his dike, and the
waters have flooded the meadow, the man in whose dike the breach
has broken out shall restore the grain he has caused to be lost. . . .

55.   If a man has opened his runnel for watering and has left
it open, and the water has flooded his neighbor's field, he shall pay
him an average crop. . . .

117.   If a man owes a debt, and he has given his wife, his son, or
his daughter [as hostage] for the money, or has handed someone over
to work it off, the hostage shall do the work of the creditor's house;
but in the fourth year he shall set them free. . . .

128.   If a man has taken a wife and has not executed a marriage-
contract, that woman is not a wife. . . .

138.   If a man has divorced his wife, who has not borne him children, he shall pay over to her as much money as was given for her
bride-price and the marriage-portion which she brought from her
father's house, and so shall divorce her. . . .

143.   If [a woman] has not been discreet, has gone out, ruined
her house, belittled her husband, she shall be drowned. . . .

168.   If a man has determined to disinherit his son and has de-

clared before the judge, "I cut off my son," the judge shall inquire into the son's past, and, if the son has not committed a grave misdemeanor such as should cut him off from sonship, the father shall [not] disinherit his son. . . .

195. If a son has struck his father, his hands shall be cut off.

196. If a man has knocked out the eye of a patrician, his eye shall be knocked out. [*For a similar law of the Hebrews, see Deuteronomy XIX:21.*]

197. If he has broken the limb of a patrician, his limb shall be broken.

198. If he has knocked out the eye of a plebeian or has broken the limb of a plebeian, he shall pay one mina of silver.

199. If he has knocked out the eye of a patrician's servant, or broken the limb of a patrician's servant, he shall pay half his value. . . .

215. If a surgeon has operated with the bronze lancet on a patrician for a serious injury, and has cured him, or has removed with a bronze lancet a cataract for a patrician, and has cured his eye, he shall take ten shekels of silver. . . .

218. If a surgeon has operated with the bronze lancet on a patrician for a serious injury, and has caused his death, or has removed a cataract for a patrician, with the bronze lancet, and has made him lose his eye, his hands shall be cut off. . . .

229. If a builder has built a house for a man, and has not made his work sound, and the house he built has fallen, and caused the death of its owner, that builder shall be put to death.

230. If it is the owner's son that is killed, the builder's son shall be put to death. . . .

237. If a man has hired a boat and boatman, and loaded it with corn, wool, oil, or dates, or whatever it be, and the boatman has been careless, and sunk the boat, or lost what is in it, the boatman shall restore the boat which he sank, and whatever he lost that was in it. . . .

245. If a man has hired an ox and has caused its death, by carelessness, or blows, he shall restore ox for ox, to the owner of the ox. . . .

251. If a man's ox be a gorer, and has revealed its evil propensity as a gorer, and he has not blunted its horn, or shut up the ox, and then that ox has gored a free man, and caused his death, the owner shall pay half a mina of silver. . . .

282. If a slave has said to his master, "You are not my master," he shall be brought to account as his slave, and his master shall cut off his ear. . . .

II

THE OLD TESTAMENT

From the Authorized King James Version of the Bible.

Exodus, *Chapter 20*

12.   Honour thy father and thy mother: that thy days may be long upon the land which the LORD thy God giveth thee.

13.   Thou shalt not kill.

14.   Thou shalt not commit adultery.

15.   Thou shalt not steal.

16.   Thou shalt not bear false witness against thy neighbour.

17.   Thou shalt not covet thy neighbour's house, thou shalt not covet thy neighbour's wife, nor his manservant, nor his maidservant, nor his ox, nor his ass, nor any thing that *is* thy neighbour's.

Exodus, *Chapter 21*

2.   If thou buy an Hebrew servant, six years he shall serve: and in the seventh he shall go out free for nothing. . . .

26.   And if a man smite the eye of his servant, or the eye of his maid, that it perish; he shall let him go free for his eye's sake.

27.   And if he smite out his manservant's tooth, or his maidservant's tooth; he shall let him go free for his tooth's sake.

28.   If an ox gore a man or a woman, that they die: then the ox shall be surely stoned, and his flesh shall not be eaten; but the owner of the ox *shall be* quit [*released from obligation*].

29.   But if the ox were wont to push with his horn in time past, and it hath been testified to his owner, and he hath not kept him in, but that he hath killed a man or a woman; the ox shall be stoned, and his owner also shall be put to death. . . .

32.   If the ox shall push a manservant or a maidservant; he shall give unto their master thirty shekels of silver, and the ox shall be stoned.

Leviticus, *Chapter 19*

9.   And when ye reap the harvest of your land, thou shalt not wholly reap the corners of thy field, neither shalt thou gather the gleanings of thy harvest.

10.   And thou shalt not glean thy vineyard, neither shalt thou gather *every* grape of thy vineyard; thou shalt leave them for the poor and stranger: I *am* the LORD your God. . . .

13.   Thou shalt not defraud thy neighbour, neither rob *him*: the wages of him that is hired shall not abide with thee all night until the morning. . . .

35.   Ye shall do no unrighteousness in judgment, in meteyard, in weight, or in measure.

36.   Just balances, just weights, a just ephah [*about a bushel*], and a just hin [*between one and two gallons*], shall ye have: I *am* the LORD your God, which brought you out of the land of Egypt.

Deuteronomy, *Chapter 19*

16.   If a false witness rise up against any man to testify against him *that which is* wrong;

17.   Then both the men, between whom the controversy *is,* shall stand before the LORD, before the priests and the judges, which shall be in those days;

18.   And the judges shall make diligent inquisition: and, behold, *if* the witness *be* a false witness, *and* hath testified falsely against his brother;

19.   Then shall ye do unto him, as he had thought to have done unto his brother: so shalt thou put the evil away from among you.

20.   And those which remain shall hear, and fear, and shall henceforth commit no more any such evil among you.

21.   And thine eye shall not pity; *but* life *shall go* for life, eye for eye, tooth for tooth, hand for hand, foot for foot.

Deuteronomy, *Chapter 24*

1.   When a man hath taken a wife, and married her, and it come to pass that she find no favour in his eyes, because he hath found some uncleanliness in her: then let him write her a bill of divorcement, and give *it* in her hand, and send her out of his house.

2.   And when she is departed out of his house she may go and be another man's *wife.*

3.   And *if* the latter husband hate her, and write her a bill of divorcement, and giveth *it* in her hand, and sendeth her out of his house; or if the latter husband die, which took her *to be* his wife;

4.   Her former husband, which sent her away, may not take her again to be his wife, after that she is defiled.

Athenian Democracy

Many of the principles and practices of Western democracy were born in the city-states of ancient Greece. To these tiny principalities we can trace the origins of much that is most cherished in our own political system. Athens was the heart of this early democratic tradition. Her people, her institutions, and her spokesmen blazed a trail that the rest of Western mankind has followed down to the present day.

What was the nature of Greek democracy? Like many similar terms, the word *democracy* has changed in meaning over the years. It had one meaning to the Greeks, another to the Romans, still a third to 19th-century Englishmen; in fact, the word has been assigned almost as many meanings as the number of nations that have adopted the system or claim to be governed under it. In order for a historian to use the word *democracy* intelligently—that is, so that it will convey one and only one meaning to his readers—he must determine (1) what all democratic systems have in common and (2) the individual peculiarities of the particular democratic system under discussion. He must then make clear which democratic system he is discussing by using suitable adjectives, such as *Athenian* democracy or *modern American* democracy. This process describes the way in which professional historians build a historical definition of a term. In addition to *democracy*, words like *socialism, nationalism,* and *imperialism* also require historical definitions before they can be used accurately.

The reading for today is from the writings of the Greek historian Thucydides, who wrote during the last half of the 5th century B.C. Thucydides, one of the world's greatest historians, participated as a general in the long struggle between Athens and Sparta. He was a stanch advocate of the Athenian side, although he was in exile when he wrote the *History of the Peloponnesian War.* The excerpt below reveals Athens in a moment of greatness. Pericles, the famous Athenian statesman, while praising the men who died defending their native city, describes the beliefs, institutions, and customs for which they fought. His speech is one of the most famous defenses of the democratic way of life in the history of mankind. Educated men throughout the centuries have read it and pondered its message. The actual words are those of Thucydides, however. In his *History* he sometimes composed speeches to put into the mouths of others. This dramatic device was used by many historians of classical times.

While you read the funeral oration, consider the following questions:

1 What were the principal characteristics of Athenian democracy, as described by Pericles? From what you have read elsewhere, do you think he represented it accurately?

2 What responsibility did individual Athenian citizens have for the maintenance of the democratic way of life?

3 Does the definition of democracy given by Pericles correspond to the way in which Americans use the word today?

4 Do you think that a funeral oration is a suitable source from which to obtain a thoroughly accurate account of Athenian democracy?

PERICLES' FUNERAL ORATION

From Thucydides, *History of the Peloponnesian War*.
Translated by Rex Warner. Penguin Books, 1954. Pp.
115-123. Reprinted by permission of The Bodley Head.

In the same winter the Athenians, following their annual custom, gave
a public funeral for those who had been the first to die in the war.
These funerals are held in the following way: two days before the
ceremony the bones of the fallen are brought and put in a tent which
has been erected, and people make whatever offerings they wish to
their own dead. Then there is a funeral procession in which coffins of
cypress wood are carried on wagons. There is one coffin for each tribe,
which contains the bones of members of that tribe. One empty bier is
decorated and carried in the procession: this is for the missing, whose
bodies could not be recovered. Everyone who wishes to, both citizens
and foreigners, ean join in the procession, and the women who are
related to the dead are there to make their laments at the tomb. The
bones are laid in the public burial-place, which is in the most beautiful quarter outside the city walls. Here the Athenians always bury
those who have fallen in war. The only exception is those who died
at Marathon, who, because their achievement was considered absolutely outstanding, were buried on the battlefield itself.

When the bones have been laid in the earth, a man chosen by the
city for his intellectual gifts and for his general reputation makes an
appropriate speech in praise of the dead, and after the speech all
depart. This is the procedure at these burials, and all through the war,
when the time came to do so, the Athenians followed this ancient
custom. Now, at the burial of those who were the first to fall in the war
Pericles, the son of Xanthippus, was chosen to make the speech.
When the moment arrived, he came forward from the tomb and,
standing on a high platform, so that he might be heard by as many
people as possible in the crowd, he spoke as follows:

"Many of those who have spoken here in the past have praised
the institution of this speech at the close of our ceremony. It seemed
to them a mark of honour to our soldiers who have fallen in war that a
speech should be made over them. I do not agree. These men have
shown themselves valiant in action, and it would be enough, I think,
for their glories to be proclaimed in action, as you have just seen it
done at this funeral organized by the state. Our belief in the courage
and manliness of so many should not be hazarded on the goodness or
badness of one man's speech. . . . However, the fact is that this

institution was set up and approved by our forefathers, and it is my
duty to follow the tradition and do my best to meet the wishes and the
expectations of every one of you.

"I shall begin by speaking about our ancestors, since it is only
right and proper on such an occasion to pay them the honour of recalling what they did. In this land of ours there have always been the
same people living from generation to generation up till now, and
they, by their courage and their virtues, have handed it on to us, a free
country. They certainly deserve our praise. Even more so do our
fathers deserve it. For to the inheritance they had received they added
all the empire we have now, and it was not without blood and toil that
they handed it down to us of the present generation. And then we ourselves, assembled here to-day, who are mostly in the prime of life,
have, in most directions, added to the power of our empire and have
organized our State in such a way that it is perfectly well able to look
after itself both in peace and war.

"I have no wish to make a long speech on subjects familiar to you
all: so I shall say nothing about the warlike deeds by which we acquired our power or the battles in which we or our fathers gallantly
resisted our enemies, Greek or foreign. What I want to do is, in the
first place, to discuss the spirit in which we faced our trials and also
our constitution and the way of life which has made us great. After that
I shall speak in praise of the dead, believing that this kind of speech is
not inappropriate to the present occasion, and that this whole assembly, of citizens and foreigners, may listen to it with advantage.

"Let me say that our system of government does not copy the institutions of our neighbours. It is more the case of our being a model to
others, than of our imitating anyone else. Our constitution is called a
democracy because power is in the hands not of a minority but of the
whole people. When it is a question of settling private disputes, everyone is equal before the law; when it is a question of putting one person before another in positions of public responsibility, what counts
is not membership of a particular class, but the actual ability which
the man possesses. No one, so long as he has it in him to be of service
to the state, is kept in political obscurity because of poverty. And,
just as our political life is free and open, so is our day-to-day life in
our relations with each other. We do not get into a state with our next-
door neighbour if he enjoys himself in his own way, nor do we give
him the kind of black looks which, though they do no real harm, still
do hurt people's feelings. We are free and tolerant in our private lives;

but in public affairs we keep to the law. This is because it commands our deep respect.

"We give our obedience to those whom we put in positions of authority, and we obey the laws themselves, especially those which are for the protection of the oppressed, and those unwritten laws which it is an acknowledged shame to break.

"And here is another point. When our work is over, we are in a position to enjoy all kinds of recreation for our spirits. There are various kinds of contests and sacrifices regularly throughout the year; in our own homes we find a beauty and a good taste which delight us every day and which drive away our cares. Then the greatness of our city brings it about that all the good things from all over the world flow in to us, so that to us it seems just as natural to enjoy foreign goods as our own local products.

"Then there is a great difference between us and our opponents, in our attitude towards military security. Here are some examples: Our city is open to the world, and we have no periodical deportations in order to prevent people observing or finding out secrets which might be of military advantage to the enemy. This is because we rely, not on secret weapons, but on our own real courage and loyalty. There is a difference, too, in our educational systems. The Spartans, from their earliest boyhood, are submitted to the most laborious training in courage; we pass our lives without all these restrictions, and yet are just as ready to face the same dangers as they are. Here is a proof of this: When the Spartans invade our land, they do not come by themselves, but bring all their allies with them; whereas we, when we launch an attack abroad, do the job by ourselves, and, though fighting on foreign soil, do not often fail to defeat opponents who are fighting for their own hearths and homes. As a matter of fact none of our enemies has ever yet been confronted with our total strength, because we have to divide our attention between our navy and the many missions on which our troops are sent on land. Yet, if our enemies engage a detachment of our forces and defeat it, they give themselves credit for having thrown back our entire army; or, if they lose, they claim that they were beaten by us in full strength. There are certain advantages, I think, in our way of meeting danger voluntarily, with an easy mind, instead of with a laborious training, with natural rather than with state-induced courage. We do not have to spend our time practising to meet sufferings which are still in the future; and when they are actually upon us we show ourselves just as brave as these others who are al-

ways in strict training. This is one point in which, I think, our city deserves to be admired. There are also others:

"Our love of what is beautiful does not lead to extravagance; our
love of the things of the mind does not make us soft. We regard wealth
as something to be properly used, rather than as something to boast
about. As for poverty, no one need be ashamed to admit it: the real
shame is in not taking practical measures to escape from it. Here each
individual is interested not only in his own affairs but in the affairs of
the state as well: even those who are mostly occupied with their own
business are extremely well-informed on general politics—this is a
peculiarity of ours: we do not say that a man who takes no interest in
politics is a man who minds his own business; we say that he has no
business here at all. We Athenians, in our own persons, take our decisions on policy or submit them to proper discussions: for we do not
think that there is an incompatibility between words and deeds; the
worst thing is to rush into action before the consequences have been
properly debated. And this is another point where we differ from other
people. We are capable at the same time of taking risks and of estimating them beforehand. Others are brave out of ignorance; and, when
they stop to think, they begin to fear. But the man who can most truly be accounted brave is he who best knows the meaning of what is
sweet in life and of what is terrible, and then goes out undeterred to
meet what is to come.

"Again, in questions of general good feeling there is a great contrast between us and most other people. We make friends by doing
good to others, not by receiving good from them. This makes our
friendship all the more reliable, since we want to keep alive the gratitude of those who are in our debt by showing continued goodwill to
them: whereas the feelings of one who owes us something lack the
same enthusiasm, since he knows that, when he repays our kindness,
it will be more like paying back a debt than giving something spontaneously. We are unique in this. When we do kindnesses to others,
we do not do them out of any calculations of profit or loss: we do them
without afterthought, relying on our free liberality. Taking everything
together then, I declare that our city is an education to Greece, and I
declare that in my opinion each single one of our citizens, in all the
manifold aspects of life, is able to show himself the rightful lord and
owner of his own person, and do this, moreover, with exceptional
grace and exceptional versatility. And to show that this is no empty
boasting for the present occasion, but real tangible fact, you have only

to consider the power which our city possesses and which has been won by those very qualities which I have mentioned. Athens, alone of the states we know, comes to her testing time in a greatness that surpasses what was imagined of her. In her case, and in her case alone, no invading enemy is ashamed at being defeated, and no subject can complain of being governed by people unfit for their responsibilities. Mighty indeed are the marks and monuments of our empire which we have left. Future ages will wonder at us, as the present age wonders at us now. We do not need the praises of a Homer, or of anyone else whose words may delight us for the moment, but whose estimation of facts will fall short of what is really true. For our adventurous spirit has forced an entry into every sea and into every land; and everywhere we have left behind us everlasting memorials of good done to our friends or suffering inflicted on our enemies.

"This, then, is the kind of city for which these men, who could not bear the thought of losing her, nobly fought and nobly died. It is only natural that every one of us who survive them should be willing to undergo hardships in her service. And it was for this reason that I have spoken at such length about our city, because I wanted to make it clear that for us there is more at stake than there is for others who lack our advantages; also I wanted my words of praise for the dead to be set in the bright light of evidence. And now the most important of these words has been spoken. I have sung the praises of our city; but it was the courage and gallantry of these men, and of people like them, which made her splendid. Nor would you find it true in the case of many of the Greeks, as it is true of them, that no words can do more than justice to their deeds.

"To me it seems that the consummation which has overtaken these men shows us the meaning of manliness in its first revelation and in its final proof. Some of them, no doubt, had their faults; but what we ought to remember first is their gallant conduct against the enemy in defence of their native land. They have blotted out evil with good, and done more service to the commonwealth than they ever did harm in their private lives. No one of these men weakened because he wanted to go on enjoying his wealth; no one put off the awful day in the hope that he might live to escape his poverty and grow rich. More to be desired than such things, they chose to check the enemy's pride. This, to them, was a risk most glorious, and they accepted it, willing to strike down the enemy and relinquish everything else. As for success or failure, they left that in the doubtful hands of Hope, and when the reality of battle was before their faces, they put their trust in their own selves. In the fighting, they thought it more honourable to stand their ground and suffer death than to give in and save their lives. So they fled from the reproaches of men, abiding with life and limb the brunt of battle; and, in a small moment of time, the climax of their lives, a culmination of glory, not of fear, were swept away from us.

"So and such they were, these men — worthy of their city. We who remain behind may hope to be spared their fate, but must resolve to keep the same daring spirit against the foe. It is not simply a question of estimating the advantages in theory. I could tell you a long story (and you know it as well as I do) about what is to be gained by beating the enemy back. What I would prefer is that you should fix your eyes every day on the greatness of Athens as she really is, and should fall in love with her. When you realize her greatness, then reflect that what made her great was men with a spirit of adventure, men who knew their duty, men who were ashamed to fall below a certain standard. If they ever failed in an enterprise, they made up their minds that at any rate the city should not find their courage lacking to her, and they gave to her the best contributions that they could. They gave her their lives, to her and to all of us, and for their own selves they won praises that never grow old, the most splendid of sepulchres — not the sepulchre in which their bodies are laid, but where their glory remains eternal in men's minds, always there on the right occasion to stir others to speech or to action. For famous men have the whole earth as their memorial: it is not only the inscriptions on their graves in their own country that mark them out; no, in foreign lands also, not in any visible form but in people's hearts, their memory abides and grows. It is for you to try to be like them. Make up your minds that happiness depends on being free, and freedom depends on being courageous. Let there be no relaxation in face of the perils of the war. The people who have most excuse for despising death are not the wretched and unfortunate, who have no hope of doing well for themselves, but those who run the risk of a complete reversal in their lives, and who would feel the difference most intensely, if things went wrong for them. Any intelligent man would find a humiliation caused by his own slackness more painful to bear than death, when death comes to him unperceived, in battle, and in the confidence of his patriotism."

Life Among Rome's Barbarian Neighbors

Publius Cornelius Tacitus was one of Rome's greatest historians, but we know very little about the details of his life. Born about 55 A.D., he was married in the year 77 to the daughter of a successful statesman. Twenty years later Tacitus himself had risen to a prominent official position, serving for a year as consul. He died sometime after 116, but we do not know exactly when or where.

Tacitus' most ambitious writings were his *Annals*, dealing with Roman history from 14 to 68 A.D., and the *Histories*, covering the period from 69 to 96. His shorter works include a biography of his father-in-law and his famous description of Germany, parts of which you will read today. The latter, titled *On the Origin, Geography, Institutions, and Tribes of the Germans* (but usually called the *Germania*), was written in 98.

Tacitus probably never visited Germany, but it is possible that he may have spent a short time there. His information about the Germans came from works of earlier writers, including Julius Caesar, and from reports of soldiers and merchants who had returned from the Roman frontier. Although he was a relatively careful reporter, Tacitus may have permitted events in Rome to influence his selection of material and the language he used. He lived through the reign of the cruel emperor Domitian and during these hard years he saw a number of his friends put to death on false charges of treason. He also witnessed the decline of moral standards in Rome. Thus he may have emphasized the freedom, democracy, and high moral standards of the German tribes in order to teach his fellow citizens a lesson by implication. In any event, *Germania* remains the best surviving description of the barbarians north of the Roman Empire.

From the pages of Tacitus, we can investigate the character traits of the Germans, an important historical understanding because it sheds light on why these barbarians were able to conquer Rome. Although Tacitus may have exaggerated their virtues, their undoubted courage and military ability made them formidable foes.

As you read, consider the following questions:

1 How credible is Tacitus?
   a. Do you find evidence that he was an eyewitness?
   b. Do you find incorrect statements of fact or credulous acceptance of statistics or opinions?
   c. Does Tacitus indicate his sources plainly?
   d. Does he clearly distinguish between evidence and inference?

2 How did Tacitus' moral outlook affect his writing? What aspects of Roman life come under implied criticism?

3 Generations of German schoolboys have read — and believed — Tacitus. How may this possibly have influenced German history?

GERMANIA / by Tacitus

From *The Complete Works of Tacitus*, translated by Alfred John Church and William Jackson Brodribb, edited by Moses Hadas. Copyright 1942 by Random House, Inc. Pp. 709-718, 719-722. Reprinted by permission.

The Germans . . . I should regard as aboriginal, and not mixed at all with other races through immigration . . . . For, in former times, it was not by land but on shipboard that those who sought to emigrate would arrive; and the boundless and, so to speak, hostile ocean beyond us, is seldom entered by a sail from our world. And, beside the perils of rough and unknown seas, who would leave Asia, or Africa, or Italy for Germany, with its wild country, its inclement skies, its sullen manners and aspect, unless indeed it were his home? . . .

They say that Hercules . . . once visited them; and when going into battle, they sing of him first of all heroes. They have also those songs of theirs, by the recital of which ("baritus," they call it), they rouse their courage, while from the note they augur the result of the approaching conflict. For, as their line shouts, they inspire or feel alarm. It is not so much an articulate sound, as a general cry of valour. They aim chiefly at a harsh note and a confused roar, putting their shields to their mouth, so that, by reverberation, it may swell into a fuller and deeper sound. Ulysses, too, is believed by some, in his long legendary wanderings, to have . . . visited German soil, to have founded and named the town of Asciburgium, which stands on the bank of the Rhine, and is to this day inhabited [*possibly the present-day town of Asperg, near Düsseldorf*]. They even say that an altar dedicated to Ulysses, with the addition of the name of his father, Laertes, was formerly discovered on this same spot, and that certain monuments and tombs, with Greek inscriptions, still exist on the borders of Germany and Rhaetia. These statements I have no intention of sustaining by proofs, or of refuting; every one may believe or disbelieve them as he feels inclined.

. . . I agree with those who think that the tribes of Germany . . . appear as a distinct, unmixed race, like none but themselves. Hence, too, the same physical peculiarities throughout so vast a population. All have fierce blue eyes, red hair, huge frames . . . .

. . . Silver and gold the gods have refused to them, whether in kindness or in anger I cannot say. I would not, however, affirm that no vein of German soil produces gold or silver, for who has ever made a search? . . .

Even iron is not plentiful with them, as we infer from the character of their weapons. But few use swords or long lances. They carry a spear (*framea* is their name for it), with a narrow and short head, but so sharp and easy to wield that the same weapon serves, according to circumstances, for close or distant conflict. As for the horse-soldier, he is satisfied with a shield and spear; the foot-soldiers also scatter showers of missiles, each man having several and hurling them to an immense distance, and being naked or lightly clad with a little cloak. There is no display about their equipment: their shields alone are marked with very choice colours. A few only have corslets, and just one or two here and there a metal or leathern helmet. Their horses are remarkable neither for beauty nor for fleetness. Nor are they taught various evolutions after our fashion, but are driven straight forward, or so as to make one wheel to the right in such a compact body that none is left behind another. On the whole, one would say that their chief strength is in their infantry, which fights along with the cavalry; admirably adapted to the action of the latter is the swiftness of certain foot-soldiers, who are picked from the entire youth of their country, and stationed in front of the line. Their number is fixed,—a hundred from each canton; and from this they take their name among their countrymen, so that what was originally a mere number has now become a title of distinction. Their line of battle is drawn up in a wedge-like formation. To give ground, provided you return to the attack, is considered prudence rather than cowardice. The bodies of their slain they carry off even in indecisive engagements. To abandon your shield is the basest of crimes; nor may a man thus disgraced be present at the sacred rites, or enter their council; many, indeed, after escaping from battle, have ended their infamy with the halter.

They choose their kings by birth, their generals for merit. These kings have not unlimited or arbitrary power, and the generals do more by example than by authority. If they are energetic, if they are conspicuous, if they fight in the front, they lead because they are admired. But to reprimand, to imprison, even to flog, is permitted to the priests alone, and that not as a punishment, or at the general's bidding, but, as it were, by the mandate of the god whom they believe to inspire the warrior. They also carry with them into battle certain figures and images taken from their sacred groves. And what most stimulates their courage is, that their squadrons or battalions, instead of being formed by chance or by a fortuitous gathering, are composed of families and clans. Close by them, too, are those dearest to them, so that they hear the shrieks of women, the cries of infants. *They* are to every man the most sacred witnesses of his bravery—*they* are his most generous applauders. The soldier brings his wounds to mother and wife, who shrink not from counting or even demanding them and who administer both food and encouragement to the combatants.

Tradition says that armies already wavering and giving way have been rallied by women who, with earnest entreaties . . . have vividly represented the horrors of captivity, which the Germans fear with such extreme dread on behalf of their women, that the strongest tie by which a state can be bound is the being required to give, among the number of hostages, maidens of noble birth.

. . . The Germans . . . do not consider it consistent with the grandeur of celestial beings to confine the gods within walls, or to liken them to the form of any human countenance. They consecrate woods and groves, and they apply the names of deities to the abstraction which they see only in spiritual worship. . . .

About minor matters the chiefs deliberate, about the more important the whole tribe. Yet even when the final decision rests with the people, the affair is always thoroughly discussed by the chiefs. They assemble, except in the case of a sudden emergency, on certain fixed days, either at new or at full moon; for this they consider the most auspicious season for the transaction of business. . . . When the multitude think proper, they sit down armed. Silence is proclaimed by the priests, who have on these occasions the right of keeping order. Then the king or the chief, according to age, birth, distinction in war, or eloquence, is heard, more because he has influence to persuade than because he has power to command. If his sentiments displease them, they reject them with murmurs; if they are satisfied, they brandish their spears. The most complimentary form of assent is to express approbation with their weapons. . . .

They transact no public or private business without being armed. It is not, however, usual for anyone to wear arms till the state has recognised his power to use them. Then in the presence of the council one of the chiefs, or the young man's father, or some kinsman, equips him with a shield and a spear. These arms are what the toga is with us, the first honour with which youth is invested. Up to this time he is regarded as a member of a household, afterwards as a member of the commonwealth. . . .

When they go into battle, it is a disgrace for the chief to be surpassed in valour, a disgrace for his followers not to equal the valour of the chief. And it is an infamy and a reproach for life to have survived the chief, and returned from the field. To defend, to protect him, to ascribe one's own brave deeds to his renown, is the height of loyalty. The chief fights for victory; his vassals fight for their chief. If their native state sinks into the sloth of prolonged peace and repose, many of its noble youths voluntarily seek those tribes which are waging some war, both because inaction is odious to their race, and because they win renown more readily in the midst of peril, and cannot maintain a numerous following except by violence and war. Indeed, men look to the liberality of their chief for their war-horse and their blood-stained and victorious lance. Feasts and entertainments, which, though inelegant, are plentifully furnished, are their only pay. . . .

Whenever they are not fighting, they pass much of their time in the chase, and still more in idleness, giving themselves up to sleep and to feasting, the bravest and the most warlike doing nothing, and surrendering the management of the household, of the home, and of the land, to the women, the old men, and all the weakest members of the family. . . .

Their marriage code . . . is strict, and indeed no part of their manners is more praiseworthy. Almost alone among barbarians they are content with one wife. . . . The wife does not bring a dower to the husband, but the husband to the wife. The parents and relatives are present, and pass judgment on the marriage-gifts, gifts not meant to suit a woman's taste, nor such as a bride would deck herself with, but oxen, a caparisoned steed, a shield, a lance, and a sword. With these presents the wife is espoused, and she herself in turn brings her husband a gift of arms. This they count their strongest bond of union, these their sacred mysteries, these their gods of marriage. Lest the woman should think herself to stand apart from aspirations after noble deeds and from the perils of war, she is reminded by the ceremony which inaugurates marriage that she is her husband's partner in toil and danger, destined to suffer and to dare with him alike both in peace and in war. . . .

Thus with their virtue protected they [the women] live uncorrupted by the allurements of public shows or the stimulant of feastings. Clandestine correspondence is equally unknown to men and women. . . . No one in Germany laughs at vice, nor do they call it the fashion to corrupt and to be corrupted. . . .

One and the same kind of spectacle is always exhibited at every gathering. Naked youths who practise the sport bound in the dance amid swords and lances that threaten their lives. Experience gives them skill, and skill again gives grace; profit or pay are out of the question; however reckless their pastime, its reward is the pleasure of the spectators. Strangely enough they make games of hazard a serious occupation even when sober, and so venturesome are they about gaining or losing, that, when every other resource has failed, on the last and final throw they stake the freedom of their own persons. The loser goes into voluntary slavery; though the younger and stronger, he suffers himself to be bound and sold. Such is their stubborn persistency in a bad practice; they themselves call it honour. Slaves of this kind the owners part with in the way of commerce, and also to relieve themselves from the scandal of such a victory. . . .

Of lending money on interest and increasing it by compound interest they know nothing,—a more effectual safeguard than if it were prohibited. . . .

In their funerals there is no pomp; they simply observe the custom of burning the bodies of illustrious men with certain kinds of wood. They do not heap garments or spices on the funeral pile. The arms of the dead man and in some cases his horse are consigned to the fire. A turf mound forms the tomb. Monuments with their lofty elaborate splendour they reject as oppressive to the dead. Tears and lamentations they soon dismiss; grief and sorrow but slowly. It is thought becoming for women to bewail, for men to remember the dead.

Such on the whole is the account which I have received of the origin and manners of the entire German people.

Roman Law and Christian Citizens

The Greek city-states were never able to achieve political unity, but the Romans learned to govern a large empire and to govern it well. The foundations for their imperial system were laid in the days of the Republic, when many sound and effective features of government were developed. Notable among Roman contributions to political organization were its legal codes, which protected citizens from arbitrary rule. As the boundaries of the empire expanded, Romans took their laws and customs with them, organizing stable government for the entire Mediterranean world. The Roman legal system is still the basis of law codes in many countries, including France, Spain, and much of Latin America.

The Roman Empire included peoples of many races, religions, and cultural traditions. Late in the 1st century A.D., the government faced the challenge of dealing with a new minority group, the Christians. In general, the Romans were tolerant of all religions and quite willing to admit the gods of subject peoples to Roman shrines on an equal basis. But Christians refused to acknowledge the existence of other gods and, more important, to recognize the emperor as divine. They set themselves apart in small communities where they shared their earthly goods in common. Unlike the Jews, they were full of missionary zeal and attempted to convert nonbelievers to the new faith. Rumors began to circulate that Christian groups held secret rites in which atrocities were committed. For example, their Communion service brought accusations of cannibalism against them.

Because Christians would not submit to Roman authority, they were regarded as dangerous and subversive, and persecuted from time to time. The persecutions were not continuous, but usually occurred during periods of national crisis when the government needed scapegoats on whom to blame disasters. Even at these times, however, Roman law defended Christian citizens. It did not always protect them from arbitrary punishment, but it did provide a framework whereby responsible government officials could see to it that their rights were respected. For example, Christians — like all citizens — had a right to appeal for a hearing in the emperor's court; there they might receive a fairer hearing than in the provinces. This right of appeal was a treasured one and usually respected, even by the more autocratic emperors.

Today's Problem includes four documents. The first consists of verses 1-21 from Chapter 25 of the Acts of the Apostles in the New Testament. It tells the story of St. Paul, who was accused of a number of misdeeds by Jewish leaders in Palestine and appealed to the emperor to assure himself a fair trial. The second, an excerpt from the historical writings of Tacitus, describes Nero's persecutions in 64 A.D. Next follows correspondence between Pliny the Younger and the Emperor Trajan about the treatment of Christians in the province of Bithynia in Asia Minor, where Pliny was the emperor's representative. Here the student can find a description of the way in which the principles of Roman law worked in practice. Finally, a decree of the Emperor Hadrian written about 124 A.D. in the form of a letter to an official reveals the attitude of the emperor toward men who accused others falsely.

From these four documents, a student should be able to generalize about the way in which Roman law protected the rights of all citizens. Scholars have often been forced to generalize from even less evidence. Think how risky it was for Howells (Problem 1) to generalize from the few artifacts that had been found. In the present Problem, you have evidence from four independent witnesses, each of whom looked at Roman law from a somewhat different point of view. Since the witnesses were independent and since their vantage points differed substantially, their combined testimony is more reliable than if all of them had written out of the same context. Historians always look for corroborating evidence when they make conclusions, but they also seek just as avidly for contrary evidence that might cause them to alter an existing interpretation.

As you read, think about the following questions:

1 What does Festus (in the reading from Acts) indicate was an important right of Roman citizens?

2 What do Trajan and Hadrian say about the kind of evidence allowed in Roman courts? Why is this an important issue?

3 According to Tacitus, why did Nero persecute the Christians? What was the attitude of this Roman historian to the Christians? to their punishment?

4 Do you think that the evidence from these sources is sufficiently reliable and drawn from a diverse enough sampling to lead to valid conclusions? What sort of evidence would you seek to make your conclusions more reliable?

I

ACTS OF THE APOSTLES

From *The Bible: An American Translation*, translated by J. M. Powis and Edgar J. Goodspeed. Reprinted by permission of the University of Chicago Press. Copyright 1935 by the University of Chicago. Pp. 137-138.

Three days after his arrival in the province, Festus went up from Caesarea to Jerusalem, and the high priests and Jewish leaders presented their charges against Paul, and begged him as a favor to order Paul to come to Jerusalem, plotting to kill him on the way. Festus answered that Paul was being kept in custody at Caesarea, and that he himself was going there soon.

"So have your principal men go down with me," he said, "and present charges against the man, if there is anything wrong with him."

After staying only eight or ten days there, he went down to Caesarea, and the next day took his place in the judge's chair, and ordered Paul brought in. When he came, the Jews who had come down from Jerusalem surrounded him, and made a number of serious charges against him, which they could not substantiate. Paul said in his own defense,

"I have committed no offense against the Jewish Law or the Temple or the emperor."

Then Festus, wishing to gratify the Jews, said to Paul,

"Will you go up to Jerusalem and be tried there before me on these charges?"

But Paul said,

"I am standing before the emperor's court, where I ought to be tried. I have done the Jews no wrong, as you can easily see. If I am guilty and have done anything that deserves death, I do not refuse to die; but if there is no truth in the charges that these men make against me, no one can give me up to them; I appeal to the emperor."

Then Festus after conferring with the council answered, "You have appealed to the emperor, and to the emperor you shall go!"

Some time after, King Agrippa and Bernice came to Caesarea on a state visit to Festus, and as they stayed there several days, Festus laid Paul's case before the king.

"There is a man here," he said, "who was left in prison by Felix, and when I was at Jerusalem the Jewish high priests and elders presented their case against him, and asked for his conviction. I told them that it was not the Roman custom to give anybody up until the accused met his accusers face to face and had a chance to defend himself against their accusations. So they came back here with me and the next day without losing any time I took my place in the judge's chair and ordered the man brought in. But when his accusers got up, they did not charge him with any such crimes as I had expected. Their differences with him were about their own religion and about a certain Jesus who had died but who Paul said was alive. I was at a loss as to how to investigate such matters, and I asked him if he would like to go to Jerusalem and be tried on these charges there. But Paul appealed to have his case reserved for his Majesty's decision, and I have ordered him kept in custody until I can send him to the emperor."

II

THE ANNALS / by Tacitus

From Book 15. Translated by Edwin Fenton.

But no routine efforts, lavish gifts to the populace by the emperor, or ceremonies to placate heaven, would quell the rumors that the burning of Rome had been due to imperial order. So to scotch such stories, Nero falsely named as culprits, and then subjected to the most extreme punishments, those people hated for their shameful behavior who are commonly called Christians. The man who gave the sect its name, Christus, was executed by authority of procurator Pontius Pilate during the time of emperor Tiberius, but the pernicious superstition was repressed only temporarily. It broke out again not only in Judea, where this disease began, but also in Rome itself, where all things from everywhere that are atrocious and disagreeable come together and become all the fashion.

At first those who confessed to being Christians were arrested. Then from information extracted from them a huge number were convicted, not as much on the charge of setting the fire as simply on the charge of hating the human race. And their deaths were embellished by the cruelest mockery, for they were wrapped in the skins of wild beasts and then torn to death by dogs, or were nailed to crosses, or were burned in flames, if the day had ended, to serve as lamps for the night. Nero provided his own gardens for this spectacle and produced a show like a circus. He even mingled with the crowd, disguised as a charioteer, or stood up in his chariot. And so, even though these Christians were malefactors who deserved severe punishment as public examples, general sympathy grew up for them, since they seemed punished not to protect the public welfare but simply to satisfy the ferocity of one man.

III

PLINY-TRAJAN CORRESPONDENCE

From *The Letters of the Younger Pliny*, edited by J. D. Lewis. London: Kegan Paul, Trench, Trubner and Company, 1879.

[*Letter from Pliny to Trajan*] It is with me, sir, an established custom to refer to you all matters on which I am in doubt. Who, indeed, is better able, either to direct my scruples or to instruct my ignorance?

I have never been present at trials of Christians, and consequently do not know for what reasons, or how far, punishment is usually inflicted or inquiry made in their case. Nor have my hesitations been slight; as to whether any distinction of age should be made, or persons however tender in years should be viewed as differing in no respect

from the full-grown: whether pardon should be accorded to repent-
ance, or he who has once been Christian should gain nothing by
having ceased to be one: whether the very profession itself if unat-
tended by crime, or else the crimes necessarily attaching to the profession, should be made the subject of punishment.

Meanwhile, in the case of those who have been brought before
me in the character of Christians, my course has been as follows: — I
put it to themselves whether they were or were not Christians. To
such as professed that they were, I put the inquiry a second and a third
time, threatening them with the supreme penalty. Those who per-
sisted, I ordered to execution. For, indeed, I could not doubt, whatever might be the nature of that which they professed, that their
pertinacity, at any rate, and inflexible obstinacy, ought to be punished.
There were others afflicted with like madness, with regard to whom,
as they were Roman citizens, I made a memorandum that they were
to be sent for judgment to Rome. Soon, the very handling of this matter causing, as often happens, the area of the charge to spread, many
fresh examples occurred. An anonymous paper was put forth containing the names of many persons. Those who denied that they either
were or had been Christians, upon their calling on the gods after me,
and upon their offering wine and incense before your statue, which
for this purpose I had ordered to be introduced in company with the
images of the gods, moreover upon their reviling Christ — none of
which things it is said can such as are really and truly Christians be
compelled to do — these I deemed it proper to dismiss. Others named
by the informer admitted that they were Christians, and then shortly
afterwards denied it, adding that they had been Christians, but had
ceased to be so, some three years, some many years, more than one
of them as much as twenty years, before. All these, too, not only
honoured your image and the effigies of the gods, but also reviled
Christ. They affirmed, however, that this had been the sum, whether
of their crime or their delusion; they had been in the habit of meeting
together on a stated day, before sunrise, and of offering in turns a form
of invocation to Christ, as to a god; also of binding themselves by an
oath, not for any guilty purpose, but not to commit thefts, or robberies,
or adulteries, not to break their word, not to repudiate deposits when
called upon; these ceremonies having been gone through, they had
been in the habit of separating, and again meeting together for the
purpose of taking food — food that is, of an ordinary and innocent kind.
They had, however, ceased from doing even this, after my edict, in

which, following your orders, I had forbidden the existence of Fraternities. This made me think it all the more necessary to inquire, even by torture, of two maid-servants, who were styled deaconesses, what the truth was. I could discover nothing else than a vicious and extravagant superstition: consequently, having adjourned the inquiry, I have had recourse to your counsels.

[*Letter from Trajan to Pliny*] You have followed the right mode of procedure, my dear Secundus, in investigating the cases of those who had been brought before you as Christians. For, indeed, it is not possible to establish any universal rule, possessing as it were a fixed form. These people should not be searched for; if they are informed against and convicted they should be punished; yet, so that he who shall deny being a Christian, and shall make this plain in action, that is by worshipping our gods, even though suspected on account of his past conduct, shall obtain pardon by his penitence. Anonymous informations, however, ought not to be allowed a standing in any kind of charge; a course which would not only form the worst of precedents, but which is not in accordance with the spirit of our time.

IV

DECREE OF HADRIAN

From Eusebius, *History of the Christian Church*, Book IV, Chapter 9. Translated by Edwin Fenton.

To Minucius Fundanus [*proconsul of Asia*]. I have received a letter written to me by Serennius Granianus, a most illustrious man, whom you have succeeded. It does not seem right to me to pass over the matter [*of the trials of Christians*] without investigation, because men can be persecuted without cause and informers can be given too many chances to practice evil ways. Therefore if witnesses can support this petition against the Christians and make their case stand up in a court of law, let them have recourse to this method, but not to mere hearsay evidence. It is quite proper, if anyone makes an accusation, for you to investigate the matter. If anyone therefore accuses Christians and shows that they are breaking the law, pass judgment according to the seriousness of the crime. But, by Hercules, if anyone accuses another falsely to do him injury, arrest the accuser and see to it that you punish him.

13th-Century France as Seen Through a Medieval Romance

Aucassin and Nicolette is a classic example of the stories told and sung by 13th-century French minstrels. In manor houses and at fairs in medieval towns, groups of people gathered around traveling singers to hear the old familiar tales. These sessions were the medieval movie, radio, and television rolled into one. They were a window to the outside world, to romance, and to the secret thoughts of men and women.

But they were fiction. The events described probably never took place; even if their origins were factual, retelling by generations of minstrels probably distorted fact until it became fiction. Nevertheless, historians have used minstrels' tales to learn more about the Middle Ages. One aspect of life they illuminate is the development of romantic love and its importance in marriage. For hundreds of years, marriage had been largely a business matter. Then, about the 12th century, there developed the chivalric ideal of courtly love — the devotion of a knight to the lady of the castle. The lyrics of the troubadours show that at first this sentiment had little to do with man and wife. Over the years, however, the attitude began to change. If a knight should love the lady he served, why not also love his wife? The delightful romance that follows presents, among other things, a 13th-century picture of love and marriage. It develops the theme of the conflict between the young, who want to marry for love, and the old, who emphasize family, wealth, and status.

Aucassin and Nicolette was written down in the early 1200's. Like most minstrel romances, it was not an original composition, but a reworked version of earlier material. Some scholars believe it may have been based on a Moorish tale. Its form of alternating prose and verse is oriental, and its hero's name may derive from the Arabic Alcazin or al-Kasim. The work survived in a single manuscript, which was rediscovered in 1752.

As you read the selections below, think about the following questions:

1 The word-portraits of Aucassin and Nicolette were probably stereotypes, not real-life descriptions. Is distortion such as this common in literature? What does it reveal about the way men often think? About what the nobility thought of themselves?

2 What can you infer about the class structure of the Middle Ages from this story?

3 What does this account reveal about the attitude of the nobility toward religion? See particularly Aucassin's remarks to the Viscount beginning "In Paradise what have I to do?"

4 What does the attitude of the vassals to Aucassin's leadership in battle indicate about the nature of personal relationships in feudalism?

5 For what type of evidence is fiction particularly useful to historians? For what should it not be used?

AUCASSIN AND NICOLETTE

From *Aucassin & Nicolette and Other Medieval Romances and Legends.* Translated by Eugene Mason. Dutton Paperback and Everyman's Library, pp. 1-3, 5-10, 13-14, 35-38. Reprinted by permission of E. P. Dutton & Co., Inc., New York, and J. M. Dent & Sons, Ltd., London.

Who will deign to hear the song
Solace of a captive's wrong,
Telling how two children met,
Aucassin and Nicolette;
How by grievous pains distraught,
Noble deeds the varlet wrought
For his love, and her bright face!
Sweet my rhyme, and full of grace,
Fair my tale, and debonair.
He who lists — though full of care,
Sore astonied, much amazed,
All cast down, by men mispraised,
Sick in body, sick in soul,
Hearing shall be glad and whole,
So sweet the tale.

Now they say and tell and relate:

How the Count Bougars of Valence made war on Count Garin of Beaucaire, war so great, so wonderful, and so mortal, that never dawned the day but that he was at the gates and walls and barriers of the town, with a hundred knights and ten thousand men-at-arms, on foot and on horse. So he burned the Count's land, and spoiled his heritage, and dealt death to his men. The Count Garin of Beaucaire was full of years, and frail; he had long outworn his day. He had no heir, neither son nor daughter, save one only varlet, and he was such as I will tell you. Aucassin was the name of the lad. Fair he was, and pleasant to look upon, tall and shapely of body in every whit of him. His hair was golden, and curled in little rings about his head; he had grey and dancing eyes, a clear, oval face, a nose high and comely, and he was so gracious in all good graces that nought in him was found to blame, but good alone. But Love, that high prince, so utterly had cast him down, that he cared not to become knight, neither to bear arms, not to tilt at tourneys, not yet to do aught that it became his name to do.

His father and his mother spake him thus — "Son, don now thy mail, mount thy horse, keep thy land, and render aid to thy men. Should they see thee amongst them the better will the men-at-arms defend their bodies and their substance, thy fief and mine."

"Father," said Aucassin, "why speakest thou in such fashion to me? May God give me nothing of my desire if I become knight, or mount to horse, or thrust into the press to strike other or be smitten down, save only that thou give me Nicolette, my sweet friend, whom I love so well."

"Son," answered the father, "this may not be. Put Nicolette from mind. For Nicolette is but a captive maid, come hither from a far country, and the Viscount of this town bought her with money from the Saracens, and set her in this place. He hath nourished and baptized her, and held her at the font. On a near day he will give her to some .young bachelor, who will gain her bread in all honour. With this what hast thou to do? Ask for a wife, and I will find thee the daughter of a king, or a count. Were he the richest man in France his daughter shalt thou have, if so thou wilt."

"Faith, my father," said Aucassin, "what honour of all this world would not Nicolette, my very sweet friend, most richly become! Were she Empress of Byzantium or of Allemaigne, or Queen of France or England, low enough would be her degree, so noble is she, so courteous and debonair, and gracious in all good graces."

Now is sung:

> Aucassin was of Beaucaire,
> Of the mighty castle there,
> But his heart was ever set
> On his fair friend, Nicolette.
> Small he heeds his father's blame,
> Or the harsh words of his dame.
> "Fool, to weep the livelong day,
> Nicolette trips light and gay.
> Scouring she from far Carthage,
> Bought of Paynims for a wage.
> Since a wife beseems thee good
> Take a wife of wholesome blood."
> "Mother, naught for this I care,
> Nicolette is debonair;
> Slim the body, fair the face,
> Make my heart a lighted place;

Love has set her as my peer,
Too sweet, my dear."

[*In the passage that follows, Count Garin, Aucassin's father, threatens the Viscount, Nicolette's guardian, and demands that she be sent away. The Viscount, in order to protect his ward, locks her in a tower of his palace. Aucassin then seeks out the Viscount, and asks for Nicolette.*]

"Fair sire," answered the Viscount, "put this from mind. Nicolette is a captive maid whom I brought here from a far country. For her price I trafficked with the Saracens, and I have bred and baptized her, and held her at the font. I have nourished her duly, and on a day will give her to some young bachelor who will gain her bread in honourable fashion. With this you have nought to do; but only to wed the daughter of some count or king. Beyond this, what profit would you have, had you become her lover, and taken her to your bed? Little enough would be your gain therefrom, for your soul would lie tormented in Hell all the days of all time, so that to Paradise never should you win."

"In Paradise what have I to do? I care not to enter, but only to have Nicolette, my very sweet friend, whom I love so dearly well. For into Paradise go none but such people as I will tell you of. There go those aged priests, and those old cripples, and the maimed, who all day long and all night cough before the altars, and in the crypts beneath the churches; those who go in worn old mantles and old tattered habits; who are naked, and barefoot, and full of sores; who are dying of hunger and of thirst, of cold and of wretchedness. Such as these enter in Paradise, and with them have I nought to do. But in Hell will I go. For to Hell go the fair clerks and the fair knights who are slain in the tourney and the great wars, and the stout archer and the loyal man. With them will I go. And there go the fair and courteous ladies, who have friends, two or three, together with their wedded lords. And there pass the gold and the silver, the ermine and all rich furs, harpers and minstrels, and the happy of the world. With these will I go, so only that I have Nicolette, my very sweet friend, by my side."

"Truly," cried the Viscount, "you talk idly, for never shall you see her more; yea, and if perchance you spoke together, and your father heard thereof, he would burn both me and her in one fire, and yourself might well have every fear."

"This lies heavy upon me," answered Aucassin.

Thus he parted from the Viscount making great sorrow.

Now is sung:

Aucassin departed thus
Sad at heart and dolorous;
Gone is she his fairest friend,
None may comfort give or mend,
None by counsel make good end.
To the palace turned he home,
Climbed the stair, and sought his room.
In the chamber all alone
Bitterly he made his moan,
Presently began to weep
For the love he might not keep.
"Nicolette, so gent, so sweet,
Fair the faring of thy feet,
Fair thy laughter, sweet thy speech,
Fair our playing each with each,
Fair thy clasping, fair thy kiss,
Yet it endeth all in this.
Since from me my love is ta'en
I misdoubt that I am slain;
Sister, sweet friend."

Now they say and tell and relate:

Whilst Aucassin was in the chamber lamenting Nicolette, his
friend, the Count Bougars of Valence, wishful to end the war, pressed
on his quarrel, and setting his pikemen and horsemen in array, drew
near the castle to take it by storm. Then the cry arose, and the tumult;
and the knights and the men-at-arms took their weapons, and hastened to the gates and the walls to defend the castle, and the burgesses
climbed to the battlements, flinging quarrels and sharpened darts
upon the foe. Whilst the siege was so loud and perilous the Count
Garin of Beaucaire sought the chamber where Aucassin lay mourning,
assotted upon Nicolette, his very sweet friend, whom he loved so well.

"Ha, son," cried he, "craven art thou and shamed that seest thy
best and fairest castle so hardly beset. Know well that if thou lose it
thou art a naked man. Son, arm thyself lightly, mount to horse, keep
thy land, aid thy men, hurtle into the press. Thou needest not to strike

another, neither to be smitten down, but if they see thee amongst
them, the better will they defend their goods and their bodies, thy
land and mine. And thou art so stout and strong that very easily thou
canst do this thing, as is but right."

"Father," answered Aucassin, "what sayest thou now? May God
give me nought that I require of Him if I become knight, or mount to
horse, or thrust into the press to strike knight or be smitten down, save
only thou givest me Nicolette, my sweet friend, whom I love so well."

"Son," replied the father, "this can never be. Rather will I suffer
to lose my heritage, and go bare of all, than that thou shouldest have
her, either as woman or as dame."

So he turned without farewell. But when Aucassin saw him part
he stayed him, saying—

"Father, come now, I will make a true bargain with thee."

"What bargain, fair son?"

"I will arm me, and thrust into the press on such bargain as this,
that if God bring me again safe and sound, thou wilt let me look on
Nicolette, my sweet friend, so long that I may have with her two
words or three, and kiss her one only time."

"I pledge my word to this," said the father.

Of this covenant had Aucassin much joy.

Now is sung:

> Aucassin the more was fain
> Of the kiss he sought to gain,
> Rather than his coffers hold
> A hundred thousand marks of gold.
> At the call his squire drew near,
> Armed him fast in battle gear;
> Shirt and hauberk donned the lad,
> Laced the helmet on his head,
> Girt his golden-hilted sword,
> Came the war-horse at his word,
> Gripped the buckler and the lance,
> At the stirrups cast a glance;
> Then most brave from plume to heel
> Pricked the charger with the steel,
> Called to mind his absent dear,
> Passed the gateway without fear
> Straight to the fight.

Now they say and tell and relate:

Aucassin was armed and horsed as you have heard. God! how bravely showed the shield about his neck, the helmet on his head, and the fringes of the baldric upon his left thigh. The lad was tall and strong, slender and comely to look upon, and the steed he bestrode was great and speedy, and fiercely had he charged clear of the gate. Now think not that he sought spoil of oxen and cattle, nor to smite others and himself escape. Nay, but of all this he took no heed. Another was with him, and he thought so dearly upon Nicolette, his fair friend, that the reins fell from his hand, and he struck never a blow. Then the charger, yet smarting from the spur, bore him into the battle, amidst the thickest of the foe, so that hands were laid upon him from every side, and he was made prisoner. Thus they spoiled him of shield and lance, and forthwith led him from the field a captive, questioning amongst themselves by what death he should be slain. When Aucassin marked their words,

"Ha, God," cried he, "sweet Creature, these are my mortal foes who lead me captive, and who soon will strike off my head; and when my head is smitten, never again may I have fair speech with Nicolette, my sweet friend, whom I hold so dear. Yet have I a good sword, and my horse is fresh. Now if I defend me not for her sake, may God keep her never, should she love me still."

The varlet was hardy and stout, and the charger he bestrode was right fierce. He plucked forth his sword, and smote suddenly on the right hand and on the left, cutting sheer through nasal and headpiece, gauntlet and arm, making such ruin around him as the wild boar deals when brought to bay by hounds in the wood; until he had struck down ten knights, and hurt seven more, and won clear of the melee, and rode back at utmost speed, sword in his hand.

The Count Bougars of Valence heard tell that his men were about to hang Aucassin, his foe, in shameful wise, so he hastened to the sight, and Aucassin passed him not by. His sword was yet in hand, and he struck the Count so fiercely upon the helm, that the headpiece was cleft and shattered upon the head. So bewildered was he by the stroke that he tumbled to the ground, and Aucassin stretched forth his hand, and took him, and led him captive by the nasal of the helmet, and delivered him to his father.

[*In the passages that follow, Count Garin refuses to keep his promise to Aucassin, who releases his captive, Count Bougars. Aucassin's father casts him into prison, where he is visited by Nicolette.*]

. . . . Her hair was golden, with little love-locks; her eyes blue and laughing; her face most dainty to see, with lips more vermeil than ever was rose or cherry in the time of summer heat; her teeth white and small; . . . so frail was she about the waist that your two hands could have spanned her, and the daisies that she brake with her feet in passing, showed altogether black against her instep and her flesh, so white was the fair young maiden.

[*Aucassin and Nicolette flee the country, but they become separated. Aucassin returns to his home to find his father, the Count, dead, and assumes his rightful place as Count. Nicolette is captured and taken to the court of Carthage where she discovers that she is the daughter of the king. Making her way back to Beaucaire, she arrives disguised as a minstrel, to sing to Aucassin.*]

> "Now I sing, for your delight,
> Aucassin, that loyal knight,
> And his fond friend, Nicolette.
> Such the love betwixt them set
> When his kinsfolk sought her head
> Fast he followed where she fled.
> From their refuge in the keep
> Paynims bore them o'er the deep.
> Nought of him I know to end.
> But for Nicolette, his friend,
> Dear she is, desirable,
> For her father loves her well;
> Famous Carthage owns him king,
> Where she has sweet cherishing.
> Now, as lord he seeks for her,
> Sultan, Caliph, proud Emir.
> But the maid of these will none,
> For she loves a dansellon,
> Aucassin, who plighted troth.
> Sworn has she some pretty oath
> Ne'er shall she be wife or bride,
> Never lie at baron's side
> Be he denied."

Now they say and tell and relate:
When Aucassin heard Nicolette sing in this fashion he was glad

at heart, so he drew her aside, and asked —

"Fair sweet friend," said Aucassin, "know you naught of this Nicolette, whose ballad you have sung?"

"Sire, truly, yes; well I know her for the most loyal of creatures, and as the most winning and modest of maidens born. She is daughter to the King of Carthage, who took her when Aucassin also was taken, and brought her to the city of Carthage, till he knew for certain that she was his child, whereat he rejoiced greatly. Any day he would give her for husband one of the highest kings in all Spain; but rather would she be hanged or burned than take him, however rich he be."

"Ah, fair sweet friend," cried the Count Aucassin, "if you would return to that country and persuade her to have speech with me here, I would give you of my riches more than you would dare to ask of me or to take. Know that for love of her I choose not to have a wife, however proud her race, but I stand and wait; for never will there be wife of mine if it be not her, and if I knew where to find her I should not need to grope blindly for her thus."

"Sire," answered she, "if you will do these things I will go and seek her for your sake, and for hers too; because to me she is very dear."

He pledged his word, and caused her to be given twenty pounds. So she bade him farewell, and he was weeping for the sweetness of Nicolette. And when she saw his tears —

"Sire," said she, "take it not so much to heart; in so short a space will I bring her to this town, and you shall see her with your eyes."

When Aucassin knew this he rejoiced greatly. So she parted from him, and fared in the town to the house of the Viscountess, for the Viscount her god-father, was dead. There she lodged, and opened her mind fully to the lady on all the business; and the Viscountess re-called the past, and knew well that it was Nicolette whom she had cherished. So she caused the bath to be heated, and made her take her ease for fully eight days. Then Nicolette sought a herb that was called celandine, and washed herself therewith, and became so fair as she had never been before. She arrayed her in a rich silken gown from the lady's goodly store; and seated herself in the chamber on a rich stuff of broidered sendal; then she whispered the dame, and begged her to fetch Aucassin, her friend. This she did. When she reached the palace, lo, Aucassin in tears, making great sorrow for the long tarrying of Nicolette, his friend; and the lady called to him, and said —

"Aucassin, behave not so wildly; but come with me, and I will show you that thing you love best in all the world; for Nicolette, your sweet friend, is here from a far country to seek her love."

So Aucassin was glad at heart.

Now is sung:

> When he learned that in Beaucaire
> Lodged his lady, sweet and fair,
> Aucassin arose, and came
> To her hostel, with the dame;
> Entered in, and passed straightway
> To the chamber where she lay.
> When she saw him, Nicolette
> Had such joy as never yet;
> Sprang she lightly to her feet
> Swiftly came with welcome meet.
> When he saw her, Aucassin
> Oped both arms, and drew her in,
> Clasped her close in fond embrace,
> Kissed her eyes and kissed her face.
> In such greeting sped the night,
> Till, at dawning of the light,
> Aucassin, with pomp most rare,
> Crowned her Countess of Beaucaire.
> Such delight these lovers met,
> Aucassin and Nicolette.
> Length of days and joy did win,
> Nicolette and Aucassin,
> Endeth song and tale I tell
> With marriage bell.

The Medieval Cathedral
in its Cultural Setting

The medieval cathedral is considered to be one of the world's artistic master-pieces. Each year thousands of American tourists stand in awe beneath the magnificent buildings of Notre Dame de Paris or Mont Saint Michel. They admire the soaring arches, the flying buttresses, and the stained glass windows which sweep the eye toward heaven. Yet many of these tourists are unaware of the vital and unique place of the cathedral in the life of the Middle Ages.

Like other artistic masterpieces, the cathedral grew out of a particular cultural setting. Its development and many of its special features were out-growths of the era that gave it birth. In order to understand the cultural significance of the cathedral, the student must know the political, economic, social, aesthetic, and religious environment in which it grew. Once this setting is understood, the cathedral takes on added meaning as an aesthetic experi-ence. The cathedral becomes an expression of its age.

As you read, consider the following questions:

1 How was the medieval cathedral related to its political, economic, social, and religious setting?

2 Would you say that contemporary architecture is as closely related to its environment as the cathedral was?

3 Do you feel that the author is correct in attributing American sky-scrapers only to youthful enthusiasm?

4 Do you see any relationship between our approach to the study of the cathedral and the manner in which Howells analyzed the Neolithic Revolution?

THE CATHEDRAL BUILDERS / by Jean Gimpel

Translated by Carl F. Barnes, Jr. Published by Grove Press, Inc.,
1961. Pp. 37-52. Reprinted by permission of Éditions du Seuil.

There is no need to emphasize that the true point of departure of the cathedral crusade is to be found in the religious faith of the Middle Ages. Circumstances were particularly favorable to the flowering of such architectural manifestations of piety. It goes without saying that if the Middle Ages had not been pre-eminently a pious age, the builders' genius and the merchants' money would have been used in other ways, and there would be no Chartres, no Amiens, no Strasbourg. . . .

The enthusiasm for cathedral building began during the second thirty years of the twelfth century: at Sens about 1130, Noyon in 1151, in Laon in 1160, in Paris in 1163. It reached its maximum intensity in the last three decades of the century and the first three of the thirteenth: Chartres in 1194, Bourges by 1195, Rouen in 1200, Mans in 1217, Reims in 1211, Amiens in 1221, and Beauvais in 1247. This enthusiasm sustained itself for one generation, long enough for the work on these buildings to get well under way; then, little by little, the passionate interest in construction fell off and, although work continued, it was less active in the last third of the thirteenth century and the first decades of the fourteenth. For all practical purposes, the Hundred Years' War, beginning in 1337, closed the workshops, and despite renewed efforts at the end of the war, in 1453, no French cathedral was ever completely finished. . . .

The history of cathedral construction and the builders is directly related to the revival of free cities and commerce, to the birth of a middle class and the first urban freedoms. In the early Middle Ages, urban life diminished, little by little, merchants disappeared, municipal organization died. Technical knowledge that had survived from antiquity fell into disuse; if only a few men had carefully preserved the secret of stonecutting, it would not have taken several centuries of groping to discover a satisfactory new system.

Strictly speaking, there were no cities left, only fortified castles. Europe became an agricultural continent in which all wealth lay in the land. Western economy bogged down and national income reached its lowest ebb. Then, beginning in the tenth century, a relative peace was established: profit-seeking vagabonds and displaced adventurers began transporting goods from one corner of Europe to the other, thus reestablishing commerce. These men installed themselves at the confluences of rivers or at important crossroads, and their activity helped cities to revive. Farsighted landowners contacted these energetic groups and encouraged them to establish towns. . . .

From the first, the mode of life in these urban groups contrasted with that of a society living solely from the land. Laws that regulated an agrarian society were unsatisfactory controls over these commercial newcomers, who frequently rioted with arms to set up a municipal organization and win legal and administrative autonomy. Out of these riots came the first communes — legal associations sanctioned by royal charters. The oldest commune north of the Alps is Cambrai, dating from 1077, and the communal movement extended to other cities such as Sens, Noyon, Laon, Rouen, Reims, Amiens, and Beauvais. Other cities (Paris, for example) were not subject to taxation. And all these cities built great cathedrals.

As noted above, there was a close relationship between the

commercial strength of the cities, their independence, and ecclesiastical construction. Nearly all the cities that gained urban independence were located on important overland or river trade routes.
In the Massif Central, a region relatively difficult to cross, there were
few communes or large cathedrals. The situation was similar in
Brittany, which lay outside the important trade routes and in which
no communes or cathedrals were found in the twelfth and thirteenth
centuries.

The spirit of the medieval bourgeois played a decisive role in the
cathedral crusade because it was inspired by a deep local patriotism.
Proud of having wrested his freedom from the feudal lord, he wanted
the Church and city to know his joy — nothing was so marvelous or so
important! The city was his, and he wanted to impress strangers with
the magnificence of his churches. A young nation's enthusiasm is
often expressed in colossal and immeasurable ways. It was young
Egypt that built the pyramids, works of the first dynasties. The
United States has surpassed all previous records [for tall buildings]
by building skyscrapers higher and higher. The Empire State Building culminated this drive for height with its 102 floors, a total height
of 1472 feet.

This young medieval society was symbolized by its bourgeois.
His enthusiasm permeated by a desire to break records, he constantly
raised his cathedral naves higher and higher. In 1163, Notre-Dame de
Paris began its record construction to result in a vault 114 feet 8
inches from the floor. Chartres surpassed Paris in 1194, eventually
reaching 119 feet 9 inches. In 1212 Reims started to rise to 124 feet
3 inches, and in 1221 Amiens reached 138 feet 9 inches. This drive to
break records reached its climax in 1247 with the project to vault the
choir of Beauvais 157 feet 3 inches above the floor — only to have the
vaults collapse in 1284.

By this time the Middle Ages was reaching maturity. The middle
class was becoming less dynamic, the desire to break records burned
out. When Saint-Urban de Troyes — a glass building — was built, it was
conceived in a new spirit. Today the United States is in the same
situation. The industrial middle class, although unwilling to admit it,
is lethargic. A new nation's desire to set records no longer interests
it. The celebrated Lever Building, constructed on New York's Park
Avenue in 1953, is a glass structure, but only thirty stories high. It
symbolizes a turning point in the American psychology.

Bourgeois civic pride, the desire to conquer new worlds, and merchants' vexed souls all contributed to the success of the cathedral crusade. But there were other factors that contributed to the financing of these edifices. From the middle of the twelfth century, the idea of going to the Holy Land was no longer as popular as it had been earlier. Why? Because Jerusalem had been in Christian hands since 1099? Because no one realized the constant menace the Moslems presented to France? Because everyone remembered the difficulties of the First Crusade? Because the taste for luxury and riches began to spread? The Church always authorized those in charge of the fabric to grant indulgences to anyone helping to build God's House. It was no longer necessary to go on a crusade to atone for sins. The cathedral crusade took form, and the entire ecclesiastical hierarchy from Pope to simple parish priest contributed to it spiritually and financially. . . .

God's House was the earthly image of the Heavenly Jerusalem, and it was a beautiful thing: it was the house of adoration, the house of the people. In most ancient religions, the people did not have access to the sanctuary. But the Christian church, by contrast, demanded that her faithful contribute to the construction of churches large enough for the populace to have access. Ecclesiastical law emphasized the difference between the sanctuary and the remaining area of the cathedral. During the Middle Ages, Notre-Dame de Paris belonged not to the bishop, but to the chapter whose jurisdiction ended at the sanctuary, which was reserved for the bishop, as was true for all cathedral sanctuaries. Naves and side aisles were reserved especially for worshipers, that is, for the people. This distinction is important because, otherwise, the twentieth-century spirit is likely to be offended by the worldly activities that went on inside these medieval churches. People slept, ate, talked openly, and brought animals—dogs and falcons—inside. Circulation was much freer than now because there were no chairs. Often the most secular matters were discussed inside the churches. Communal representatives met in the cathedral to discuss city business, and it has been noted that in some of the communes with large cathedrals the burghers did not even build a city hall. There is at least one text forbidding a commune to use the cathedral as a meeting hall, proof enough that it was a common occurrence. It was evidently not a right in itself, but simply tolerated by the Church. At Marseille, meetings of the guild masters, councils, and business leaders were regularly held in the Church of the Major. Presumably, communal representatives helped finance the city cathedral with the idea of holding their meetings there.

If this supposition is disturbing it must be remembered that these men lived in daily contact with the divinity. They were probably much less intimidated by the Lord than the modern Christian who encounters God at best every Sunday morning in his parish church.

Following this line of thought, account must be taken of professional organizations that did not consider it disrespectful to make announcements in the Cathedral of Chartres. Examining the church closely, it becomes evident that the guilds obtained the best possible placement for their windows. They are installed along the side aisles or in the ambulatory nearest the public, while glass donated by bishops and lords was relegated to the clerestory windows of the nave and choir. The cloth merchant, the stonecutter, the wheelwright, and the carpenter each had himself depicted in a medallion in the lower part of the window donated by his guild, as close as possible, as it were, to future clients.

Numerous feasts increased the contact between God and medieval man, explaining in part the latter's passion for enlarging and beautifying his church. Never has a civilization offered so many holidays to its peasants and workers. In February, 1956, France voted three weeks of annual vacation plus ten legal feast days for every citizen, and in so doing became the world's first country to give its citizens anything approximating what was granted by the Church in the Middle Ages. It should be remembered that in former times the working day was much longer than today. Frequently it began at dawn and ended at sundown. The number of annual feasts varied according to the year and town in question. In fifty-two weeks, there was an average of thirty feast days, noted in workshop accounts. In the accounts of the Cistercian abbey at Vale Royal, England, in 1280, twenty-nine feast days are specified. Idle days brought no pay in the Middle Ages, although today employers are legally bound to give pay on some feast days. . . .

. . . the medieval working population was not overburdened with work. Indeed, it ought to be envied rather than pitied, for its leisure was magnificently organized by the authorities and absolutely free. It is not unlikely that the medieval laborer's leisure had a considerable influence on the cathedral crusade and the work of enlarging the churches.

The Church masterfully organized ceremonies and processions. One can only try to imagine the splendor of medieval religious feasts. Probably only the services in St. Peter's in Rome adequately recall those of the past. On important feast days, ecclesiastical authorities concentrated their efforts on ceremonies in the cathedral, to the detriment of those taking place in parish churches. The congregations from various parishes usually wanted to attend the services in the cathedral. This is analogous to the situation today when it is announced that an international soccer match is to be played in a city's largest stadium. On the big day, the population rushes to the game *en masse*, abandoning local stadiums in which matches of only sectional importance are being played. Thus those stadiums scheduling international matches must be as large as possible. For comparable reasons . . . the medieval cathedral had to be sufficiently large to accommodate crowds coming from every part of the city. Faced with an influx of the faithful, authorities were constantly pressed to enlarge their cathedrals. The area of some was increased to handle a larger number of worshipers than the total inhabitants of the city, space being opened for peasants from neighboring parish churches. . . .

The curious or devout passer-by, approaching the portal, enjoyed recognizing sculptured figures of Old and New Testament characters close to his heart and soul. The thing that made the Middle Ages moving and amicable was this: the lettered and the ignorant had the same book of images, and they received the same education, the only difference being one of degree. Several centuries later it was different. The educated man of the Renaissance, in cultivating antiquity to excess, had mythological scenes painted and sculpted that were simply incomprehensible to the general public. The introduction of the humanities abruptly separated the masses from men of learning —a situation that to this day has not been completely rectified in western Europe.

Advancing into the church, the bourgeois found other familiar scenes. Until about the middle of the twelfth century, the book of images opened itself on frescoed walls and vaults, as in Saint-Savin, for example. Then, little by little, windows become larger as wall space contracted, providing light but limiting the opportunity to paint large frescoes. After that time, the book of images was inscribed in the beautiful stained glass windows.

Under the cathedral vaults—another aspect of medieval harmony —men of all social conditions met side by side. The bourgeois found the peasant as well as the bishop, the nobleman, and even the king. The great men of the realm came to pray in the cathedral and gave generously for its munificence.

Mohammed as a Man
of his Time

In this volume we have already examined some aspects of Judaism, Christianity, and the religion of the ancient Babylonians; we shall focus our attention on religion again in later readings. When historians study religions, they should not try to answer questions about the truth of religious doctrines. Such questions cannot be proved to the satisfaction of all men by using the discipline of the historian. They depend upon faith for their answers and so cannot be proved true or false by factual evidence.

When a historian examines a religious institution or set of beliefs, he often looks for connections between the religion and the culture of which it is a part. Such relationships can be seen between the religion and the life of the Babylonians, the Jews, and the Christians. However, historians have much more evidence about both Islam and its setting than they have about most earlier religions. Your reading today indicates the conclusions a skilled historian can draw from such information. It should be read carefully to see whether Muller gives sufficient evidence to support his interpretation.

Islam has been and still is one of the most vital forces in the world. The followers of Islam swept over Africa and much of Asia in great religious wars during and after the time of Mohammed. During the early Middle Ages, Moslem centers of learning preserved much of the knowledge accumulated by the Greeks and Romans. Renaissance scholars often found priceless remnants of classical manuscripts only in Arab libraries. In our own day, Islam is the religious faith of millions of men, particularly in North Africa and Asia.

As you read, consider the following questions:

1 What were some of the influences of time and place upon Mohammed? Would you expect other religious leaders to come under similar influences?

2 In the sixth paragraph, the author writes that Mohammed "was a great man, superior to his time and place." What standards of judgment for greatness is he employing here? Are these standards good ones?

3 In the fifth paragraph from the end of the essay, the author advances several possible explanations for the fact that Mohammed retained the sacred Black Stone. Why would the author do this?

4 Do you feel that Muller's comparisons between Islam and Christianity are valid? Note particularly the quotation in the next-to-last paragraph.

THE LOOM OF HISTORY / by Herbert J. Muller

Pp. 264-273 from The Loom of History by Herbert J. Muller. Copyright © 1958 by Herbert Joseph Muller. Reprinted with the permission of Harper & Row, Publishers, Incorporated.

As an avowed mortal, Mohammed was naturally influenced by his time and place. The religion of the Arabs before him was a very primi-

tive one. Their holy of holies was the Kaaba—the Black Stone of
Mecca. . . . Together with nature spirits, the Arabs worshiped
various goddesses. . . . Allah himself was ancient—a thousand
years before Mohammed the Persians wrote that "Allah is exalted"—
but he was only one of many deities. All this refutes the seductive and
popular idea of [*French historian Ernest*] Renan that monotheism is
the "natural religion of the desert." Mohammed himself was not a
man of the desert. He was a man of Mecca: a busy, prosperous city
on a caravan route (like Petra and Palmyra before it), which largely
controlled the overland trade between the Indian and the Mediterranean oceans, and which confronted the Prophet with the familiar
problem of the rich and the poor. He shared in the chief spiritual
possession of the Arabs aside from the Kaaba—their poetry. In their
passion for poetry and their common illiteracy, the Arabs developed
a prodigious capacity for memorizing that enabled them to preserve
the Koran. The scattered verses of the Prophet had been inscribed
not only on date leaves and shreds of leather but on "the hearts of
men."

On his own heart had been inscribed more than Arab tradition.
There were large numbers of Jews and Christians in Arabia, including
many converted Arabs . . . . Mohammed had direct relations with
colonies of Jews in and about Medina. In the Koran he displayed an
acquaintance with their Scriptures, if an imperfect one (he declared
that the Jews worshiped Ezra as the son of God); often he used
Biblical characters to preach his doctrines. Of Christian Scriptures he
had a more limited, garbled knowledge, or at least he felt freer to
reinterpret them, in an original and somewhat incongruous fashion.
Thus he denied the divinity of Christ and rejected the Crucifixion as a
Jewish falsehood, while for some reason he accepted the miraculous
birth (perhaps because there were paintings of Jesus and Mary on the
inner walls of the Kaaba). But he identified Allah with the God of
Judaism and Christianity. He borrowed other ideas foreign to Arab
tradition, notably the Last Judgment and the resurrection of the flesh,
which the Arabs of Mecca thought ridiculous and revolting. We cannot
know to what extent he consciously borrowed, and may assume that
he was more deeply indebted than he realized. . . . In any case, his
basic teaching is unmistakably in the line of Judaism and Christianity.

The key events of Mohammed's career are also beyond dispute.
After some forty years of respectable but obscure life, during which
his abilities in business won him the confidence and the hand of a

rich widow, he felt his calling as a prophet. In his belief, the Angel
Gabriel appeared to him and dictated this calling . . . . His subsequent career supports the tradition that he was at first appalled by
God's orders, knowing that there would be no more sleep or rest for
him. Like Jesus, he was from the beginning opposed by the most
powerful, respectable, God-fearing members of his community.
Men said: "Shall we forsake our gods for a mad poet?" Although he
won over a few influential men, most of his early converts came from
among the poor people and the slaves of Mecca. The mockery of the
respectable turned to violent hostility when his preaching threatened
the profitable business of Mecca as the sanctuary of all Arabia, the
hostelry for the annual pilgrimage. The persecution of Mohammed
was so effective that conceivably his mission might have failed had
not a few men come from Medina one year to hear his message, and
returned home as missionaries. Finally, in A.D. 622, after thirteen
years of generally disheartening and increasingly dangerous obedience to God's orders, he fled in the night and sought refuge in Medina
— the hegira that marks the beginning of the Mohammedan era with
a certainty that cannot be claimed for the beginning of the Christian
era.

   At Medina the Prophet entered the triumphant phase of his
career, and the most dubious for a man of God. He became the
political as well as spiritual leader of a community. He waged war
against the Meccans, initiating hostilities by raiding one of their
caravans in the holy month of pilgrimage, when war was banned in
Arabia; to justify his aggression, he preached war against idolaters as
a sacred duty (jihad). With a force of only three hundred, he routed
some thousand Meccans in the piddling but momentous battle of
Badr, and later proved his generalship by holding off much larger
forces sent against him. He also attacked several wealthy Jewish
communities, which had refused to recognize him as a prophet. When
one of them surrendered after a short siege, he had all its men put
to death and its women and children sold into slavery. By these
campaigns he won much booty as well as prestige; one may suspect
that it was not so much his spiritual message as his worldly success
that now drew the Arabs to Allah. At length the Meccans gave in:
eight years after the hegira, Mohammed returned to his native city
in triumph. As he then proved his wisdom and clemency by putting
only four people to death, the Meccans accepted him as the apostle
of Allah and joined his army. In the short time left to him he sent an

expeditionary force to attack a Byzantine outpost in Syria. In the year 632 Mohammed shocked and confused his followers by dying. Most had refused to take his own word that he was a mortal.

Now Mohammed had certainly not lived like an angel. While often preaching an otherworldly gospel, he was a worldly man, with a shrewd eye to both political and economic interests. He enjoyed the company of a number of concubines in addition to his eleven wives. Most troublesome is his addiction to war. One may argue that in the Arabia of his time he could not have succeeded except by war . . . but the fact remains that his was no gospel of love, no message of peace and good will on earth. In preaching the holy war he could sound very naïve: the special rewards in Paradise he promised to martyrs who fell in battle included marriage to "seventy dark-eyed virgins." His preaching involved some bloody texts as well: "It is not for a Prophet to hold captives till he hath dealt slaughter through the earth." To all but pious Moslems Mohammed is bound to seem a distinctly fallible mortal, limited by his time and place. If his is indeed God's final revelation to man, the Lord have mercy on us.

Yet as certainly Mohammed was a great man, superior to his time and place. He not only preached but practiced a morality that was lofty for his society. If he could be ruthless, he was more often gentle, kind, generous, magnanimous. He could be Christlike in his sympathy for the weak and poor. Through the pious fog of tradition one catches many glimpses of an attractive humanity, as in his unfailing courtesy touched by shyness, his fondness for jokes and fun, his humble sharing of the household chores, his wry indulgence of the frailties of his womenfolk, his tolerance of the foibles of the companions. One can understand why he was so deeply loved by those around him. As one reads of his death and of the quiet unaffected way in which he met it, one may almost share the grief of the companions, if not their bewilderment. Say the worst about his human limitations, and there remain a heroic and inspired life, a complete dedication to the service of his God, and a power of personality that made as deep an impression on his followers as Jesus made on his, in some ways a more lasting impression. . . .

The Koran is much harder for Westerners to admire. In Arabic, one gathers, it makes a magnificent music that still moves its readers to tears and ecstasy. In translation it strikes most Westerners as an uninspired work, occasionally eloquent but more often dully didactic, and on the whole loose, incoherent, and insufferably repetitious. The

Angel Gabriel who dictated it to Mohammed seems most prosaic when he retells Biblical stories, as in the whole sura (chapter) on Joseph and his brethren. There are dull enough passages in the Old Testament, but few — even among unbelievers — would call it a mediocre book, as many do the Koran.

Our major concern, however, is the teaching of the Koran. Here the difficulty is that Mohammed was hardly a clear, consistent thinker, if a thinker at all. He did not reason — he merely preached or revealed, as the spirit dictated. The difficulty is aggravated by the lack of logical or chronological order in the suras of the Koran. Although Moslems make out a subtle sequence, to outsiders the only apparent principle is the arbitrary one of putting first the longer suras, which are generally the later ones chronologically. We must remember, at any rate, that Mohammed at first spoke as the prophet of a weak minority sect in Mecca, unable to enforce his will, given to calling himself the "Warner"; then as leader of an independent, increasingly strong community in Medina, and in this capacity both as prophet and statesman; and finally as the triumphant ruler of a temporal kingdom — the one great religious leader whose career ended in worldly success, rather than sacrifice or renunciation. . . .

Even so, his basic teaching is clearer and more nearly uniform than that attributed to Jesus by the diverse authors of the New Testament. The theme of more than half of the Koran is an insistence on an absolutely pure monotheism, a denunciation of all forms of polytheism and idolatry. "There is no god but God." Allah is the God preached by the prophets, from Abraham and Ishmael through Moses to Jesus, and revealed in the Scriptures of the Jews and the Christians; Abraham was the true founder of the faith, Mohammed the last prophet, and the Koran the final, complete, perfect revelation, correcting the false beliefs that had corrupted Judaism and Christianity. In particular Mohammed repudiated the ideas that Allah had a Son and a Mother, or was part of a Trinity, and with them all the elaborate theology that Christianity had spun around its Godhead. While admitting angels and the old Arabian jinn, the bad ones of whom were led by "the Satan" or Eblis, he rejected all human intermediaries between Allah and man — the priests and monks whom men "have taken as lords beside Allah." Like Yahweh, Allah strictly banned all images, which might also become objects of worship. . . .

For the rest, Mohammed spelled out in minute detail the ceremonial and ethical requirements of Allah, many of them drawn from

Arab custom. The major ceremonial duties were the daily prayers, fasting during the holy month of Ramadan (in which the Koran had been revealed), and the pilgrimage to Mecca. The latter involved a major concession to pagan idolatry — the retention of the sacred Black Stone. Possibly Mohammed felt obliged to make this concession, or shrewdly calculated it as a means of uniting the Arabs behind him and making Islam a national crusade; just as possibly he had a sincere reverence for the ancient shrine of his people, in the belief that it had been set up by Abraham. He was not free from superstition. He also retained the jinn, and his prescriptions included some primitive taboos, such as those on the eating of pork and strangled animals. . . .

Otherwise both the strength and the weakness of Mohammedan ethics derive from the definiteness of the Prophet. A practical, literal-minded man, addressing a relatively rude, lawless people, he was more specific than Jesus in condemning current evils, such as idolatry and infanticide, and in defining humane conduct, as in the treatment of women and slaves. Moslems could not so easily distort his teachings, rationalize their violation of them, as Christians could take liberties with the Gospels. But in his definiteness he tied his ethical system to the peculiar customs and limited ideals of his age. He positively legalized slavery, for instance, as he did polygamy and war. His prescriptions were likely to be unsuited to the needs of a developed civilization, while the more general teaching of Jesus could always remain a guide and inspiration. And both the strength and the weakness were more pronounced because Mohammed was laying down the law for a kingdom of this world, laying the foundations of a theocratic state.

Christianity grew up under a highly developed political state with a complete system of law. When it triumphed, the Church had to adjust itself to this state; later Christian nations would continue to operate on the basis of a secular law. In Mohammed's Arabia there was no state — there were only scattered independent tribes and towns. The Prophet formed his own state, and he gave it a sacred law prescribed by Allah. Moslem nations would continue to base their law on their religion; in theory there was no confusion between the things that are Caesar's and the things that are God's. Still, a system designed for the small cities of Mecca and Medina was scarcely adequate for great nations and empires, and there would in fact be considerable confusion. . . .

In one view, Mohammed unquestionably purified Judaism and in
particular Christianity. Allah was a truly universal God, with no
chosen people, no feelings about race, and he shared the Godhead
with no one; there was no metaphysical nonsense about him. Likewise Mohammed purified the worship of the One God. He abolished
the hierarchical priesthood, the monkery, the sacraments, and the
elaborate ceremonials that had got between the simple worshiper and
God. He made the daily prayers a pure act of adoration, not a petition
for special favors or a bribe. Even in the most splendid mosques the
worshipers of Allah perform their individual devotions with a modest
piety and decorum that might justify Byron's saying, that the calls of
the muezzin were preferable to all the bells of Christendom. The
mosque is neither a place of mystery nor a social center for the
Sabbath. "Islam set the terms of a new experiment in human religion,"
concluded Professor Gibb, "an experiment in pure monotheism,
unsupported by any of the symbolism or other forms of appeal to the
emotions of the common man, which had remained embedded in the
earlier monotheistic religions." . . .

All this is by no means the whole truth about Islam. It is an important part of the truth, however, and historically the most enduring
part. It must be kept in mind as we consider the actual influence of
the Koran on history. Islam inspired new peoples, such as the Seljuk
Turks, and embarked on new adventures, especially when it discovered the thought and learning of the Greeks.

A Hindu View of Life

Americans living in the 20th century have found that many people in the world do not believe as they do. Foreigners often act in ways we find bewildering. They seem to live according to a completely different set of assumptions about the nature of man and the universe. How can we understand peoples whose customs and traditions are so unlike our own? Can the study of history help us to know the way they think? The reading below provides insights into some of the customs of India quite different from our own.

India was conquered by northern invaders known as Aryans around 1500 B.C. The Aryan conquerors sought to maintain their identity in the midst of millions of Dravidian natives with whom they came into daily contact and whom they regarded as inferiors. Thus they regulated social and cultural relationships, rigorously discriminating against the Dravidians.

During the period between 1500 and 500 B.C., there evolved a four-part system with the priests (Brahmans, or Brahmins) at the top and the nobles, farmers, and serfs (Sudras) beneath them. Gradually this division, as well as numerous other circumstances, led to an elaborate caste system with hundreds of different castes. Rules of conduct forbade an upper-caste Indian to touch food prepared by one of a lower caste, or to speak to him. One was also expected to marry within one's own caste.

Closely connected with the caste system was the idea, derived from Hindu religious beliefs, that the individual soul would be reincarnated, or reborn into a new life in this world. Only by living a good life could one hope to climb the social ladder through reincarnation. Thus Brahmans, enjoying the highest status in society, came to believe that they had earned their position in earlier incarnations. Each individual enjoyed the station in life which his previous existences merited. These beliefs implied that everyone should be satisfied with his station and should attempt to live such an exemplary existence that there would be hope for advancement in his next life. The ultimate goal of a Hindu was release from the cycle of reincarnation and absorption into the world-soul.

The following reading is taken from a story in the *Upanishads*, a group of writings believed to have been composed around 500 B.C. The word means "to sit down near something" and relates to the idea of learning at the feet of a teacher and meditating to acquire knowledge of the Self (Brahma, or Brahman).

As you read, keep in mind the following questions:

1 What do these passages lead you to believe concerning the Hindu attitude toward life?

2 What did Nachiketa ask of the King of Death? Why did he desire these things?

3 How did the King of Death try to trick Nachiketa? How does the speech of the King of Death exemplify the statements concerning Hinduism found in the introduction and in your text readings?

4 How do the value systems of the Hindus differ from those implied in the Code of Hammurabi and the Old Testament? from your own value system?

"KATHA," from THE UPANISHADS

The Upanishads, Breath of the Eternal, edited by Swami Prabhavananda and Frederick Manchester. New York: Mentor Books, New American Library, 1948. Copyright Vedanta Society of Southern California. Pp. 14-20.

On a certain occasion Vajasrabasa, hoping for divine favor, performed a rite which required that he should give away all his possessions. He was careful, however, to sacrifice only his cattle, and of these only such as were useless—the old, the barren, the blind, and the lame. Observing this niggardliness, Nachiketa, his young son, whose heart had received the truth taught in the scriptures, thought to himself: "Surely a worshiper who dares bring such worthless gifts is doomed to utter darkness!" Thus reflecting, he came to his father, and cried:

"Father, I too belong to thee: to whom givest thou *me*?"

His father did not answer; but when Nachiketa asked the question again and yet again, he replied impatiently:

"Thee I give to Death!"

Then Nachiketa thought to himself: "Of my father's many sons and disciples I am indeed the best, or at least of the middle rank, not the worst; but of what good am I to the King of Death?" Yet, being determined to keep his father's word, he said:

"Father, do not repent thy vow! Consider how it has been with those that have gone before, and how it will be with those that now live. Like corn, a man ripens and falls to the ground; like corn, he springs up again in his season."

Having thus spoken, the boy journeyed to the house of Death.

But the god was not at home, and for three nights Nachiketa waited. When at length the King of Death returned, he was met by his servants, who said to him:

"A Brahmin, like to a flame of fire, entered thy house as guest, and thou wast not there. Therefore must a peace offering be made to him. With all accustomed rites, O King, thou must receive thy guest, for if a householder show not due hospitality to a Brahmin, he will lose what he most desires—the merits of his good deeds, his righteousness, his sons, and his cattle."

Then the King of Death approached Nachiketa and welcomed him with courteous words.

"O Brahmin," he said, "I salute thee. Thou are indeed a guest worthy of all reverence. Let, I pray thee, no harm befall me! Three nights hast thou passed in my house and hast not received my hospitality; ask of me, therefore, three boons—one for each night."

"O Death," replied Nachiketa, "so let it be. And as the first of these boons I ask that my father be not anxious about me, that his anger be appeased, and that when thou sendest me back to him, he recognize me and welcome me."

"By my will," declared Death, "thy father shall recognize thee and love thee as heretofore; and seeing thee again alive, he shall be tranquil of mind, and he shall sleep in peace."

Then said Nachiketa: "In heaven there is no fear at all. Thou, O Death, are not there, nor in that place does the thought of growing old make one tremble. There, free from hunger and from thirst, and far from the reach of sorrow, all rejoice and are glad. Thou knowest, O King, the fire sacrifice that leads to heaven. Teach me that sacrifice, for I am full of faith. This is my second wish."

Whereupon, consenting, Death taught the boy the fire sacrifice, and all the rites and ceremonies attending it. Nachiketa repeated all that he had learned, and Death, well pleased with him, said:

"I grant thee an extra boon. Henceforth shall this sacrifice be called the Nachiketa Sacrifice, after thy name. Choose now thy third boon."

And then Nachiketa considered within himself, and said:

"When a man dies, there is this doubt: Some say, he is; others say, he is not. Taught by thee, I would know the truth. This is my third wish."

"Nay," replied Death, "even the gods were once puzzled by this mystery. Subtle indeed is the truth regarding it, not easy to understand. Choose some other boon, O Nachiketa."

But Nachiketa would not be denied.

"Thou sayest, O Death, that even the gods were once puzzled by this mystery, and that it is not easy to understand. Surely there is no teacher better able to explain it than thou—and there is no other boon equal to this."

To which, trying Nachiketa again, the god replied:

"Ask for sons and grandsons who shall live a hundred years. Ask for cattle, elephants, horses, gold. Choose for thyself a mightly kingdom. Or if thou canst imagine aught better, ask for that—not for sweet pleasures only but for the power, beyond all thought, to taste their sweetness. Yea, verily, the supreme enjoyer will I make thee of every good thing. Celestial maidens, beautiful to behold, such indeed as were not meant for mortals—even these, together with their bright chariots and their musical instruments, will I give unto thee, to serve thee. But for the secret of death, O Nachiketa, do not ask!"

But Nachiketa stood fast, and said: "These things endure only till the morrow, O Destroyer of Life, and the pleasures they give wear out the senses. Keep thou therefore horses and chariots, keep dance and song, for thyself! How shall he desire wealth, O Death, who once has seen thy face? Nay, only the boon that I have chosen—that only do I ask. Having found out the society of the imperishable and the immortal, as in knowing thee I have done, how shall I, subject to decay and death, and knowing well the vanity of the flesh—how shall I wish for long life?

"Tell me, O King, the supreme secret regarding which men doubt. No other boon will I ask."

Whereupon the King of Death, well pleased at heart, began to teach Nachiketa the secret of immortality.

King of Death

The good is one thing; the pleasant is another. These two, differing in their ends, both prompt to action. Blessed are they that choose the good; they that choose the pleasant miss the goal.

Both the good and the pleasant present themselves to men. The wise, having examined both, distinguish the one from the other. The wise prefer the good to the pleasant; the foolish, driven by fleshly desires, prefer the pleasant to the good.

Thou, O Nachiketa, having looked upon fleshly desires, delightful to the senses, hast renounced them all. Thou hast turned from the miry way wherein many a man wallows.

Far from each other, and leading to different ends, are ignorance and knowledge. Thee, O Nachiketa, I regard as one who aspires after knowledge, for a multitude of pleasant objects were unable to tempt thee.

Living in the abyss of ignorance yet wise in their own conceit, deluded fools go round and round, the blind led by the blind.

To the thoughtless youth, deceived by the vanity of earthly possessions, the path that leads to the eternal abode is not revealed. *This world alone is real; there is no hereafter*—thinking thus, he falls again and again, birth after birth, into my jaws.

To many it is not given to hear of the Self. Many, though they hear of it, do not understand it. Wonderful is he who speaks of it. Intelligent is he who learns of it. Blessed is he who, taught by a good teacher, is able to understand it.

The truth of the Self cannot be fully understood when taught by an ignorant man, for opinions regarding it, not founded in knowledge, vary one from another. Subtler than the subtlest is this Self, and beyond all logic. Taught by a teacher who knows the Self and Brahman as one, a man leaves vain theory behind and attains to truth. . . .

The goal of worldly desire, the glittering objects for which all men long, the celestial pleasures they hope to gain by religious rites, the most sought-after of miraculous powers — all these were within thy grasp. But all these, with firm resolve, thou hast renounced.

The ancient, effulgent being, the indwelling Spirit, subtle, deep-hidden in the lotus of the heart, is hard to know. But the wise man, following the path of meditation, knows him, and is freed alike from pleasure and from pain.

The man who has learned that the Self is separated from the body, the senses, and the mind, and has fully known him, the soul of truth, the subtle principle — such a man verily attains to him, and is exceeding glad, because he has found the source and dwelling place of all felicity. Truly do I believe, O Nachiketa, that for thee the gates of joy stand open. . . .

Know that the Self is the rider, and the body the chariot; that the intellect is the charioteer, and the mind the reins.

The senses, say the wise, are the horses; the roads they travel are the mazes of desire. The wise call the Self the enjoyer when he is united with the body, the senses, and the mind.

When a man lacks discrimination and his mind is uncontrolled, his senses are unmanageable, like the restive horses of a charioteer. But when a man has discrimination and his mind is controlled, his senses, like the well-broken horses of a charioteer, lightly obey the rein.

He who lacks discrimination, whose mind is unsteady and whose heart is impure, never reaches the goal, but is born again and again. But he who has discrimination, whose mind is steady and whose heart is pure, reaches the goal, and having reached it is born no more . . . .

Brahman is the end of the journey. Brahman is the supreme goal. This Brahman, this Self, deep-hidden in all beings, is not revealed to all; but to the seers, pure in heart, concentrated in mind — to them is he revealed.

The senses of the wise man obey his mind, his mind obeys his intellect, his intellect obeys his ego, and his ego obeys the Self.

Arise! Awake! Approach the feet of the master and know *THAT*. Like the sharp edge of a razor, the sages say, is the path. Narrow it is, and difficult to tread!

Soundless, formless, intangible, undying, tasteless, odorless, without beginning, without end, eternal, immutable, beyond nature, is the Self. Knowing him as such, one is freed from death.

Confucius on Good Government

Although wave after wave of conquerors have swept across China, the essential elements of ancient Chinese culture remained unchanged until recent years. Centuries before the birth of Christ, Chinese culture had sunk its roots deep into the soil of its venerable villages. The invaders, simple and crude in comparison, generally climbed to the Chinese cultural level after a few generations in the new land. The long and continuous life of Chinese culture and its ability to absorb invaders rested upon an entrenched set of traditions stretching back 2500 years. Centuries ago the Chinese people reached general agreement about the nature of good and evil, about proper and improper behavior, and about what rules should govern personal relationships. The man who gave these principles their classic form was Confucius, who lived almost a century before the greatest days of Periclean Athens.

We know very little about the life of Confucius despite his importance to Chinese history. During his lifetime China was torn by war among a number of small states which the ruling Chou dynasty was unable to control. Disturbed by this anarchy, Confucius sought a ruler who would employ him to put his philosophy into practice. He believed that in a few short years of power he could set the entire society aright by his good example. Finding no one who would grant his wish, he retired to a life of teaching, hoping that his students would some day be able to prove that, with good men in power, oppression of man by man would cease.

Confucianism was not a religion; it was a social and political philosophy and a code of right behavior. Confucius was concerned with the relationship, not of man to God, but of man to his fellow man. The most important of human relationships was that between children and parents. According to Confucius, proper filial relations—based on the respect and obedience which everyone owed the head of his family—provided the foundation for all other human ties.

More than anything else, Confucius was concerned about good government. With it, he believed, society would be stable, the state safe and secure, and the people happy. The Confucian idea of good government was remarkably simple: let a good ruler set an example for his subjects to follow. He will thus earn their respect and they will obey him; the relationship is the political equivalent of that between father and son.

Like Thomas Jefferson, Confucius thought that government should be placed in the hands of the most able men in the country and that these men should come from all social classes, low as well as high. Real ability was not the result of birth but of character produced by excellent education. Through education and rituals, men of ability would learn and pass on the values of the past. In order to recruit an elite, the Chinese eventually set up a civil service based on examinations, an institution that lasted for centuries. The conservatism and reverence for the past which characterize Confucian thought became a part of the Chinese national character.

Many political scientists would not agree that virtuous men following moral laws make the best rulers. Niccolò Machiavelli, an Italian writer of the

Renaissance, argued that princes should obey no moral rules at all but should let the ends justify the means (see Problem 13). This issue — the relationship of moral rules and government — is one which should concern every citizen in a democracy. It should also concern young historians, who ought to investigate the merits of the issue.

Many of the sayings and rules of Confucius were recorded by his students in *The Analects*, brief discourses and dialogues. Although the ideas and the way they are expressed may strike the Western student as strange, *The Analects* provide one of the best insights available into the character of the Chinese people.

As you read these excerpts, consider the following questions:

1 Would men who studied and believed the philosophy of Confucius respect old men or young ones more? List the passages which contain evidence to answer this question.

2 According to Confucius, how should good men govern? What passages support your answer? Do you think that men who followed the advice of Confucius would be successful rulers?

3 According to Confucius, should a good ruler use force to make men obey his commands? What arguments does Confucius give to support his position? Do you agree?

4 Do you think that good rulers have been able to make good citizens by example? Have the most successful rulers refused to be bound by the rules of fair conduct that govern personal relationships?

THE ANALECTS OF CONFUCIUS

Reprinted with permission of the publishers from *The Analects of Confucius*, translated by Arthur Waley. Copyright 1939 by The Macmillan Company, New York, and George Allen & Unwin, Ltd., London. Pp. 88-89, 92-93, 102-103, 168-169.

BOOK II

1. The Master said, He who rules by moral force . . . is like the pole-star, which remains in its place while all the lesser stars do homage to it.

2. The Master said, If out of the three hundred *Songs* I had to take one phrase to cover all my teaching, I would say "Let there be no evil in your thoughts."

3. The Master said, Govern the people by regulations, keep order among them by chastisements, and they will flee from you, and lose all self-respect. Govern them by moral force, keep order among them by ritual and they will keep their self-respect and come to you of their own accord.

4. The Master said, At fifteen I set my heart upon learning.

At thirty, I had planted my feet firmly upon the ground. At forty, I no longer suffered from perplexities. At fifty, I knew what were the biddings of Heaven. At sixty, I heard them with docile ear. At seventy, I could follow the dictates of my own heart; for what I desired no longer overstepped the boundaries of right.

5. Mêng I Tzu asked about the treatment of parents. The Master said, Never disobey! When Fan Ch'ih was driving his carriage for him, the Master said, Mêng asked me about the treatment of parents and I said, Never disobey! Fan Ch'ih said, In what sense did you mean it? The Master said, While they are alive, serve them according to ritual. When they die, bury them according to ritual and sacrifice to them according to ritual.

6. Mêng Wu Po asked about the treatment of parents. The Master said, Behave in such a way that your father and mother have no anxiety about you, except concerning your health.

7. Tzu-yu asked about the treatment of parents. The Master said, "Filial sons" nowadays are people who see to it that their parents get enough to eat. But even dogs and horses are cared for to that extent. If there is no feeling of respect, wherein lies the difference?

8. Tzu-hsia asked about the treatment of parents. The Master said, It is the demeanour that is difficult. Filial piety does not consist merely in young people undertaking the hard work, when anything has to be done, or serving their elders first with wine and food. It is something much more than that. . . .

18. The Master said, Hear much, but maintain silence as regards doubtful points and be cautious in speaking of the rest; then you will seldom get into trouble. See much, but ignore what it is dangerous to have seen, and be cautious in acting upon the rest; then you will seldom want to undo your acts. He who seldom gets into trouble about what he has said and seldom does anything that he afterwards wishes he had not done, will be sure incidentally to get his reward.

19. Duke Ai asked, What can I do in order to get the support of the common people? Master K'ung [that is, K'ung-fu-tse, or Confucius] replied, If you "raise up the straight and set them on top of the crooked," the commoners will support you. But if you raise the crooked and set them on top of the straight, the commoners will not support you.

20. Chi K'ang-tzu asked whether there were any form of encouragement by which he could induce the common people to be respectful and loyal. The Master said, Approach them with dignity,

and they will respect you. Show piety towards your parents and kindness towards your children, and they will be loyal to you. Promote those who are worthy, train those who are incompetent; that is the best form of encouragement.

22. The Master said, I do not see what use a man can be put to, whose word cannot be trusted. How can a waggon be made to go if it has no yoke-bar or a carriage, if it has no collar-bar?

23. Tzu-chang asked whether the state of things ten generations hence could be foretold. The Master said, We know in what ways the Yin [*Shang*] modified ritual when they followed upon the Hsia. We know in what ways the Chou modified ritual when they followed upon the Yin. And hence we can foretell what the successors of Chou will be like, even supposing they do not appear till a hundred generations from now.

24. The Master said, Just as to sacrifice to ancestors other than one's own is presumption, so to see what is right and not do it is cowardice.

BOOK IV

1. The Master said, It is Goodness that gives to a neighborhood its beauty. One who is free to choose, yet does not prefer to dwell among the Good—how can he be accorded the name of wise?

2. The Master said, Without Goodness a man

    Cannot for long endure adversity,

    Cannot for long enjoy prosperity.

The Good Man rests content with Goodness; he that is merely wise pursues Goodness in the belief that it pays to do so.

3, 4. Of the adage "Only a Good Man knows how to like people, knows how to dislike them," the Master said, He whose heart is in the smallest degree set upon Goodness will dislike no one.

5. Wealth and rank are what every man desires; but if they can only be retained to the detriment of the Way he professes, he must relinquish them. Poverty and obscurity are what every man detests; but if they can only be avoided to the detriment of the Way he professes, he must accept them. The gentleman who ever parts company with Goodness does not fulfil that name. Never for a moment does a gentleman quit the way of Goodness. He is never so harried but that he cleaves to this; never so tottering but that he cleaves to this.

6. The Master said, I for my part have never yet seen one who really cared for Goodness, nor one who really abhorred wickedness.

One who really cared for Goodness would never let any other consideration come first. One who abhorred wickedness would be so constantly doing Good that wickedness would never have a chance to get at him. Has anyone ever managed to do Good with his whole might even as long as the space of a single day? I think not. Yet I for my part have never seen anyone give up such an attempt because he had not the *strength* to go on. It may well have happened, but I for my part have never seen it.

7.   The Master said, Every man's faults belong to a set. If one looks out for faults it is only as a means of recognizing Goodness.

8.   The Master said, In the morning, hear the Way; in the evening, die content! . . .

BOOK XII

19.   Chi K'ang-tzu asked Master K'ung about government, saying, Suppose I were to slay those who have not the Way in order to help on those who have the Way, what would you think of it? Master K'ung replied saying, You are there to rule, not to slay. If you desire what is good, the people will at once be good. The essence of the gentleman is that of wind; the essence of small people is that of grass. And when a wind passes over the grass, it cannot choose but bend.

20.   Tzu-chang asked what a knight must be like if he is to be called "influential." The Master said, That depends on what you mean by "influential." Tzu-chang replied saying, If employed by the State, certain to win fame, if employed by a Ruling Family, certain to win fame. The Master said, That describes being famous; it does not describe being influential. In order to be influential a man must be by nature straightforward and a lover of right. He must examine men's works and observe their expressions, and bear in mind the necessity of deferring to others. Such a one, whether employed by the State or by a Ruling Family, will certainly be "influential"; whereas the man who wins fame may merely have obtained, by his outward airs, a reputation for Goodness which his conduct quite belies. Anyone who makes his claims with sufficient self-assurance is certain to win fame in a State, certain to win fame in a Family.

21.   Once when Fan Ch'ih was taking a walk with the Master under the trees at the Rain Dance altars, he said, May I venture to ask about "piling up moral force," "repairing shortcomings" and

"deciding when in two minds"? The Master said, An excellent question. "The work first; the reward afterwards"; is not that piling up moral force? "Attack the evil that is within yourself; do not attack the evil that is in others." Is not this "repairing shortcomings"?

"Because of a morning's blind rage

To forget one's own safety

And even endanger one's kith and kin"

is that not a case of "divided mind"?

22.   Fan Ch'ih asked about the Good (ruler). The Master said, He loves men. He asked about the wise (ruler). The Master said, He knows men. Fan Ch'ih did not quite understand. The Master said, By raising the straight and putting them on top of the crooked, he can make the crooked straight. Fan Ch'ih withdrew, and meeting Tzu-hsia said to him, Just now I was with the Master and asked him about the wise (ruler). He said, By raising the straight and putting them on top of the crooked he can make the crooked straight. What did he mean?

Tzu-hsia said, Oh, what a wealth of instruction is in those words! When Shun had all that is under Heaven, choosing from among the multitude he raised up Kao Yao, and straightway Wickedness disappeared.

The Case for Cultural Diffusion

Anthropologists—those who study man and his works from earliest times to the present—have always been especially interested in peoples who have no written history, such as the American Indians. Scholars agree that the Indians are descended from peoples that crossed the Bering Strait from Asia thousands of years ago. What happened after they arrived, however, is a matter of great controversy. Anthropologists used to assume that Indian civilizations developed by independent invention—that is, that the Indians climbed the ladder from Stone Age culture to the complex civilizations of the Incas and Mayas in isolation from other peoples. Similarities in the cultures of the Indians and those of the peoples of Asia, the Pacific islands (Oceania), and the Mediterranean world were explained by the argument that cultures everywhere developed in approximately the same way, passing through the same stages. The "psychic unity" of mankind produced similar "elementary ideas," which in turn led to the growth of similar cultural patterns without transplanting ideas or institutions from one culture to another. This is somewhat like saying, "Necessity is the mother of invention."

In recent years, a few anthropologists have attacked this explanation. Arguing that the societies of Central and South America seem to have developed at a remarkable rate of speed and in patterns common in Asia and the Pacific islands, these scholars believe that some diffusion must have taken place. Diffusion means that traits of one culture are transmitted to another; this process, of course, requires cultural contact. But how could this contact be made? Some of the diffusionists argue that Melanesians and Polynesians, many of whom had been in contact with Asian and even with Mediterranean peoples, sailed across the broad Pacific and landed in the Americas, bringing with them many of the culture traits later observed by European explorers.

The reading below, excerpts from Harold S. Gladwin's book *Men Out of Asia*, is an example of this point of view. Although the author is not a professional anthropologist, he is thoroughly trained in scientific techniques and has written widely in the field. Not all anthropologists have been won over to Gladwin's position. In his foreword to the book, Earnest A. Hooton, a Harvard anthropologist, states his position on the matter: "I, myself, do not agree with all Gladwin's theories and conclusions hereinafter set forth. In fact, I am profoundly skeptical of some of them . . . . I think that Harold Gladwin is at times resoundingly right, and at other times magnificently wrong."

Hooton's statements make it clear that the particular subject you are about to explore is a controversial one. But the general idea of cultural diffusion is important for historians to understand because so many basic ideas and institutions have been spread in this way. Think, for example, about the manner in which industrialism traveled from one Western nation to another and from the West to the underdeveloped world.

As you read, think about the following issues:

1 What evidence does Gladwin present to support his argument for diffusion? Make a list of the major pieces of evidence. Is it convincing?

2 If diffusion does not explain this evidence, can you develop another explanation?

3 What additional evidence bearing on the hypothesis of diffusion would you look for to help you make up your mind about this problem? For example, how can a diffusionist explain the fact that American Indians never knew about the potter's wheel until white explorers came?

4 How should a historian or an anthropologist decide when a hypothesis has been proved? Should he expect to find final proof or should his explanations remain tentative in case further evidence shows up?

MEN OUT OF ASIA / by Harold S. Gladwin

The landing on the west coasts of Middle and South America of Melanesians who later turned out to be Caribs, and of Polynesians who later turned out to be Arawaks, is such an obvious and logical explanation for the presence of Oceanian culture traits in these regions that you may be making the mistake of thinking that this explanation solves all of our problems. It doesn't. There are some things such as polished red pottery, metallurgy and fancy textile techniques which were characteristic of some of the advanced cultures from Mexico down to Peru and which were not known in Polynesia.

For these we must go even farther west, to the sources of the Polynesians themselves—to Indonesia, India and the Near and Middle East. Fortunately the trail is clear and it is simply a case of following your nose, if you happen to have one that is built on the generous lines of the Armenoid model.

When Alexander's fleet left Susa in 323 B.C. the ships were manned by men from the Near East. They wore the costumes with which we are all familiar—short tunics, a fez or else a Grecian crested helmet, quilted armor—and for weapons they used slings, short stabbing clubs, and broad-bladed spears.

Inside their broad, flattened skulls they carried the knowledge of their day, and what with their different nationalities—Greek, Armenian, Syrian, Persian, Cretan, Egyptian; their campaigns in Greece, Asia Minor, Palestine, Egypt, Mesopotamia, Afghanistan and India, and particularly their intermingling in Alexander's many and various Alexandrias, their knowledge, collectively, was comprehensive. And, of equal or even greater importance, they had picked up a large following of natives from India who could be expected to know their stuff.

So from the center of the splash in western Asia, it is simply a case of picking up the intermediate ripples until the last little wavelet laps the beach in the Gulf of Panama.

You will have no trouble picking out your own ripples . . . . First, you ask yourself if there is any evidence of the means by which culture could have been diffused from Polynesia to South America, and you look over your shelves and take down anything that has a bearing on the subject. If you happen to have Nordenskiöld's *Ethnographical Studies* you are off to a good start, as these are a gold mine of information even if they were written to disprove what you intend to prove. Here are plenty of facts and these are what we need; everyone is entitled to his own opinions of what such facts may mean.

You begin by looking for some sort of a craft that would be capable of making the voyage across the Pacific, and you can at once rule out rafts and coracles as being impractical. So you look up "canoes" in any good index—such as in Dixon's *Building of Cultures*, Wissler's *American Indian,* or Linton's *Study of Man*—and you will probably find that they have listed bark canoes, dugouts and plank canoes as too flimsy for your purpose. An ordinary dugout, made by hollowing out a large log by the use of fire and an adz, is good and sturdy but would have too low a freeboard for a long ocean voyage unless the sides could be raised.

Plank canoes are more what you are looking for. . . . In Polynesia, where boatbuilding has always been a fine art, even from early times, someone conceived the brilliant idea of making a dugout and then raising the sides by adding planks. The joints were covered with battens, sewed and caulked, and the bow and stern were further strengthened with solid pieces of wood, usually carved with elaborate patterns. This, of course, was a great improvement as the dugout base gave greater stability than a plank bottom, and the plank sides raised the freeboard, which had been the chief weakness of the dugout.

Another contraption adding immeasurably to the seaworthiness of a canoe was the outrigger. This was a device consisting of two booms lashed horizontally across the sides, amidship, and projecting outward to a cigar-shaped float parallel to the canoe. In some cases, a double outrigger was used with a float on either side, but the single type appears to have been more popular and was known throughout the southwestern Pacific and westward into the Indian Ocean. It was undoubtedly this combination of dugout, plank sides and outrigger that made it possible for Melanesians first, and later Polynesians, to colonize the islands of the Pacific. There is no record of the outrigger in the New World, however, and our search is not yet ended.

You will find just what you are looking for in the double canoe, in which another full-sized canoe took the place of the outrigger, and this brings us around again to the great planksewn double canoes mentioned by Captain Cook in Chapter XXIII, where we were dealing with the colonization of Polynesia. Now we are primarily concerned with the voyages from outer Polynesia to the Americas, and it will be necessary to run down references to show that the double canoe was known in the New World if we are going to prove our case.

Nordenskiöld starts you off with the double canoe listed for Peru, Central America, Mexico, Melanesia and Polynesia. But, although this is encouraging, it may occur to you that if the double canoe was known in America and Oceania it may have had even wider distribution, and so you look up Pitt-Rivers' *Evolution of Culture*, let us say, and find that he also lists this type of craft as having been used in Melanesia and Polynesia, but adds Ceylon, Burma, the Malabar Coast of southwestern India, and the Ganges as far up as Patna. Of even greater importance, however, Pitt-Rivers also includes the Waraus of Guiana, in South America, and the Ahts of the northwest coast of North America. . . .

Now, how about a sail? You can begin in Peru where the Spaniards found them in use on boats large enough to carry 50 men. Canoes, equipped with sails, and capable of carrying 50 men, strike another familiar chord, and as there is no reason to suppose that the Spaniard who saw it was dreaming—or trying his hand at independent invention—you can chalk it up. Nordenskiöld is even more encouraging and lets you have both square and triangular sails in Peru and Central America. Pitt-Rivers, among others, will supply you with the triangular or lateen sail all the way through the South Pacific, the Indian Ocean and up to the Mediterranean.

The only other thing about a boat that you need is something with which to steer or to propel the craft for short distances if becalmed. You will not have to look farther than Nordenskiöld, who gives a paddle with a so-called crotched handle—a sort of cap for the top of the paddle, carved to fit the hand—known from Colombia, Panama,

Mexico, the Amazon and our northwest coast to Melanesia and Polynesia.

Next you ask yourself what the people could have carried as food, and Nordenskiöld tells you that there are three plants which are found to be the same in America as well as in Polynesia: coconut palms in Colombia and Panama, sweet potatoes in Peru, and a calabash known as *Lagenaria vulgaris* over most of South America. You already know that some men think that sweet potatoes were carried *from* South America to Polynesia, and as to coconuts and calabashes, it has not yet been claimed that they were independently invented. The calabash is a large hardshelled gourd which was hollowed out and used to hold lime or liquids, and, although we have never tried to eat one, it is probably as palatable, judging by our own tastes, as summer squash.

While on the subject of calabashes, there is a useful quotation from Nordenskiöld to back up our tale in an earlier chapter:

"A parallel between Chinese and [*American*] Indian culture is duckhunting with a calabash. In a place where duck are usually found, calabashes are thrown on the water and left to float about until the duck are used to them. When the duck are no longer afraid of the calabashes, the Indians cover their heads with a sort of mask made from calabash shell, and stalk the duck with only the mask showing above the water. The duck, which have lost their timidity of the empty calabashes, do not fear the hunter concealed in the calabash mask, and allow themselves to be caught with the bare hands.

"In America this strange method of hunting is known from Mojos, Maracaibo, Haiti, Chiriqui, and Mexico. Du Halde reports it from China."

You can also add to your list the same kind of fishhook in America and Polynesia, and the same method of stupefying fish by putting poison in their pools. We do not recommend this for modern practice since the game wardens might regard it as taking a rather unfair advantage, but for downright meanness we know of nothing worse than tying a string around a cormorant's neck, letting him catch a fish, and then taking it away from him, as they did in China and Peru. . . . One other labor-saving device was employed in the West Indies and also on the coasts of India, where they used sucking fish on the end of a string to catch turtles, all according to Nordenskiöld. . . .

Then you can ask yourself what may have happened when land was reached and the men went ashore. If they were as smart as we think they were, they would undoubtedly have made ready for a scrap.

Some would don their helmets—and here we pause to say that these must be seen to be believed. They were tight-fitting caps of wickerwork, surmounted by a curved crest, the whole covered with feathers and exactly the same shape as the Greek helmet of the days of Alexander. The resemblance is so perfect that the question has been raised as to whether they were not copies from late European models, but this idea was scotched by Captain Cook who found them in fashion in Hawaii when this first European contact with Polynesia was made. The same type of helmet has been reported from Melanesia and you will also find illustrations of crested helmets on Mochica pottery in Peru.

Some wore fezzes, as in the Near East, Polynesia and Peru. Others wore turbans around their heads, and it would be difficult to tell whether they came from India or Mexico. You need only to glance at some of the turbaned figurines from Arbolillo, in the valley of Mexico, to realize how deeply such evidence would affect us.

Some men wore bark corsets. Others protected their tummies with quilted or rod armor. Some used slings, as in South America and Polynesia; some had blowguns, as in Colombia, Panama, Mexico, Peru and Oceania; all probably used the short stabbing clubs so suggestive of Greek models, which were used in Polynesia and also profusely illustrated in Mexican codices and on old Peruvian pottery.

Both round and square shields were carried, and some men may have tried to raise themselves above the din of battle by climbing on stilts—if they were fighting in Central America or Oceania. Those who were fussy about their hands used knuckle-dusters, as in Peru, Central America and Polynesia. A nasty piece of work, in the form of a club, was the stone macehead shaped like a five-pointed star— presumably to prevent skidding off thick skulls—from Peru, Central America and Melanesia. There was also the wicked-looking wooden sword of Polynesia which had cutting edges of inlaid shark's teeth; in Mexico they substituted obsidian, more in the style of the old, Egyptian flint-edged swords. . . .

Bamboo was also used for daggers in Colombia, Panama and Oceania; perhaps men were called to battle with the conch trumpets of Colombia, Panama, Peru, Mexico and Oceania; and they may have flashed back the news of how things were going on the same kind of signal gong in Colombia, Panama and Melanesia.

Then, when the shouting and tumult had died down, by listening carefully one might have heard a simple tune played on Panpipes in either Melanesia, Colombia, Panama, or Peru. In case you do not know them by name, Panpipes are ingenious little musical instruments which came originally from Greece. . . . It is interesting, and some may regard it as significant, that the pipes in Melanesia and those in South America have been shown by Hornbostel to have tonal identity and the same pitch.

Some of the women might have settled down on the same wooden stools and started weaving on the same Arawak looms or on the same lattice baskets, whether they were in Colombia, Panama or Melanesia. Other women would take care of the wounded by putting wooden pillows under their heads, cooling them by waving plaited fans, boiling water in bamboo sections, or maybe sending out a call for a Medicine Man to come and do a job of bloodletting with the same venesection bow used in Colombia, Panama and Melanesia. If skulls needed a little attention, the treatment might call for trepanning if the patient happened to be in Peru, Central America or Oceania.

Those men who had survived without injury might decide to relax, and taking their calabashes filled with lime they would first remove the swizzle stick which also served as a stopper, lick off some lime, and chew a plant — tobacco, if in Mexico; coca, if in South America; or betel, if in Oceania. Then, while they were reclining, a fellow might draw near in a grotesque mask and offer to do a quick job of tattooing, or piercing a septum for a nose plug or the lobe of an ear for an earplug, or punch a hole in a cheek for a lip stud, or drill a few teeth for fancy inlays — the job would have been the same in either South America or Oceania.

Chasing down analogies is fun, but we don't want to run them into the ground; it is even more fun to dig them up. . . . you may be growing weary of hearing that the ways and means of life were so much the same in Colombia, Panama, Mexico, Peru and Oceania.

You may also be thinking that what we have been saying sounds good enough for an episode, like a battle and its aftermath, but what did they do afterward? Did they settle down and go to work?

They did.

A Milestone in
Constitutional Government

Magna Charta is one of the most famous documents in all history. Written in 1215 by feudal barons and accepted at the point of the sword by King John of England, this famous pact has often been viewed as the source of almost all British freedoms. However, students of history should understand its limitations and should be careful not to distort its meaning.

Magna Charta was a feudal document; in no sense did it signal the advent of democracy in England. It came as the result of a long series of events which revealed John as untrustworthy, cruel, and greedy. The English barons, having inherited rights from their ancestors, resisted the king's attempts to violate these rights and run the country as he pleased. In forcing the king to sign the charter, the nobles sought only specific remedies for particular abuses.

The chronological chart shows the major events of John's reign. These are divided into three categories, according to whether they were concerned with France, internal affairs (particularly taxation), or the Church. Study the chart carefully before reading excerpts from Magna Charta itself, so that you can place this document in its proper historical setting.

Pay close attention to the following questions:

1   Was Magna Charta confined to granting privileges only to the barons?

2   What possible beginnings of constitutional government do you detect in these excerpts from Magna Charta? Can you find specific references that seem to suggest the following: (a) limitations on executive power; (b) no taxation without representation; (c) trial by jury; (d) respect for property rights; (e) supremacy of national law.

3   What seems most significant about Clause 61? Is it a clear-cut right to revolt?

4   Is it possible to discern from this reading the form of future parliamentary institutions?

MAGNA CHARTA

From "Magna Carta (1215)" in *Sources of English Constitutional History*, edited and translated by Carl Stephenson and Frederick George Marcham. Copyright 1937 by Carl Stephenson and Frederick George Marcham. Reprinted with the permission of the publishers, Harper & Row, Publishers, Incorporated. Pp. 115-121, 125-126.

John, by the grace of God king of England, lord of Ireland, duke of Normandy and of Aquitaine, and count of Anjou, to his archbishops, bishops, abbots, earls, barons, justiciars, foresters, sheriffs, reeves, ministers, and all his bailiffs and faithful men, greeting. Know that, through the inspiration of God, for the health of our soul and [the

RELATIONS WITH FRANCE	INTERNAL EVENTS	CHURCH AFFAIRS

1199 John becomes King of England

1200 John acknowledges Philip Augustus of France as overlord of his French possessions.	**1200** John offends English barons by divorcing Isabella of Gloucester.	
1202 John angers French nobles by marrying Isabella of Angouleme, betrothed to one of his French vassals.		
Philip Augustus deprives John of French lands for his failure to do homage.		
	1203 John's nephew murdered; John suspected.	
1204 Philip gains Normandy from John.		
1204-1206 John loses Maine, Touraine, Anjou, Poitou, and Brittany to Philip.	**1205** John assesses duty of 1/15 on exports and imports.	**1205** Office of Archbishop of Canterbury becomes vacant. Monks choose one candidate; John, another. Pope Innocent III refuses to recognize either.
	1207 Special tax of 1/13 levied on all movable property.	**1207** Special tax assessed on Church.
		Pope names Stephen Langton Archbishop of Canterbury; John refuses to accept him.
		1208 Pope places England under interdict.
		John seizes Church revenues.
		1209 John excommunicated.
	1210 Jews taxed £44,000.	
	1212-1213 Great inquiry conducted into feudal dues.	**1213** Innocent asks Philip Augustus to invade England; John submits to Pope and accepts him as feudal lord of England. John recognizes Langton.
		Langton proposes reforms to check royal despotism.
1214 French defeat English at Battle of Bouvines.	**1214** John levies heavy scutage to pay for French expedition.	

1215 Magna Charta

souls] of all our ancestors and heirs, for the honour of God and the
exaltation of Holy Church, and for the betterment of our realm, by
the counsel of our venerable fathers . . . of our nobles . . . and of
our other faithful men . . . .

2.   If any one of our earls or barons or other men holding of us
in chief dies, and if when he dies his heir is of full age and owes
relief [*sum paid to the lord of an estate by an heir when the latter
takes possession*], [that heir] shall have his inheritance for the ancient
relief: namely, the heir or heirs of an earl £100 for the whole barony
of an earl; the heir or heirs of a baron £100 for a whole barony; the
heir or heirs of a knight 100s, at most for a whole knight's fee [*fief*].
And let whoever owes less give less, according to the ancient custom
of fiefs. . . .

12.   Scutage [*tax paid by tenant of a knight's fief, usually instead
of military service*] or aid shall be levied in our kingdom only by the
common counsel of our kingdom, except for ransoming our body,
for knighting our eldest son, and for once marrying our eldest daughter; and for these [purposes] only a reasonable aid shall be taken. The
same provision shall hold with regard to the aids of the city of London.

13.   And the city of London shall have all its ancient liberties
and free customs, both by land and by water. Besides we will and
grant that all the other cities, boroughs, towns, and ports shall have
all their liberties and free customs.

14.   And in order to have the common counsel of the kingdom
for assessing aid other than in the three cases aforesaid, or for assessing scutage, we will cause the archbishops, bishops, abbots, earls,
and greater barons to be summoned by our letters individually; and
besides we will cause to be summoned in general through our sheriffs
and bailiffs, all those who hold of us in chief—for a certain day,
namely at the end of forty days at least, and to a certain place. And
in all such letters of summons we will state the cause of the summons;
and when the summons has thus been made, the business assigned
for the day shall proceed according to the counsel of those who are
present, although all those summoned may not come. . . .

17.   Common pleas [*civil lawsuits*] shall not follow our court, but
shall be held in some definite place. . . .

20.   A freeman shall be amerced [*fined*] for a small offence only
according to the degree of the offence; and for a grave offence he shall
be amerced according to the gravity of the offence, saving his con-
tenement [*except for his land*]. And a merchant shall be amerced in

the same way, saving his merchandise; and a villein [*serf*] in the same way, saving his wainage [*farm implements*] – should they fall into our mercy. And none of the aforesaid amercements shall be imposed except by the oaths of good men from the neighbourhood. . . .

28.   No constable or other bailiff of ours shall take grain or other chattels of anyone without immediate payment therefor in money, unless by the will of the seller he may secure postponement of that [payment]. . . .

35.   There shall be one measure of wine throughout our entire kingdom, and one measure of ale; also one measure of grain, namely, the quarter of London; and one width of dyed cloth, russet [cloth], and hauberk [cloth], namely, two yards between the borders. With weights, moreover, it shall be as with measures. . . .

39.   No freeman shall be captured or imprisoned or disseised [*dispossessed*] or outlawed or exiled or in any way destroyed, nor will we go against him or send against him, except by the lawful judgment of his peers or by the law of the land.

40.   To no one will we sell, to no one will we deny or delay right or justice. . . .

51.   And immediately after the restoration of peace we will remove from the kingdom all alien knights, crossbowmen, serjeants, and mercenaries, who have come with horses and arms to the injury of the kingdom. . . .

61.   Since moreover for [the love of] God, for the improvement of our kingdom, and for the better allayment of the conflict that has arisen between us and our barons, we have granted all these [liberties] aforesaid, wishing them to enjoy those [liberties] by full and firm establishment forever, we have made and granted them the following security: namely, that the barons shall elect twenty-five barons of the kingdom, whomsoever they please, who to the best of their ability should observe, hold, and cause to be observed the peace and liberties that we have granted to them and have confirmed by this our present charter; so that, specifically, if we or our justiciar or our bailiffs or any of our ministers are in any respect delinquent toward any one or transgress any article of the peace or the security, and if the delinquency is shown to four barons of the aforesaid twenty-five barons, those four barons shall come to us, or to our justiciar if we are out of the kingdom, to explain to us the wrong, asking that without delay we cause this wrong to be redressed. And if within a period of forty days, counted from the time that notification is made to us,

or to our justiciar if we are out of the kingdom, we do not redress the wrong, or, if we are out of the kingdom, our justiciar does not redress it, the four barons aforesaid shall refer that case to the rest of the twenty-five barons, and those twenty-five barons, together with the community of the entire country, shall distress and injure us in all ways possible — namely, by capturing our castles, lands, and possessions and in all ways that they can — until they secure redress according to their own decision, saving our person and [the person] of our queen and [the persons] of our children. And when redress has been made, they shall be obedient to us as they were before. . . . And neither of ourself nor through others will we procure from any one anything whereby any of these concessions and liberties may be revoked or diminished; and should anything of the sort be procured, it shall be null and void, and we will never make use of it either of ourself or through others. . . .

63.   Wherefore we wish and straitly enjoin that the English Church shall be free and that the men in our kingdom shall have and hold all the aforesaid liberties, rights, and grants well and in peace, freely and quietly, full and completely, for themselves and their heirs from us and our heirs, in all things and in all places forever, as aforesaid. Moreover, it has been sworn both on our part and on the part of the barons that all the aforesaid [provisions] shall be observed in good faith and without malicious intent. . . .

By the witness of the aforesaid men and of many others. Given by our hand in the meadow that is called Runnymede between Windsor and Staines, June 15, in the seventeenth year of our reign.

Machiavelli and Realistic Politics

Niccolò Machiavelli taught the world a lesson in practical politics. He was born in 1469, the son of a lawyer, and grew up in the Italian city of Florence. In 1498 he obtained a minor clerical post in the Florentine government, a job he held for fourteen years. He became a trusted public servant and eventually a diplomat, traveling to every important city-state in the peninsula and to several foreign courts as well.

Everywhere Machiavelli observed politicians and their ways; he became an analyst of power. Above all, he loved Italy and longed to see it united under one monarch. In 1512, he lost his position because of a change in the Florentine government. He then settled in a small community outside the city and took up writing. The most famous of all his works is The Prince, a handbook containing the rules he had developed through his observations, rules which he hoped a monarch would use to unite Italy. Machiavelli died in 1527 and The Prince was published five years later.

Machiavelli, like other Italian humanists of the Renaissance, had always been an avid reader. His reading included a number of traditional books addressed to rulers and containing advice on how to run their governments. The authors had written in idealistic terms guided by medieval religious beliefs. Machiavelli turned their maxims upside down. To him there were no means which the ends did not justify, no moral codes which could not be broken, no religious principles binding a ruler. Distinguishing between what man was and what he ought to be, he aligned himself with reality as he saw it and struck "ought" from his vocabulary.

As you read these excerpts from The Prince, consider the following questions:

1   According to Machiavelli, what is the purpose of government?

2   By what standards should we judge rules such as those that Machiavelli supports?

3   What is Machiavelli's opinion of the role of the individual in history? Consider particularly the last three paragraphs, in which he discusses this matter explicitly.

4   How do Machiavelli's beliefs regarding government compare with those of Confucius?

THE PRINCE / by Niccolò Machiavelli

Florence: G. C. Sausoni, 1899. Translated by Edwin Fenton.

I shall now explore the methods and rules which a prince should follow in regard to the treatment of his subjects and his friends. I know that many other men have written about this matter, and I fear that some people may think my writing about it presumptuous because my opinion differs so much from the opinions of others. But

I intend to write something useful. I shall look at the facts of politics rather than take my evidence from imaginary governments which have never really existed. There is a big difference between how we live and how we ought to live. In politics a man should be guided by what is, rather than by what ought to be. A man who did only what was right would soon fail among so many who are untrustworthy. Therefore, a prince who wishes to remain in power must learn how not to be good and must also learn to use this knowledge, or not use it, depending upon the circumstances. . . .

It is a good thing to be considered generous. But if liberality is not openly displayed for all to see, no one will ever hear about it, and under these circumstances a person would soon become known as a miser. For this reason many men who wish to earn a reputation for liberality depend upon lavish displays or costly shows which are easily seen. If a prince does this, he is likely to spend most of his money on display, and if he wishes to keep his reputation for liberality he will have to impose heavy taxes and do everything possible to obtain more funds. This course of action will make his subjects begin to hate him; they will not even respect him because he will be poor. His liberality will have injured many and benefited only a few. So many of his subjects will grow angry with him that his position will be endangered by any little incident. If he recognizes this fact and tries to spend less money, people will notice the change and accuse him of being a miser.

Since a prince cannot exercise the virtue of liberality without risking his position, he must not object too much to being called miserly. In the long run he will be thought more liberal when his subjects see that his income is sufficient to keep the government going. Without raising taxes, he will be able to defend himself against his enemies and undertake new enterprises without burdening his people with additional taxes. In this way he is really being liberal to all those from whom he does not collect higher taxes.

In our own times we have seen nothing great done except by those who have seemed miserly; the others have all been ruined. Pope Julius II used his reputation for liberality in order to get elected to the papacy, but he did not try to keep this reputation afterward, so that he might have enough money to wage war. The king of France has fought a number of wars without increasing taxes because his extra expenses were covered by the money he saved by being stingy. The king of Spain would not have been able to engage in so many successful enterprises if he had spent money in order to be thought liberal.

For these reasons a prince must not worry if he becomes known as a miser. He must be a miser if he wishes to be able to defend himself and to avoid becoming disliked, robbing his subjects, and exploiting his citizens. Thus miserliness is one of those vices which enables a prince to reign. . . .

Is it better to be loved more than feared or feared more than loved? Ideally, one ought to be both feared and loved, but it is difficult for the two sentiments to go together. If one of the two must be sacrificed, it is much safer to be feared than loved. In general men are ungrateful, dishonest, cowardly, and covetous. As long as you help them, they will do your bidding. They will offer you their blood, their goods, their lives, and their children when it appears that you will not need to take them up on the offer. But when you try to collect, they often go back on their word. If a prince has relied solely on the good faith of others, he will be ruined. Men are less afraid to offend a prince they love than one they fear. They feel free to break the obligation which they owe for love whenever it suits them to do so. But they will do their duty if they fear, for the threat of punishment never fails to bring them to heel.

Still a prince should be careful to make himself feared in such a way that if men do not love him, they at least do not hate him. Fear and the absence of hatred can go together. Both can be won by a prince as long as he does not interfere with the property of his subjects or with their women. When he has to take anyone's life, let him be sure to make the reasons for doing it plain. Above all he must not seize their property, for men will more easily forget the death of their father than the loss of their worldly goods. . . .

I conclude, therefore, with regard to being feared or loved that men have control of their love but the prince controls fear. The wise prince will rely on what he can control and not on what is in the control of others. He must be careful, however, not to make men hate him.

Everyone knows that it is a good thing for a prince to keep his word and live a faithful life. The history of our own times shows, however, that those princes who have done great things have had little regard for keeping faith. They have in the long run been able to overcome those who have made loyalty and honesty the basis of their rule.
. . . a successful prince must imitate both the fox and the lion, for the lion cannot protect himself from traps, and the fox cannot defend

himself from wolves. He must, therefore, be at the same time a fox to recognize traps, and a lion to frighten off wolves. Those who wish to be only lions do not understand this important fact. A prince ought not to keep his word when doing so would go against his best interest, and when the reasons which originally motivated him no longer exist. If men were all good, this rule would not be a sound one. But because they are bad and would not honor their word to the prince, he is not bound to keep faith with them. In addition a prince can always find an excuse for breaking his word. Anyone can supply a number of modern examples of this statement, and can demonstrate how many times peace has been broken and promises scrapped by dishonest princes. Those who have been able to imitate the fox have been most successful. But a prince should be careful to disguise these characteristics well. Men are so simple-minded that anyone who wants to be deceitful can always find those who will allow themselves to be deceived.

I will only mention one modern instance. Alexander VI always deceived men; he thought of nothing else. No man was ever more able to give assurances or to swear on a stack of Bibles that such and such would be done, but no one broke his word more easily. However, he always got away with things because he knew how to manage them.

It is not at all necessary for a prince to have all the good qualities which I have named, but it is necessary to seem to have them. I will even go so far as to say that to actually have these qualities and to be guided by them always is dangerous, but to appear to possess them is useful. Thus it is well to seem merciful, faithful, sincere, religious, and also to be so. But a prince must always be ready to embrace the opposite qualities if the occasion demands it. New princes particularly are unable to live by these fine qualities. They are often obliged, in order to maintain their position, to act against faith, against charity, against humanity, and against religion. A prince must be ready to shift with the wind as the ups and downs of fortune dictate. He should not deviate from what is good if he can avoid it, but he should be ready and able to do evil when it is necessary.

A prince must be careful to say nothing which is not full of the above-named five qualities. He should leave the impression that he is all mercy, faith, integrity, humanity, and religion. Of these, none is more necessary than to seem to be religious, for men usually judge by what they see rather than by what actually is. Everyone sees what you appear to be; few know what you really are, and those few will not dare to set themselves up in opposition to the many. In the affairs of men, and especially in the affairs of princes, the end justifies the means. Let a prince, therefore, aim at conquering and maintaining the state and the means by which he does this will always be praised by everyone. The world consists mainly of vulgar people and the few who are honorable can safely be ignored when so many vulgar rally around the prince. A certain contemporary prince, whom I will not name, never does anything but preach peace and good faith, but he is really a great enemy to both. If he had kept the peace and observed good faith, he would have lost his position and his reputation on many occasions.

Nothing increases the reputation of a prince so much as great enterprises. For example, we have in our own day Ferdinand, King of Aragon, the present king of Spain. Starting as a weak king, he has become the most famous and glorious in Christendom, and his actions have been universally great. At the beginning of his reign he attacked Granada, and that enterprise laid the foundation for his state. He kept the minds of the barons of Castile occupied with his attack on Granada so that they did little to draw the attention of the public to themselves. He was therefore able to acquire a fine reputation and to gain power over them almost before they knew what was happening. Money from the Church and the people maintained his armies; the war against Granada let him lay the foundations of the military power that has made him famous. In order to gain an even greater reputation, he drove the Moors from his kingdom and took their property under the pretext of protecting religion. He also attacked Africa using the same excuse. Since then he has attacked both Italy and France. For years he has contrived great things which have kept his subjects' minds astonished. Men have spent so much time watching these great enterprises that they have had no occasion to settle down and act in concert against him. . . .

I know many people who believe that events in this world are so governed by fortune and by God and that mere man can do nothing to control them. This opinion is held increasingly in our own day; at times even I am partly inclined to share it. But upon examination I have come to the conclusion that fortune rules only about half our actions, and that she allows the other half, or thereabouts, to be governed by us. . . .

Some princes, despite the fact that their characters remain the same, are successful today and ruined tomorrow. I believe this reversal of fortune arises from some of the causes that we have already discussed. Any prince who gambles entirely on fortune is ruined when fortune changes. That prince will be successful whose method of procedure fits the needs of the times, and similarly a prince will be unfortunate if the way in which he customarily works is out of keeping with the times. Men who seek glory and riches operate in various ways — one very carefully, another impetuously, one by violence, another with cunning, one with patience, another impatient to an extreme. Each man may arrive at his goal by a different path. We can see two cautious men, one of whom succeeds while the other fails. In the same way, we can see two men succeed equally well by employing different methods, one being cautious, perhaps, and the other impetuous. This result comes from the nature of the times and not from the method which the men employ. We can conclude that sometimes two men acting differently attain the same goal while of two others who act in the same way, one may reach his goal and the other fall short. A man must always shift his tactics with the times. If he is always cautious when the times demand sudden action, he will be ruined. If a man could change his tactics with time and circumstances, fortune might never frown upon him. . . .

I conclude, then, that if fortune varies and men remain fixed in their ways, they will be successful so long as these ways fit the circumstances of the moment, but when the times call for other tactics they will fail. I certainly think that it is better to be impetuous than cautious, for fortune is a woman, and it is necessary, if you wish to master her, to conquer her by force. It can be seen that she lets herself be overcome by the bold rather than by those who proceed coldly. And therefore, like a woman, she is always a friend to the young, because they are less cautious, more fierce, and master her with greater audacity.

Causes of the Reformation

The Reformation was one of the most significant developments of modern history. It ended the dominion of a universal religion in the Western world and helped release forces long dormant in European society. No course in world history can ignore its effects on intellectual life, the status of individuals, and the growth of political institutions. Hence the causes of the Reformation are of vital importance to the entire West.

The readings in this volume have been concerned with interpretations of the past. We are now prepared to deal explicitly with one important aspect of interpretation, the problem of causation in history. Students often believe that an event or movement was the result of a single circumstance. Such interpretations are almost always too simplified to be accurate. The reading for today describes the manner in which one contemporary historian analyzes the causes of the Reformation. The general technique he employs can be used in any historical investigation.

As you read this passage, consider the following questions:

1 What technique does the author suggest for examining causation? Does this technique imply that he agrees with the definition of history given in the first reading in this book, "What Is History?"

2 Many historians use the term "multiple causation." After reading this article, what do you think the term means?

3 What is the difference between immediate and long-range causes?

4 What tentative generalization would you be willing to make about the role of individuals as causative factors in history?

A PREFACE TO HISTORY / by Carl G. Gustavson

Copyright © 1955 by the McGraw-Hill Book Company, Inc. Used by permission. Pp. 53-64.

Sooner or later in a course dealing with European history, the question "What caused the Reformation?" is almost certain to appear. Confronted with this crisis, some people have been known to profane their bluebooks with the assertion "Martin Luther—he did it," in whatever verbose lengths they are able to contrive. Another popular aphorism that is frequently used is "The Church was corrupt," followed by a similar plethora of words. The old favorite (for certain questions), "The King was weak," is less frequently attempted here, probably because the person who can see how this one applies to the Reformation is already capable of a more intelligent type of answer. . . .

In the heat of conflict, the temptation to ascribe malignant characters and purposes to one's adversaries is often irresistible. This is as true now as in the time of Luther. The political party finds it a highly useful technique to blame all the misfortune of the time upon the other party or its leaders. . . . Even in those cases where there may be a kernel of truth to the charges, these explanations are all vastly oversimplified. . . . No man in a public movement is a free agent or can act entirely according to his own free will. Although he seeks certain objectives and will strive toward them, he must take into consideration other forces or speedily come to an impasse. All the factors in his time condition the way in which he shapes his destinies and help to determine the success of his policies. . . .

Another type of error is committed by persons who overrate one single social force in a situation at the expense of other factors. While this may win temporary political advantage, in the long run serious damage may flow from such a misconception of causation. Prior to the Second World War a group of people became convinced that the United States had entered the First World War primarily because of the activities of the munitions makers; some of these zealots argued that the economic interests of the "merchants of death" were the chief cause of war. This argument, reinforced by isolationist feelings, became so popular that Congress passed laws to prevent our shipment of munitions overseas in case of hostilities. Subsequent events proved that the munitions factor was a relatively inconsequential fragment of the whole picture. Meantime, the focusing of attention on a minor cause, to the exclusion of more potent factors, weakened the American position in time of crisis.

One more instance of an inadequate conception of causation may be mentioned at this time. Very often the *immediate* cause — whether seen in terms of a person or of an event — receives greater emphasis than it deserves. Recognition of the event (or person) which precipitated the larger sequence of happenings does not in itself explain why the chain of development occurred. Most of us have, as children, placed a set of dominoes on end in such a way that each falling domino would trip the next one. Although the pushing of the first domino was the immediate cause for all of them toppling, the sequence would not have been possible if the set had not first been placed on end. The more remote causes in history establish the particular situation which makes the whole historical sequence possible.

No single cause ever adequately explains a historical episode. A "cause" is a convenient figure of speech for any one of a number of factors which helps to explain why a historical event happened. The analogy of the dominoes is misleading to the extent that we may think of the events as following mechanically upon the original act. The direction that the medley of causes will precipitate events can never be precisely gauged while the event is occurring.

The problem of causation is inextricably connected with the whole question of movement and change in history, and some facility in dealing with it is indispensable for an understanding of the course of events. While studying several such historical episodes as the Reformation, the student should be training himself to see the various factors, the multiple causation, that enter into these situations until he learns to use this approach with present-day problems also. When a more advanced student is confronted with a question of causation, he can frequently hazard a fairly good response, even though he may not yet have learned the accepted explanation. He can do so because he has met somewhat similar instances before and will have a general idea of what the possibilities are. He has a certain fund of wisdom, a certain know-how in selecting pertinent factors, and will know which possibilities are likely, which unlikely, and which totally irrelevant. The purpose of this chapter is to provide an outline of causation in a major historical development, the beginnings of the Reformation, as an example of the type of reasoning which must go into the analysis of any such phenomenon. The same sort of approach should be used in connection with the Puritan Revolution and the French Revolution, as well as with lesser, and more simple, developments.

Quite obviously the immediate cause for the Reformation is to be found in the activity of Luther between 1517 and 1521, although the selection of a specific event may bring differences of opinion; the most likely choices would be the nailing of the ninety-five theses, the Diet of Worms, or the famous disputation with Eck, in which Luther first clearly crossed the line between Catholicism and heresy. Identifying the initial spark, however, by no means explains the enormous extent of the conflagration which followed.

Luther's ninety-five theses immediately became the best seller of that day. Great crowds gathered to applaud him as he went to the Diet of Worms. If we can decide why he suddenly experienced this popularity, we may also gain some idea of the reason for his success. First of all, anyone who champions a cause and defies authority will attract a crowd of supporters, if only for the sake of the show. Luther had been denouncing the outrageous methods used in the sale of indulgences, an issue everyone could understand far better than discussions of abstruse theology. He was hitting out at unpopular figures, always a good way to attract a following. The friar of Wittenberg was a German, a son of the people, courageously talking up to pope and emperor, speaking for the common people and expressing what many of them felt.

Could any deeper reasons be at work that produced the quick acclaim for Luther's stand? Could it be that such a sudden blaze was generated because the inflammable materials had already been gathered by others? Had there been any earlier instances of men who preached the same viewpoint as this reformer? (Remember that the mind of the historian inevitably gravitates in the direction of the past, seeking origins, relationships, and comparisons.) If so, this must indicate a general trend of the time in the direction of the reform which the Protestants were to take.

The career of John Hus of Prague is apt to come to mind. His life story bears several marked resemblances to that of Luther, and his proposals were very similar to those of his successors; there was a major difference however—he was burned for his temerity. A whole century before the Lutheran Reformation some of its principles were already widely approved, as witness the obstinate refusal of the Bohemians to give up the reforms of Hus. (Note, also, that Bohemia borders on Saxony, Luther's home district.) Other reformers had also preceded Luther: Peter Waldo, Wyclif, Savonarola, to mention the most prominent. Nor should the criticism of the Church by such writers as Erasmus and Valla be forgotten. . . . Consequently, the historian may fairly assume that whatever the reasons for the Reformation were, they were operative to a considerable degree long before Luther. The Reformation could, conceivably, have begun in 1415, and it might have been postponed beyond 1520.

One point to note is that the criticism of the Church usually did not carry with it a threat to leave the institution. It was criticized, its officials castigated, its practices and policies assailed in the same spirit in which Americans treat their governmental institutions. The object was reform, not separation, the attacks representing no more a desire to destroy the Church than we expect to abolish Congress. Some people might dislike papal authority in much the same way as some Americans suspect the power of a strong President. When Luther appeared at Worms, he had no expectation of founding a

separate church, and in fact he may have gone to the diet with a
lurking hope of converting Charles V to his own viewpoint. . . .

Luther dared to go to Worms. Powerful reasons must have driven
him to risk the fate of Hus by making this journey. The assurance
that his own prince, the Elector of Saxony, was on his side and the
boisterous plaudits of the multitudes undoubtedly emboldened him,
but beyond all this was an inner necessity, a personal conviction of a
spiritual mission, that forced him to speak his mind. Luther's actions
were indubitably born of motives other than personal ambition or
opportunism: biographies of the reformer fully document the gradual
development of his convictions from the time he became a friar until
he stood in full defiance against the existent ecclesiastical authorities.
This must be accounted as an instance where spiritual force acted as
a primary impulse in history.

Only a rugged, roughhewn, obstinate man could have shouldered
his way to success in the circumstances — the looming figure of Luther
makes the personal factor important in the causation of the Reformation. Unless the odds are too great, the victory is likely to go to the
side inspired by genuine zeal for a cause. Historical movements,
however much they are impelled by economic and social factors,
after all are carried through by men. Their states of mind are important. Even Luther, however, could have accomplished little more
than propagate his ideas if he had not found many others in the same
mood. Had Luther alone, or a small circle of disciples only, held
Protestant ideas, no social force of sufficient magnitude to create
historical events would have existed. When tens of thousands, however, were possessed of the same general outlook, the scene was set
for action, and it took only Luther's words and actions to precipitate
the formation of a spiritual force of enormous extent and potency.
We are dealing with a large-scale example of a social force of a spiritual nature such as was described in the preceding chapter. In time,
also, the Reformation stimulated an equally powerful reaction to it in
Catholicism, a renewed spiritual vigor on the Catholic side . . . .

The circumstances were ready for the man, and his religious zeal
furnished a focal point for the hitherto diffused causes for the Reformation. One may legitimately question if any one single force, albeit
as powerful as this one, could in itself have altered the course of
history. From our perspective, at least, a number of social forces seem
to converge upon the developing events and carry them forward.

We have seen gunpowder and the better ocean-going vessels

make possible the expansion of the European into other parts of the world. The printing press, another technological advance, served as a tool of incalculable importance in the Reformation. Someone might argue very plausibly that no Reformation could have occurred had it not been for the invention of the printing press. Without this method of spreading ideas, the Lutheran doctrines could not have been disseminated so rapidly, and, if support had not quickly manifested itself, the emperor and Church might have succeeded in suppressing the movement. The press also aided the reformers by undermining the claim of the Church to pose as the custodian of final truth, since it was now becoming possible for more persons to acquire a copy of the Bible.

Social forces emerging from economic motives, powerful as they were, must have exercised an important influence on these events. The kind of merchant that we encountered in Florence or in sixteenth-century England, and who was also active in Germany, would deplore the constant flow of money to Rome. Most people, indeed, would feel indignation at this continual drain on the national wealth, and any rebel against papal authority would find useful ammunition here. The incessant sniping at the wealth of the bishops and the monasteries was partly due to the unfortunate contrast with the early ideal of the Church, but the criticisms were also likely to remind people that their contributions were not always usefully applied. Especially would the growing middle class deplore the drag on productivity caused by the clerical possession of land, the numerous church festivals, and the presumed idleness of the monks. With their ideals of thrift and industry, the middle class found many church habits irritating. Luther appealed to these feelings, with violent and exaggerated words, in his *Address to the Christian Nobility of the German Nation:* "What has brought us Germans to such a pass that we have to suffer this robbery and this destruction of our property by the pope? . . . Do we still wonder why princes, cities, foundations, convents, and people grow poor? We should rather wonder that we have anything left to eat."

We know that the nobles were always eager to expand their holdings. They had long eyed the lands of the Church, and the Reformation, with its expropriation of clerical wealth, offered the awaited opportunity. Many of England's noble families had their origin in grants of this kind, and these were likely to remain Protestant, since any reversion to the old order would jeopardize their new acquisitions. The princes of Germany likewise benefitted in this fashion, and the Crown in England and the Scandinavian countries added to its wealth at the expense of the Church.

After this brief survey of the impact of social forces studied earlier, let us see what other factors were influential in the situation. For instance, the thought must occur to one that the incipient restlessness should have been crushed by the imperial regime. Why did Luther "get away with it" when others before him had failed? The truth is that Charles V was in a dilemma. New on the throne, he was uncertain of his support and would hesitate before alienating his German subjects. Luther's own prince, the Elector of Saxony, was friendly to the reformers and possessed the force and prestige to raise a rebellion. The loud acclaim of the friar must have alarmed Charles and dissuaded him from a highly unpopular move. He undoubtedly underestimated the potentialities of the movement, the more so since he had grave political problems to grapple with elsewhere. The Ottoman Turks were approaching the far-flung borders of his realm, and Charles needed German unity in order to meet this threat. All in all, "the king was weak," not so much because of his own personality as in his inheritance of an enfeebled government from his predecessors.

The Crown was one of the institutions which should have suppressed the rebellion. The other was the Church itself. After many centuries as the universal Church of Western Europe, it had undergone both a loss of positive vitality and a diminishing strength in comparison with new emerging forces. It had failed to suppress the Hussite heretics. The internecine struggle between two organs of the Church, the papacy and the council, in the conciliar movement might be seen as a portent of disruption. Perhaps most significant of all, the Renaissance was having a debilitating spiritual effect upon the papacy; popes who were using spiritual resources for temporal ends were blunting their own swords. Having centralized the Church, they failed to live up to their responsibilities. By making the papacy synonymous with the Church, they drew upon the Church itself a shower of invective. The fact that many believed the Church to be corrupt shook the all-important allegiance of the great masses of the people.

The Church no longer possessed as much power, proportionately, either. New forces were rising which had long challenged the Church and which now overwhelmed it. One of these was the national state.

Even at the height of the Middle Ages potent secular authorities had challenged the papacy. A king might possess the men and swords, the brute force, which could humiliate a pope, as Philip IV's men did Boniface VIII.

Inasmuch as the Church itself could not muster a physical force to resist the state, the king's chief anxiety in such a conflict concerned the question whether his men would follow him against the Bishop of Western Christendom. As long as men were, in the last analysis, more loyal to the Church than to the Crown, the universal Church retained its power. The medieval sovereigns who defied the papacy were not attempting to rebel against the Church for the purpose of setting up a separate one. They continued to work within the framework of the older institutions.

During the fourteenth and fifteenth centuries, national kings continued to add to their power, and in France, England, and Spain these rulers arrogated to themselves increasing control over the national churches. Seen in the light of later events, the rivalry of nations during the Avignon period, the schism, and the conciliar movement betoken a growing national feeling which would burst asunder the ancient bonds. The Catholic Church was faced with its perennial problem, how to keep its international character although threatened by national feelings and provincial attachments. The Church, after all, was essentially an institution of the southland. From thence it had come, there it had matured and built up its customs and symbols. At one time, the cultural inferiority of the north caused these peoples to accept southern leadership as natural; as the northern peoples developed, however, the subservience to the south began to rankle.

In the northern countries, a sense of nationalism was a strong factor in the break with Rome. In Germany, where other national aspirations went unsatisfied, this was particularly true. The Reformation passed into effect in Sweden coincident with the overthrow of Danish rule. The English struggle against Spain would tend to associate the state church with national existence in that country. The native language was substituted for Latin in the churches of these regions. In nearly all instances, the advent of the Reformation brought added power and wealth to the kings or territorial princes. The institutional factor is a powerful one in the causation of the Reformation; one institution, the Church, was losing ground to another institution, the national monarchy, and the spiritual crisis precipitated by Luther offered the territorial princes of Germany and the kings of northern Europe a splendid opportunity to establish state control over the Church.

The foregoing outline, which by no means exhausts the possibilities of causation in the Reformation, does provide a check list of factors likely to be important in such a phenomenon. When a student is faced with a problem of this nature, a few general questions are of great assistance in analyzing the situation. When these are "tried on for size," some will immediately suggest causes, while others may have little relevance. The following nine should prove helpful: (1) What was the immediate cause for the event? (2) Had there been a background of agitation for the principles victorious during this episode? (3) Were personalities involved on either side whose strengths or weaknesses may have helped to determine the outcome of the struggle? (4) Were any new and potent ideas stimulating the loyalty of a considerable number of people? (5) How did the economic groups line up on the issue? (6) Were religious forces active? (7) Did any new technological developments influence the situation? (8) Can the events be partially explained by weakened or strengthened institutions? (9) Was the physical environment itself a factor in the situation? (It will be noticed that questions four through eight relate to various social forces already enumerated.) A systematic analysis of a problem of causation with the aid of these questions will ensure that all the major historical factors have been taken into consideration.

The factors in the above list obviously do not carry equal weight in the causation of the Reformation. Nor will they do so when applied to other historical events. Attempting to assess their proportionate importance, in any given case, is an excellent exercise in reasoning for the beginning student. Some individuals, reading the textual account of the theology, are apt to regard this as unimportant and will assert that the real reasons lie in the social and economic sphere. Others, of a more religious nature, are likely to take the religious ideas seriously, and in so doing probably better appreciate the motives by which the reformers believed themselves guided. Some will feel that the personality of the leading reformers bulk large in the outcome; others regard them as the puppets of more impersonal forces. Geographical influences will receive greater emphasis from some than from others. Unfortunately, no method exists for measuring these causes or for attaining a final verifiable evaluation. One possible empirical test which may help to weigh the respective merits of each cause is to imagine the Reformation with that specific factor omitted; would its absence have changed the course of events? It is in the interpretation of history that perplexity begins, but also much of the fascination.

Some perspicacious individuals may decide the proportionate values of the factors vary with the country. Certain reasons may not apply at all in England or the Netherlands. Then, too, how account for Italy and Spain, where the Reformation made little headway? Were the factors listed above too weak in these countries, or did still other considerations enter the picture in these regions? The same causes may have different effects in different circumstances. In certain states with relatively strong central governments, such as England, Sweden, and Denmark, the Crown itself took the lead in severing relations with Rome, while in others, France, Spain, and Austria, the ruling dynasties opposed the religious changes. Ideas of the Renaissance undoubtedly helped to stimulate Protestant ideas in Germany, yet the Renaissance equally surely was a factor militating against the success of the Reformation in France. . . .

One warning needs to be added. The foregoing represents an attempt to provide a systematic approach to causation for the beginner. Reasoning, however, cannot be effective without the facts. A student is using facts from a textbook, class notes, and whatever other reading is provided. The historian, while using a basically similar approach, cannot be satisfied until he finds genuine evidence upon which to base his conclusions. There is only one way to achieve this: go to the evidence itself, which is made up of the records of that age. A reading of a few of Luther's pamphlets is apt to be revealing. The historian will want to read the opinions of many people who were contemporaries of Luther and Calvin. He will examine the declarations from the Roman Catholic side of the controversy. Other factors must be investigated. If he carefully examines the record in a spirit of humility, prepared to recognize tenacious reality rather than what he wishes to find, he is then prepared to formulate a worthwhile interpretation of the events.

Why English Settlers
Came to America

Following the discoveries of the 15th and 16th centuries, a great number of people migrated to the open spaces of the New World. Many students in American schools believe that the majority of the early immigrants braved the stormy Atlantic solely to obtain religious liberty. Additional settlers are supposed to have left their homes only to establish free governments in a world unsullied by king and aristocracy. Any student who has used this volume carefully has a right to question the accuracy of these interpretations. The excerpts below deal with the motives of early immigrants to the New England area, and will help the reader to make his own judgment.

Today's Problem is in three parts. The first is an excerpt from a propaganda pamphlet written by Sir George Peckham in 1583 to encourage settlers to move to the coast of what is now the northeastern United States and southeastern Canada. The second, a selection from George F. Willison's book *Saints and Strangers*, analyzes the reasons why the Pilgrims left their settlement at Leyden in the Netherlands. (Quotations within this reading are from *Of Plimoth Plantation*, by William Bradford, governor of the Pilgrims at Plymouth.) The third selection, John Winthrop's "Reasons," contains a list of the motives for colonizing compiled about 1629 by one of the founders of the Massachusetts Bay Company. The three excerpts record quite different points of view regarding settlement.

As you read, consider the following questions:

1   What were the motives of each group represented here? Were motives in each case mixed or was a single motive always more important than all the others? What are some useful ways of classifying motives?

2   Do you think these three sources are varied enough so that you can safely generalize from them? How would you evaluate their reliability?

3   How would Gustavson handle the problem of investigating the motives of English settlers?

I

A DISCOURSE . . . UPON THE NORTH PARTS OF AMERICA
by Sir George Peckham

From Richard Hakluyt, *The Principal Navigations, Voyages, Traffiques and Discoveries of the English Nation.* London, 1600. Language simplified and spelling modernized by Edwin Fenton.

The fourth chapter shows how the trade, traffic, and planting in those countries is likely to prove very profitable to the whole realm in general.

Now to show how the same is likely to prove very profitable and beneficial generally to the whole realm: it is very certain that the greatest jewel of this realm and the chief strength and force of the same, for defence or offence in martial matter and manner, is the multitude of ships, masters, and mariners ready to assist the most stately and royal navy of her Majesty, which by reason of this voyage shall have both increase and maintenance. And it is well known that in sundry places of this realm ships have been built and set forth of late days for the trade of fishing only: yet notwithstanding, the fish which is taken and brought into England by the English navy of fishermen would not suffice for the expense of this realm four months if there were none else brought by strangers. And the chief cause why our Englishmen do not go so far westerly as the special fishing places do lie, both for plenty and greatness of fish, is that they have no aid and known safe harbor in those parts. But if our nation were once planted there, or near thereabouts, whereas they now fish but for two months in the year, they might then fish for so long as they pleased, or rather, at their coming find such plenty of fish already caught, salted, and dried, as might be sufficient to bring them home without long delay (God granting that salt may be found there) whereof David Ingram (who traveled in those countries before mentioned) says that there is great plenty: and certainly the climate gives great hope that though there be none there naturally, yet it may be manufactured as it is both at Rochelle and Bayonne, or elsewhere. And this being brought to pass shall increase the number of our ships and mariners, if only in respect of fishing: but much more in regard of the sundry merchandises and commodities which are there found and had in great abundance.

Moreover, it is well known that all savages, as well those that dwell in the South as those that dwell in the North, so soon as they shall begin but a little to taste of civility, will take marvelous delight in any garment, be it ever so simple; as a shirt, a blue, yellow, red, or green cotton coat, a cap, or such like, and will take incredible pains for such a trifle.

For I myself have heard this report made sundry times by various of our countrymen who have dwelt in the southerly parts of the West Indies, some as long as twelve years, and some for a shorter time; that the people in those parts are easily reduced to civility both in manners and garments. Which being so, what a market for our English clothes will thereby develop, and how great a benefit to all such persons and artificers, whose names are quoted in the margin [*clothiers, woolmen, carders, spinners, weavers, fullers, sheermen, dyers, drapers, cappers, hatters, etc.*], I do leave to the judgment of such as are discerning.

And there is no question that by this means it will also come to pass that all such towns and villages as both have been, and now are utterly decayed and ruined . . . shall by this means be restored to their pristine wealth and estate: all of which does likewise tend to the enlargement of our navy and the maintenance of our navigation.

Why do I need by arguments to prove that by this voyage our navy and navigation shall be enlarged, when no reason is needed other than the manifest and late example of the near neighbors of this realm, the kings of Spain and Portugal, who since the first discovery of the Indies have not only mightily enlarged their dominions and greatly enriched themselves and their subjects, but have also by just account trebled the number of their ships, masters, and mariners — a matter of no small moment and importance.

Besides this, it will prove a general benefit to our country that through this occasion not only a great number of men who now live idly at home and are burdensome, unprofitable, and a charge to this realm shall hereby be set to work, but also children of twelve or fourteen years of age or under may be kept from idleness, in making a thousand kinds of trifling things which will be good merchandise for that country. And moreover, our idle women (which the realm may well spare) shall also be employed in plucking, drying, and sorting feathers; in pulling, beating, and working hemp; and in gathering cotton and various things necessary for dyeing. All which things are to be found in those countries most plentifully. And the men may employ themselves in dragging for pearl, working mines, and in matters of husbandry, and likewise in hunting the whale for oil, and making casks to put the same in: besides in fishing for cod, salmon, and herring, drying, salting, and barrelling the same, and felling of trees, hewing and sawing them, and such work suitable for those persons that are no men of art or science.

Many other things may be found to the great relief and good employment of no small number of the natural subjects of this realm, who do now live here idly to the common annoyance of the whole state. Neither may I here omit the great hope and likelihood of a passage . . . into the South Seas, confirmed by sundry authors to be found leading to Cathay [*China*], the Moluccas, and Spiceries, whereby may ensue as general a benefit to the realm, or greater than yet

hath been spoken of, without either such charges or other incon-
veniences as the peril and tedious passage of time which the ordinary
voyage to those parts now requires.

And to conclude this argument, it is well known to all men of
sound judgment that this voyage is of greater importance and will be
found more beneficial to our country than all other voyages now
common among us.

II

SAINTS AND STRANGERS / by George F. Willison

Copyright 1941 by George F. Willison. Reprinted by
permission of the author. Pp. 102-103.

The leaders of the group [*of Pilgrims at the Green Gate, Leyden*]
were worried — above all, by the poverty in which most of the congregation lived. Many were getting on in years, feeling old age stealing
upon them, and their "great & continuall labours, with other crosses
and sorrows, hastened it before ye time." Even worse, they were
compelled by their need to put their children to work, and the latter
were "so oppressed by their hevie labours that, though their minds
were free and willing, yet their bodies bowed under ye weight of ye
same and became decreped in their early youth, the vigour of nature
being consumed in ye very bud, as it were." Their situation aroused
an uneasy fear that within a few years they would either scatter by
reason of necessity or "sinke under their burdens, or both." Aware of
their hardships, friends in England hesitated to come to them, and
some at Leyden had already given up the bitter struggle and returned
home. "Yea," said Bradford, they "preferred & chose ye prisons in
England rather than this libertie in Holland, with these afflictions."

Many began to argue not unreasonably that if they could find a
place where they might live more comfortably and still enjoy freedom
of religion, they would have greater success in spreading the glad
tidings of salvation. They could then hope to make converts of all
those who "desired to injoye ye ordinances of God in their puritie."
Then, too, they wished to retain their identity as an English group,
having no desire to be absorbed by the Dutch, which was not a
fanciful danger, for in the end that was the fate of the larger part of
this and every other Separatist congregation in exile. But a more

immediate danger was the seduction of their children by "ye great licentiousness of youth in that countrie and ye manifold temptations of ye place." The younger "Saincts" had developed as yet no great resistance to the lures of Satan, allowing themselves to slide with alarming ease "into extravagante & dangerous courses, getting ye raines off their neks, & departing from their parents." But that was one of the penalties of living among the jolly, pleasure-loving Dutch. It surprised and pained those at the Green Gate to observe that, do what they would in a friendly way to reform them, the Dutch remained incorrigibly lighthearted. This was bad enough on week days, but it was intolerable on the Sabbath, which the Dutch insisted upon celebrating as a holiday (holy day), simply laughing and tossing off another pot of beer when told it should be endured grimly as a penance.

III

REASONS TO BE CONSIDERED FOR JUSTIFYING THE UNDERTAKERS OF THE INTENDED PLANTATION IN NEW ENGLAND / by John Winthrop

From *Life and Letters of John Winthrop.* Boston, 1864. Language simplified and spelling modernized by Edwin Fenton.

1.   It will be a service to the Church of great consequence to carry the Gospel into those parts of the world . . . and to raise a bulwark against the kingdom of antichrist which the Jesuits labor to rear up in those parts.

2.   . . . our sins, for which the Lord begins already to frown upon us . . . do threaten evil times to be coming upon us, and who knows but that God has provided this place to be a refuge for many whom he means to save out of the general calamity, and seeing the Church has no place left to fly into but the wilderness, what better work can there be than to go and provide tabernacles and food for her in case she must flee.

3.   This land grows weary of her inhabitants, so that man, who is the most precious of all creatures, is here more vile and base than the earth we tread upon, and less valued among us than a horse or a sheep: masters are forced by authority to care for their servants and parents to maintain their own children. All towns complain of the burden of their poor, though we have taken up many unnecessary and

even unlawful trades to maintain them . . . and thus it has come to pass that children, servants and neighbors, especially if they are poor, are counted the greatest burdens, which if things were right would be the chief earthly blessings.

4. The whole earth is the Lord's garden and he has given it to the sons of men with a general commission: increase and multiply, and replenish the earth and subdue it (Gen. 1:28), which was again renewed to Noah. The end is double and natural, that man might enjoy the fruits of the earth, and God might have his due glory from the creature; why then should we stand striving here for places of habitation, etc. . . . and in the meantime suffer a whole continent . . . to lie waste without any improvement?

5. We are grown to that height of intemperance in all excess of extravagance so that almost no man's estate will suffice to keep pace with his equals: and he who fails herein must live in scorn and contempt. Hence it comes that all arts and trades are carried in that deceitful and unrighteous course as it is almost impossible for a good and upright man to maintain his charge and live comfortably in any of them.

6. The fountains of learning and religion are so corrupted that . . . most children . . . are perverted, corrupted, and utterly overthrown by the multitude of evil examples . . . .

7. What can be a better work, and more honorable and worthy a Christian, than to help raise and support a particular Church while it is in its infancy, and to join his forces with such a company of faithful people, as by a timely assistance may grow strong and prosper, and for want of it may be put to great hazard, if not wholly ruined.

8. If any such as are known to be Godly, and live in wealth and prosperity here, shall forsake all this to join themselves with this Church and to run a hazard with them of a hard and mean condition, it will be an example of great use both for removing the scandal of worldly and sinister respects which is cast upon the Adventurers; to give more life to the faith of God's people, in their prayers for the Plantation; and to encourage others to join the more willingly in it.

9. It appears to be a work of God for the good of his Church, in that he has disposed the hearts of so many of his wise and faithful servants, both ministers and others, not only to approve of the enterprise, but to interest themselves in it—some in their persons and estates, others by their serious advice and help otherwise, and all by their prayers for the welfare of it.

Peter the Great and the Limits of Absolutism

Peter the Great tried to help Russia pull itself up by its own bootstraps. A man of abundant energies, great ability, and ruthless ambition, he made a serious attempt to catapult his backward nation into the Western world. If any man in Russia could have done the job, that man was Peter. He had a long reign, absolute power, and the resources of an entire nation. Yet some of his reforms failed to outlast his reign, others never spread throughout the nation, and still more were only moderately successful. These conclusions indicate that even absolutism has its limits, and raise the questions: how much can a ruler accomplish in the face of limited resources and the lethargy or even the opposition of many of his people? Can he hope to make reforms for which the ground has not been prepared in previous decades?

Such questions involve an important issue, the role of the individual in history. Historians have debated it for a long time. At one extreme, men like the English historian Thomas Carlyle have given the "hero" a dominant role as a major force in causation. On the other hand, determinists like Karl Marx have argued that only long-range socioeconomic forces really produce change in the world and that individuals as such can do nothing to alter the direction of history. Other historians, agreeing with neither extreme, have argued that individuals in particularly strategic positions have sometimes been able to change the course of history while others of less talent or in less promising circumstances have been unable to do anything.

Peter's reforms marked a turning point in Russian history. Although some of his predecessors had taken tentative steps toward westernization, Peter struck out boldly in this direction. If he had succeeded entirely, Russia might eventually have become a Western-style democracy. Hence the reasons for his failure are particularly significant to us.

The three readings in this problem all concern in one way or another the limits of Peter's power. The first passage is from the pen of an English engineer, John Perry, who wrote an account of his fourteen years in Russia after he returned home in 1712. The second is taken from a biography of Peter the Great written by an American historian, Eugene Schuyler. The final excerpt by an English scholar, B. H. Sumner, assesses Peter's reign from a modern perspective.

As you read, consider the following questions:

1 What characteristics distinguish the reforms Peter was able to make from those that failed?

2 What kind of methods did Peter use to achieve reforms?

3 What differences are there in the points of view of the three writers regarding Peter's role in Russian history?

4 What does Peter's reign indicate about the role of the individual in history?

I

THE STATE OF RUSSIA UNDER THE PRESENT CZAR / by John Perry

Reprinted from *Seven Britons in Imperial Russia*, edited by Peter Putnam, by permission of Princeton University. Copyright 1952 by Princeton University Press. Pp. 33-34, 39-41, 61-62.

It was a very rare thing in Russia before this present Czar's time to have found any man, even among the highest and most learned of the clergy, to have understood any language but their own; and as they were themselves void of learning, so they were wary and cautious to keep out all means that might bring it in, lest their ignorance should be discovered . . . for which reason the learning of foreign languages and books were always formerly discouraged; even as they are to this day in the Turkish Empire. . . .

There came once a press and letters out of Poland to Mosco, where a printing-house was set up with the approbation of one of the former Czars; but not long after the house was fir'd in the night-time, and the press and letters were burnt, as was thought by the procurement of the priests, they looking upon all other books except the history of their own countrey, and the exploits and victories of their Czars, and the lives and miracles of their saints, to be as dangerous as witchcraft.

This ignorance was not so much to be wonder'd at when it is consider'd that they neither suffer'd their sons to travel, nor was there ever any university in the countrey, or considerable school of any learning, till this Czar's time. . . .

. . . the Czar came down to Veronize [*Voronezh*], where I was then on service, and a great many of my men that had worn their beards all their lives, were now obliged to part with them, amongst which . . . was an old Russ carpenter that had been with me at Camishinka. . . . I jested a little with him on this occasion, telling him that he was become a young man, and asked him what he had done with his beard? Upon which he put his hand in his bosom and pull'd it out, and shew'd it to me: farther telling me, that when he came home, he would lay it up to have it put in his coffin and buried along with him, that he might be able to give an account of it to St. Nicholas, when he came to the other world; and that all his brothers (meaning his fellow-workmen . . .) had taken the same care.

The Czar . . . gave orders that all his boyars and people whatsoever, that came near his court, and that were in his pay should . . .
equip themselves with handsome cloathes made after the English
fashion. . . . And next he commanded, that a pattern of cloathes of
the English fashion should be hung up at all the gates of the city of
Mosco, and that publication should be made, that all persons (except-
ing the common peasants who brought goods and provisions into the
city) should make their cloathes according to the said patterns; and
that whosoever should disobey the said orders, and should be found
passing any of the gates of the city in their long habits, should either
pay two grevens (which is 20 pence) or be obliged to kneel down at
the gates of the city, and to have their coats cut off just even with
the ground . . . .

It had been the custom of Russia, in case of marriages, that the
match used always be made up between the parents on each side,
without any previous meeting, consent or liking of one another. . . .
But the Czar taking into his consideration this unacceptable way of
joining young people together without their own approbation, which
might in a very great measure be reckon'd to be the occasion of that
discord and little love which is shewn to one another afterwards, it
being a thing common in Russia to beat their wives in a most barba-
rous manner . . . . made an order that no young couple should be
marry'd together, without their own free liking and consent. . . .
This new order is so well approved of, and so very pleasing to the
young people, that they begin to think much better of foreigners, and
to have a better liking of such other new customs as the Czar has
introduced, than they ever did before. . . .

. . . among some other causes, one of the chief which makes the
generality of the nobility at present uneasy, is, that the Czar obliges
them against their will, to come and live at Petersburgh, with their
wives and their families, where they are oblig'd to build new houses
for themselves, and where all manner of provisions are usually three
or four times as dear, and forage for their horses, etc. at least six or
eight times as dear as it is at Mosco; which happens from the small
quantity which the countrey thereabouts produces, being more than
two thirds woods and bogs; and not only the nobility, but merchants
and tradesmen of all sorts, are oblig'd to go and live there. . . .

As for the Czar, he is a great lover of the water, and entirely
delights in ships and boats, and in sailing. . . . But his lords have no
relish nor pleasure in those things, and though they seemingly com-

pliment the Czar whenever he talks to them of the beauties and
delights of Petersburgh; yet when they get together by themselves,
they complain and say that there are tears and water enough at
Petersburgh, but they pray God to send them to live again at Mosco.

II

PETER THE GREAT / by Eugene Schuyler

London: Samson Low, Marston, Searle, & Rivington, 1884.
Vol. II.

"The Tsar, pitying the peoples of his realm, zealous to root out unjust,
disastrous, general burdens and crafty thefts from the State treasury,
having ascertained that great falsifications and thefts are increasing
the public burdens and injuring the interests of the State, and that by
this many people of every station, but most of all the peasants, are
becoming impoverished and ruined," etc., etc. So began one of the
Tsar's decrees in 1713; but the Tsar really knew very little of the
sufferings of the people. Indeed, how could he? What were the
Russian serfs at that time, that any one should interest themselves in
them except as mere draft animals, machines for labour, and objects of
taxation? The revenue of Russia which for 1709 had been calculated at
3,026,128 rubles had risen in 1725 to 10,186,707 rubles, the ruble
having depreciated fifteen per cent in value. At the end of Peter's
reign the regular army numbered 210,000 men, and the fleet contained forty-eight ships of the line and eight hundred smaller vessels,
manned by 28,000 men. This result could not have been reached without immense and oppressive taxation, and . . . nearly everything
possible was taxed. Besides that, the recruiting and the way it was
carried on, the building of St. Petersburg, the construction of the
fortresses, the digging of canals, and the opening of harbours had cost
the lives of hundreds of thousands of men. To escape harsh treatment
and death many more had run away. [*One writer*] tells us that to
escape the oppression of the tax officials, who collected the taxes in
the times of the year worst for agriculture, and seized the draft horses
of the peasants, at least a hundred thousand men had fled to Poland,
Lithuania, Turkey, and the Tartars. Others say two hundred thousand.
The figures may be doubted, but the general fact remains true. Whole
villages ran away to the frontiers or hid in the woods. As the main-

tenance of a large army rendered both men and money necessary, the pursuit of the fugitive serfs, and of unwilling and runaway conscripts, was carried on diligently throughout the whole of Peter's reign. . . .

In spite of the great increase of revenue and the constant economy practised by the Tsar, yet—owing to wars as well as bad harvests—the treasury was sometimes so low that it was necessary to resort to extraordinary measures, such as are now practised only in Turkey. In the winter of 1723 the Government officials were paid in furs and other Government wares instead of money. It was not so easy then for the Government to contract loans. A subsequent decree says that "when money is absolutely necessary, and when no other way of raising it is found, the sum must be deducted proportionately from the salaries of the officials, spiritual as well as temporal, except foreign artisans and soldiers and sailors." A few months later, besides raising the excise on spirits and the price of stamped paper, one-fourth was deducted from the pay of all officials, and the rations of officers were either reduced by half or withheld altogether.

In a decree of 1723 Peter thus explains the causes of the slow development of manufactures. "Either our decrees are not accurately observed, or there are few people who wish to go into the business. Manufactures too are ruined by goods brought from abroad. For instance, a peasant discovered a dye called 'Florence lake.' I had artists try it. They said that it was only inferior to the Venetian, and quite equal to the German; some said even better. A good deal of it was made, and no one buys it on account of the quantity brought from abroad. Other manufacturers also complain. Therefore it is necessary to look after this sharply and to communicate with the College of Commerce, and, if it does not look after it, then to protest to the Senate and state the matter to us, for other nations greatly envy our manufactories and try by all means to ruin them by bribery, as many examples show. That there are few people wishing to go into business is true, for our people are like children, who never want to begin the alphabet unless they are compelled to by their teacher. It seems very hard to them at first, but when they have learnt it they are thankful. So in manufacturing affairs we must not be satisfied with the proposition only, but we must act and even compel, and help by teaching, by machines, and other aids, and even by compulsion, to become good economists. For instance, where there is fine felt we should compel people to make hats, by not allowing the sale of felt unless a certain number of hats are made." Always force, always compulsion. Peter seems to have found no better way for dealing with even such a delicate matter as commerce, where people are governed entirely by their own interests, and where a slight fear of loss, especially if caused by Government interference, counteracts an almost certain hope of profit. Force was of little avail to promote Russian industry. High import duties, bounties, privileges and monopolies did more, but Russian manufactures never took a high rank in Peter's day nor indeed for long after.

III

PETER THE GREAT / by B. H. Sumner

From *History* magazine, Vol. XXXII, March 1947. Pp. 40-43, 47-48.

In various popular editions and in the rewritten textbooks Peter and his reign are now duly prominent, and . . . Alexis Tolstoy's remarkable novel [*Peter the Great*] . . . still further served towards his reinstatement. In the historical treatment of Peter's reign the man himself is given his due. . . . Peter is called great because he was a man of exceptional gifts and force of character who sensed many of the greatest needs of Russia and bent himself to the task of meeting them; because he appreciated certain of the most important forces or tendencies working within Muscovy of the second half of the seventeenth century; because with his tempestuous (and indeed spendthrift) energy, with his immense power of (and indeed at times immersion in) detail, with his steadfastness and courage in overcoming failures (and indeed at times recklessness and obstinacy), he hastened into being that new Russia which was in process of gestation. . . .

[*A modern Russian historian, M. M. Bogoslovsky, has written of Peter as follows:*]

"Peter was the founder of the Russian regular, national army. With masterly foresight, Peter knew how to pick out and assimilate what was useful and progressive and how to reject what was useless. By his creation of the regular army Peter the Great raised an indestructible monument to himself in the history of the Russian State. In his grandiose reorganisation of the armed forces of Russia, Peter showed himself a wise and far-sighted statesman. Under the conditions of the exhausting Northern War and of the backwardness of Russia, Peter successfully decided this historical task. . . ."

Peter was an iconoclast: he broke with many externals, and with the ritualistic, traditional orthodox manner of life that hitherto had been part and parcel of the nationalism and religion of the court and the magnates and landed families, and in some degree of the bulk of the Russian people. He was lay and secular in his interests, aims, and habit of mind and of life; rationalism and utility were uppermost. He had dynamic energy, violent unbreakable determination, and unfailing courage: therewith he triumphed in the long run over all his adversities, defeats and setbacks — except one, and that one curiously enough his defeat at the hands of the Turks, in 1711, on the Pruth. He was a patriot, devoted to Russia, not sparing his subjects, but least of all himself, in unremitting service to her. He worked upon her [in the phrase of Frederick the Great] "like nitric acid on iron." He was untiring in his plans for the development of Russia's economic resources, particularly her industries, and among those especially metallurgy. In this he had much success, and the great iron and copper industries in the Urals owe their origin to Peter. He was the initiator of what may be called modern education in Russia, not confined to one class, though mainly confined to the immediately useful and the technical. He devoted great attention to Asiatic lands and to Siberia, marched in person into Transcaucasia in war against Persia, sought out Central Asian routes to India and initiated the final successful search for a North-East passage, discovered shortly after his death by Behring. He made the Russian navy out of nothing. He re-made the Russian army, on the model of the up-to-date European armies of that day, armed for the greater part with flint-locks and bayonets, well-equipped with a varied artillery, munitioned in the end for the most part from Russian resources. With this army and navy he defeated Sweden, ultimately, after twenty-one consecutive years of war; and Sweden ranked among the foremost military powers of the day, and had in her King Charles XII, a military leader who was the compeer of Marlborough and Prince Eugene, however lacking he was as a statesman. . . . With this army and navy Peter gained for Russia the Baltic provinces and the mouth of the Neva, where he founded his new capital St. Petersburg. . . .

If you take eight essential fields in which Peter wrought profound changes, you will find that in all of these there were beginnings in the generation before him, and sometimes much further back than that. That applies to the greater part of his foreign policy, to his army reorganisation, to his reorganisation of the central government, to his reorganisation of taxation and serfdom, to his employment of foreigners in Russia and education reforms, to his insistence on compulsory service, to his economic and industrial developments, and lastly to his break with the prevailing traditional and ritualistic ordering of life typified in so much of seventeenth century orthodoxy. I can think of only four changes wrought by Peter (though they were great and lasting) which had either nothing leading towards them in the immediate past or so very little that it scarcely counts. These were the education of Russians abroad, the abolition of the Patriarchate, the creation of the navy, and the making of a new capital, St. Petersburg. Further, however much in many ways Peter was enamoured of the West and borrowed from it, he did not do so indiscriminately or wholesale, and he remained thoroughly Russian. It is a striking fact that Milyukov, who was perhaps the strongest of Peter's critics among recent historians, should sum up on Peter's reforms thus: — "Their fortuitousness, arbitrariness, individual stamp, and violence are necessary elements in them. Despite their sharply antinational externals, they are entirely rooted in the conditions of national life. The country received nothing but the reforms for which she was fitted."

Locke and Rousseau on
the Social Contract

Two scientists, Sir Isaac Newton and Charles Darwin, had particularly significant effects upon the political and social thought of the eras in which they
lived. Although Newton was primarily an astronomer and mathematician and
Darwin a biologist, their basic ideas filtered rapidly through the academic
communities of their day to be taken up and used in entirely different contexts.

The idea of natural law provides an example of this process. Newton
believed that phenomena such as planetary motion could be explained in
terms of laws expressed mathematically. Once he had proved this hypothesis
with his law of gravitation, other men began to look for laws governing
religion, economics, and politics. Motivating their search was a belief in so-
called natural law — that is, rules underlying human behavior that could be
discovered through the use of reason. The Problem for today consists of
selections from the works of two men, John Locke and Jean Jacques Rousseau,
each of whom based his political philosophy on natural law.

John Locke, a contemporary of Newton's, published *Two Treatises of
Government* in 1690. In one of the essays, entitled "Of Civil Government," he
tried to justify the action of the English parliament in the Glorious Revolution
of 1688 by arguing that James II had violated nature's laws and thus deserved
to be deposed. Locke believed that men were born into a "state of nature" in
which everyone was free and entitled to the essential natural rights of life,
liberty, and property. In order to protect these rights, men formed societies by
a "social contract" and transferred to a government the obligation of safe-
guarding them. A government was a party to the contract made with its
citizens; if it failed to protect life, liberty, and property, the people had a right
to overthrow it. This is what happened in England in 1688, according to Locke.
It is clear that Locke believed that neither the individual nor his government
could be trusted with complete power. Hence, some rights had to be protected
so that even the central government could never violate them.

Jean Jacques Rousseau was not essentially a political philosopher like
Locke, but rather a man of literature. In *The Social Contract,* first published in
France in 1762, Rousseau started with some of Locke's assumptions but came
to quite different conclusions. Like Locke, Rousseau argued that men had originally lived in a state of nature. Like Locke, Rousseau believed that men in
this state had certain rights. But here he parted company with Locke. Once
people entered a social contract to form a government, they gave all their
rights over to the control of the community. In doing so, they submitted to the
"general will" — a kind of ideal representing what was best for the whole
state, a will for the general good. According to Rousseau, men were essentially
good and the general will which grew out of their social contract could be
trusted to protect the rights of all. Clearly the general will was "right." If
someone disagreed with it, then he must be "wrong" and for his own sake
ought to be made to agree. In Rousseau's phrase, it might become necessary

to "force a man to be free," that is, to agree with the general will. In Rousseau's society no rights were sacred. The general will controlled everything.

The American Constitution is Lockean in nature. Both the Constitution itself and the Bill of Rights contain a number of provisions forbidding government to invade certain areas of individual freedom. These clauses are based on the assumption that some rights are so important that we should not risk permitting even an elected government to violate them. We assume, therefore, that we cannot always trust our government, particularly in times of crisis, to protect all the rights which we want man to enjoy.

The present government of the Soviet Union makes assumptions like those of Rousseau. It assumes that man is essentially good and that government can be trusted. Since there is only one party in Russia, that party represents the general will, and the general will is always right. If any man disagrees with party policy, he is wrong and ought for his own sake to be corrected. Hence a term in a corrective labor camp is good for him as well as for society. Thus, although Rousseau himself was an ardent believer in human freedom, some of his ideas can be used as a justification for dictatorship.

The two excerpts below contain the essence of some of the ideas discussed in this introduction. As you read, consider the following questions:

1   Did the state of nature ever really exist? Where did the idea come from? Was the social contract an actual event?

2   Why do you suppose Locke chose life, liberty, and property as natural rights? Would a contemporary Communist (if he believed in natural rights) choose these three?

3   Why does Locke think that men have a right to revolt? Why does Rousseau disagree? Upon what assumptions does Locke's justification of revolt rest? Is it similar to the idea in Clause 61 of Magna Charta?

4   How would you compare Locke's attitude toward human nature with that of Machiavelli?

I

OF CIVIL GOVERNMENT / by John Locke

From *Two Treatises of Government*. London, 1690. Language simplified and spelling modernized by Edwin Fenton.

To understand political power aright, we must consider what condition all men are naturally in, and that is, a state of perfect freedom to do as they wish and dispose of their possessions and persons as they think fit, within the bounds of the law of nature, without asking leave or depending upon the will of any other man.

A state also of equality, in which no one has more power or authority than another, there being nothing more evident than that creatures of the same species and rank born to all the same advantages of nature, and the use of the same faculties, should also be equal to each other without subordination or subjection. . . .

The state of nature has a law of nature to govern it, and reason, which is that law, teaches all mankind who will but consult it that, being all equal and independent, no one ought to harm another in his life, health, liberty, or possessions; for men being all the workmanship of one omnipotent and infinitely wise Maker; all the servants of one sovereign Master, sent into the world by His order and about His business; they are His property, whose workmanship they are, made to last during His, not one another's pleasure. All men are naturally in that state, and remain so till, by their own consents, they make themselves members of some political society. . . .

If man in the state of nature is as free as has been said, if he is absolute lord of his own person and possessions, equal to the greatest and subject to nobody, why will he part with his freedom? Why will he give up this empire, and subject himself to the dominion and control of any other power? To which it is obvious to answer, that though in the state of nature he has such a right, yet the enjoyment of it is very uncertain, and constantly exposed to the invasion of others; for all being kings as much as he, every man his equal, and most of them no strict observers of equity and justice, the enjoyment of the property he has in this state is very unsafe, very insecure; and it is not without reason that he seeks out and is willing to join in society with others who are already united, or have a mind to unite for the mutual preservation of their lives, liberties and estates, which I call by the general name—property.

The great and chief end, therefore, of men uniting into commonwealths is the preservation of their property. . . .

. . . since it can never be supposed to be the will of the society that the legislature should be able to destroy that which everyone hopes to secure by entering into society, and for which the people submitted themselves to legislators of their own making; whenever the legislators try to take away and destroy the property of the people, or to reduce them to slavery under arbitrary power, they put themselves into a state of war with the people who are thereupon freed from any further obedience, and are left to the common refuge which God hath provided for all men against force and violence. Whensoever, therefore, the legislature shall break this fundamental rule of society, and either by ambition, fear, folly, or corruption, try to grasp themselves, or put into the hands of any other, an absolute power over the lives, liberties, and estates of the people, by this breach of trust they forfeit the power the people had put into their hands for quite contrary ends, and it is the privilege of people, who have a right to resume their original liberty, to establish a new legislature and provide for their own safety and security. What I have said here concerning the legislature in general holds true also for the executive, who having a double trust put in him, both to have a part in the legislature and to carry out the law, acts against both, when he goes about to set up his own arbitrary will as the law of the society. . . .

To this perhaps it will be said, that the people being ignorant, and always discontented, to lay the foundation of government in the unsteady opinion and uncertain humour of the people, is to expose it to certain ruin: and no government will be able long to subsist, if the people may set up a new legislature whenever they take offense at the old one. To this I answer, quite the contrary. People are not so easily got out of their old forms, as some are apt to suggest. . . . The slowness of the people to quit their old constitutions has, in the many revolutions which have been seen in this kingdom, in this and former ages, still kept us to, or, after some interval of fruitless attempts, still brought us back again to our old legislature of king, lords, and commons.

But it will be said, this hypothesis may lead to frequent rebellion. To which I answer . . . . such revolutions happen not upon every little mismanagement in public affairs. . . . But if a long train of abuses, prevarications and artifices, all tending the same way, make the design visible to the people, they cannot but feel what they lie under, and see whither they are going; it is not to be wondered at that they should then rouse themselves, and endeavor to put the rule into such hands which may secure to them the end for which government was at first erected.

II

THE SOCIAL CONTRACT / by Jean Jacques Rousseau

Geneva: Marc-Michel Bousquet, 1766. Translated and adapted by Edwin Fenton.

I assume, for the sake of argument, that mankind at some time reached a point when the disadvantages of remaining in a state of nature outweighed the advantages. Under these conditions, the original state of nature could no longer endure. The human race would have perished if it had not changed its ways.

Men, being human, cannot develop new powers. But they can unite and control the powers they already have. Men in the state of nature could get together, pooling their strength in a way that would permit them to meet any challenge. They had to learn to work together under central direction.

A real concentration of human powers could be brought about only as the result of an agreement among individual men. But each individual man relies on his own strength and his own freedom of action to protect and preserve himself. How can he limit his strength and his freedom of action without injuring himself and neglecting to care for his own affairs?

Some form of association must be found which can rally the whole community for the protection of the person and property of each of its citizens in such a way that each man, because he is a voluntary member of the association, renders obedience to his own will and hence remains as free as he was before. That is the basic problem solved by the social contract.

The provisions of the social contract are determined by the nature of the act [of association] in such a way that the least modification will render them invalid. Even though the terms of association may never have been formally accepted in open meeting, they are everywhere the same and universally recognized. If the social contract were in any way broken by anyone, then each individual could at once resume all the rights which were his in the state of nature. He would regain his natural liberty by losing the liberty of the social contract for which he originally gave up his freedom of action.

The essence of the social contract can be stated simply: each individual surrenders all his rights to the community. Since each man surrenders his rights without reservation, all are equal. And because all are equal, it is to everyone's interest to make life pleasant for his fellows.

Since all rights have been surrendered to the community without reservation, no one has any claim against the group. If any rights were left to individuals and no one was given authority to decide between individual rights and the public good, then each man would try to extend the scope of those rights he had reserved for himself. This situation would mean that a state of nature still existed. All rights must be surrendered; none may be reserved. . . .

The heart of the idea of the social contract may be stated simply: Each of us places his person and authority under the supreme direction of the general will; and the group receives each individual as an indivisible part of the whole. . . .

In order that the social contract may not be a mere empty formula, everyone must understand that any individual who refuses to obey the general will must be forced by his fellows to do so. This is a way of saying that it may be necessary to force a man to be free; freedom in this case being obedience to the will of all.

A Comparison of the American and French Revolutions

With the exception of the Industrial Revolution in England, no events of the 18th century were more significant to the history of the world than the American and French revolutions. The American revolt resulted in the establishment of the United States and in the development of a democratic government on a hitherto unknown scale. The French upheaval overthrew an ancient monarchy, strengthened men's faith in the efficacy of revolutions, and stimulated nationalism and liberalism all over Europe. Without these two revolutions the entire course of modern history would have been drastically different.

Many historians have discussed the similarities and differences between the American and French revolutions. On some matters, they usually agree. For example, we know that Louis XVI increased an already huge debt by giving financial aid to American colonies; in order to raise more money he had to call a meeting of the Estates-General, an event that triggered the French Revolution. But debates are still raging about a number of other questions. Did the American Revolution provide a real source of inspiration for the French? Or was French influence on America (through the philosophers of the Enlightenment) a more powerful stimulus? Were the two revolutions inspired by similar philosophies or did they proceed from quite different assumptions? The readings for today discuss some of these issues.

Throughout this volume we have emphasized that all history is interpretation. Today you will read two interpretive excerpts about the French and American revolutions. The first is from the pen of a German writer, Friedrich Gentz, who was analyzing events of his own lifetime. As you will see, he argued that the two conflicts were quite different. The other selection was written by a contemporary American historian, Robert R. Palmer of Princeton University, one of our greatest living authorities on the French Revolution. Professor Palmer argues that the American Revolution had subtle and far-reaching effects in France and that these currents helped to touch off revolt. It is for you to decide whether these interpretations can be supported by evidence.

As you read, consider the following questions:

1   According to Gentz, how did the French and American revolutions differ? Do you agree with him?

2   Some scholars have argued that the American Revolution reflected the ideas of Locke and the French Revolution those of Rousseau. Do you agree?

3   What specific connections does Palmer find between the American and the French revolutions? What evidence does he use to support his interpretation? What do you think of the technique implied in the first sentence of his fourth paragraph?

4   Were Palmer and Gentz discussing the same issues?

I

THE FRENCH AND AMERICAN REVOLUTIONS COMPARED
by Friedrich Gentz

From *Historisches. Journal*, Vol. II, May-June, 1800. Translated by Edwin Fenton.

Throughout its history the American Revolution had a fixed and definite goal toward which it moved. The French Revolution never had a definite goal and instead of moving in one direction toward a set objective, it ran helter-skelter in a thousand directions.

From the beginning, the leaders of the American Revolution knew exactly how far they wanted to go and where they wanted to stop. The constitutions of the several colonies and even the organization of the federal government, at least in its principles, were already established. Their purpose was not to create from nothing but to preserve the best of the past, not to erect a new building but to free the old one from a confining and burdensome scaffolding built by others. It never occurred to them to reform even their own country, much less the rest of the world. So they escaped the most dangerous of all the pitfalls which in our times threaten the founders of any great revolution.

It is true that the introduction to the Declaration of Independence published by the Congress in the name of the colonies contains a reference to the natural and unalienable rights of mankind as the foundation of all government and that the right of the people to change their form of government follows logically from those rights. It is also true that most of the state constitutions are preceded by these idle declarations of rights which are so dangerous when they are applied and from which so much misery has come to France and to the rest of the civilized world. But those who have studied the American Revolution closely agree that the Americans permitted speculative ideas of natural rights to have no visible effect upon practical measures and revolutions. They only made these declarations to justify their first steps, but after the first steps speculative ideas had no marked influence upon them. Never in the whole course of the American Revolution were the rights of man appealed to in such a way that the rights of citizens were imperiled. Never was the sovereignty of the people used as an excuse to undermine the respect due to the laws or the bases of social stability. In not even one case did

an individual, a social class, or the representatives of a state appeal to
a declaration of rights to justify escaping from an obligation or re-
nouncing obedience to a common ruler. Finally, not one legislator
or statesman in America tried to undermine the lawfulness of foreign
constitutions or to set up the American Revolution as the harbinger
of a new era in society all around the world.

The contrast between the objectives of the French and American
revolutions is just as striking as the one which has resulted from com-
paring their origins and developments. The American Revolution was
characterized by the utmost precision of objectives and therefore of
principles and of means throughout its duration. But the French
Revolution has had imprecisely stated objectives and therefore the
means of attaining these objectives and the principles used to justify
action have changed constantly. The history of the revolution proves
this point over and over again, but this development should not sur-
prise a man who has thought about the origin and nature of the revolution. For as soon as a step is taken entirely outside the boundaries
of definite and acknowledged rights, and everything which imagination, necessity, or passion inspires is declared to be lawful, then
society lays itself open to the exercise of arbitrary authority. A revolution which has no other principle than to attack the existing constitution will have its limits set only by the imagination and by the sense
of guilt of the participants.

II

THE FRENCH AND AMERICAN REVOLUTIONS CONSIDERED
TOGETHER / by Robert R. Palmer

From an address given at the Eighth Annual Advanced
Placement History Conference, Carnegie Institute of
Technology, 1961. By permission of Robert R. Palmer.

While seeing the differences between the American and French
revolutions, differences which have been very fortunate for the subsequent history of the United States, we should also admit certain
resemblances, accept both of them as significant revolutions, and see
them as the two principal manifestations of an even more general
movement, which may be called the eighteenth-century democratic
revolution. This was most essentially a movement against aristocracy, in the sense of a privileged, hereditary, oligarchic and self-

perpetuating elite or ruling group; and since aristocracy in this sense was characteristic of every European country, and by no means unknown in America, the movements against it were kindred movements that could be stimulated by each other. There was something in the American Revolution that corresponded and appealed to something in Europe, and hence the impact of the American Revolution in Europe was immediate and profound. Here is another difficulty for those historians who stress the unique or nonexportable character of the American Revolution. They are obliged to believe that many people who lived at that time were mistaken. Conservatives deplored it, progressives hailed it, but there was wide agreement on the fact— the fact that the American Revolution had somehow set off a chain of revolutions in other countries. . . .

There were many reasons why the birth of the United States had a revolutionary effect in Europe. It seemed to offer dramatic proof of what Europeans of the Enlightenment already believed. The independence of a New World was taken to signify the dawn of a New Era. It confirmed the sense of progress and rapid change. The new American Constitution and Bill of Rights seemed to prove that European ideas of liberty and equality, of the social contract and the sovereignty of the people, could exist not only in books but in real life also.

.All this inspired the confident outlook on the future without which there can be no revolutionary psychology. It is also part of a revolutionary psychology to have a negative attitude, a sense of alienation or rejection of the existing order. This too was produced in Europe by the American Revolution, especially among middle-class people, who were beginning to resent the superiority of the aristocracy, and were made more dissatisfied by what they heard or read of America. It can be very unsettling for any social order, and can undermine the basis of political loyalty, when a great many people have their minds forever fixed upon another country which they believe to be free of the faults of their own, and where they think that their deepest wishes for their own country are already in process of fulfilment. Whether or not we Americans approve of this sort of thing today, the truth seems to be that the infant United States, in the critical years which preceded the French Revolution, had precisely this effect upon the existing order in France and Europe.

Endless examples could be given, of which I shall offer only two. One concerns L. G. Bourdon, an interpreter at the French Foreign

Office, where he had as a colleague the young Edmond Genet. This is the Genet, always called "citizen Genet" in American history, who so horrified the Federalists a few years later when he was minister to the United States; we catch a glimpse of what the young nobleman Genet, who soon became an ardent revolutionary, might be absorbing from his middle-class colleague, Bourdon. In 1786 Bourdon wrote a poem on America. It abounds in every cliché known to the French Enlightenment. The Americans are unspoiled children of nature, and at the same time Philosophers who follow reason and respect humanity; they enjoy equality, brotherhood, religious freedom, and happiness. . . . Perhaps Bourdon unduly idealized or even misunderstood the United States. The point, however, is the implied criticism of his own country for its lack of these qualities which he so glowingly ascribes to the new land across the sea.

The other example is that of Mme. Roland. During the French Revolution she was to figure as an important political hostess. Before the Revolution she sat at home, writing long letters to her husband, who was an inspector of manufacturers in the government service. Mostly she told him the news of servants, babies, food, visits with neighbors, and the books she had been reading, but at one point she rose to a high pitch of indignation. She was annoyed at the trouble he was having with some of his colleagues. She was outraged that this "virtuous man," as she called her worthy spouse to his face, or at least in writing, should have to deal with such vile creatures. She thought the French government "frightful" for not seeing his merits. The situation was so bad, she said, that she wished they might flee together to the wilderness of Pennsylvania. Of course Mme. Roland was too well off to have any real intention of emigrating. But it was harder for her to accept conditions in her own country when she could have such dreams of America. . . .

When the revolution came in France, in 1789, and went on with fluctuating violence for ten years, the relationship between French and Americans, on the matter of revolution, underwent a change. Absorbed now in their own affairs, the French had less interest in the American Revolution. The Americans sharply divided. Some were repelled, others attracted, by the events in France. Except as an official government policy, insisted upon by both Presidents Washington and Adams, there was very little neutrality. There was no feeling that the affairs of Europe were none of America's business. On the contrary, it was widely agreed that developments in Europe and

America were part of one great trend. For American Federalists it was evident that the rising American democrats, and the political radicals who kept arriving from England and Ireland, were the same kind of beings as French Jacobins. For the American democrats it was clear that Federalists hankered for hereditary aristocracy, lords and ladies, royal courts, a despotic executive, and special privileges for the few. The ideological excitement, by making everything seem so clear-cut, by arousing opinion among people normally apathetic, and by accentuating and generalizing such real differences as existed among Americans on concrete matters, helped to build the habit of a two-party political system in the United States. It is a wonder that the young American republic, just learning to live under a new and indeed novel kind of federal constitution, preserved even the loose and uncentralized unity that it had. Both Britain and France interfered in American politics, and both had their actively committed partisans in America. Some believed that the triumph of the French Revolution was necessary to save America from the snares of aristocracy and the clutches of England, others that the victory of England and the Coalition was necessary to save America from exploitation by France and from a descent into demagogy and ruin. It still seems . . . that the American people have never been so aroused, genuinely and in the depths, by any foreign event as by the French Revolution, precisely because Americans did not see it as wholly foreign, but identified it with live issues in the United States.

For example, in this golden age of Fourth of July oratory, right through the French Reign of Terror, Fourth of July orators continued to associate the French and American revolutions. A man by the name of Elihu Palmer delivered such an address in July 1793. He began by deploring that some signers of the Declaration of Independence now wanted to crush liberty and equality. "Beware, ye American aristocrats!" he exclaimed as he warmed to his subject. "Your principles and efforts are leading you to a precipice. . . . If the cause of France, which is the cause of human nature, should succeed, then farewell kings, aristocrats, and the long catalogue of clerical impositions." Language of this kind naturally inflamed the opposition. Fisher Ames . . . wrote extensively on, or rather against, such subjects as equality and the French Revolution. . . . Looking at the French Republic, he thought it foreshadowed what democracy would be like in the United States. "Behold France, that open hell, in which we see them in their torment, and perhaps our future state."

The Congress of Vienna

By what standards should we measure the success of a peace conference? Should we insist that the delegates make their decisions in accordance with some absolute standard of what is "right"? Should we ask them to solve the problems that caused the war? Should we expect them to set aright the numerous issues in international affairs that disturbed the peace in a particular period? Should we require them to punish the vanquished in order to teach them a lesson? Or should we merely ask them, in the process of settling one war, to avoid making mistakes that might bring on another one? Obviously, the standards we adopt will have a marked effect on our judgment of the success of a peace conference.

Whether they like to or not, historians must always establish criteria for judgment. They ought to make these criteria clear and explicit so that their readers can establish a basis for agreement or disagreement. How can a reader judge the accuracy of an interpretation if he does not know the assumptions upon which the interpretation rests? If a writer does not state his criteria expressly, a reader who wants to determine the accuracy of the interpretation should think the argument through and then state the author's criteria for himself. Developing this habit will help to make the student able to think more clearly for himself.

One peace conference which has been the subject of debate ever since it met in 1814-1815 is the Congress of Vienna, which drafted a settlement after the Napoleonic wars. Europe's most important statesmen were present at Vienna. Their deliberations lasted for months and settled a number of issues for years to come. But did they settle these issues well?

Prince Metternich, the chief Austrian delegate, played an important role in the Congress and later helped to enforce its principles. Between 1815 and 1848 he was the most influential statesman in Europe. The statement of his political "faith" in one of the selections below was written in 1820 at the time of uprisings in southern Europe, but it accurately reflects his ideas at the time of the Congress itself. In this passage Metternich makes clear the conservative philosophy that helped give the Congress of Vienna a bad reputation among liberal nationalists. Because the Congress did not produce parliamentary governments ruling over free nations, many liberals argued that the peace was a poor one. But is this a good way to measure the success of a peace treaty?

The second excerpt is from the pen of Hajo Holborn, professor of history at Yale University. Professor Holborn here judges the peace conference both from the standpoint of the issues involved and for its influence on the future. Notice the way in which he sets forth the criteria by which he will evaluate the success of the Congress.

As you read these two excerpts, consider the following questions:

1   What are the principles that seemed to guide Metternich's thinking? Did reliance on such principles doom the Congress of Vienna to failure? Would they doom it by the standards of a liberal nationalist?

2   What do you think of the comments Metternich makes in the middle

of this excerpt about the difference in the ambitions of the rich and the poor?

3   According to Holborn, what is the major measure of the success of a peace conference?

4   What was the major failure of the men who wrote the Vienna settlement, according to Holborn?

5   What areas of agreement do you find between Metternich and Holborn?

6   How should a historian judge whether a peace conference was a success or a failure?

I

METTERNICH'S CONFESSION OF FAITH

From *Memoirs of Prince Metternich*. London: Richard Bentley & Son, 1880-1882. Language simplified by Edwin Fenton.

"Europe today," a famous writer said recently, "makes an intelligent man feel sad and a decent man feel horror." It would be difficult to describe the present situation in better words.

Kings have to wonder whether they will remain on their thrones; passions are released which aim at overthrowing everything that is respected as the basis of society; religion, public morality, laws, customs, rights and duties are all being attacked. Most people are not taking part in these attacks and revolutions. Some are carried away by the flood of events but most wish simply to preserve things the way they were.

What is the cause of all these evils? How have they come about? Why are they so widespread? Can something be done about it? These are questions which every good man who loves peace and order should ask himself. Peace and order — these are really one and the same thing, which all men need and should be grateful for. . . .

. . . we must point out in particular the evil which is threatening to rob us of the real blessings and enjoyments of civilization. This evil may be described in one word — presumption, an overconfidence which comes from the rapid development of the human mind in so many directions. It is this which today leads so many men astray, because almost everybody suffers from it.

Religion, morality, legislation, economy, politics, administration, all have become the common property of every man. Knowledge seems to come by inspiration; experience has no value for our over-confident man; faith and trust is nothing to him. He puts in its place what he calls personal convictions and, to arrive at these convictions, eliminates all special study. Such application seems too petty for our modern men, who believe they are able to understand everything in a flash. Laws have no value for this modern man, simply because he has not personally had a part in making them and he is too self-important to approve of what "less gifted" men in generations before him have done. He himself is the source of power; why should he submit to things established by those who know less than he does? He may admit that certain laws were necessary in bygone, weaker days, but they are no longer suitable for an age of reason and vigor. He sees himself in a world of universal perfection, an idea which some Germans refer to in absurd terms as the Emancipation of the People! . . .

It is chiefly the middle classes which are infected with this "moral gangrene" and it is only among them that the real leaders of the movement are to be found. It can really have no attraction for the great mass of the people. They must spend too much of their lives working for a living to waste time on such dreams. The people know what is the happiest thing for them: this is to be able to count on the next day, for it is the next day which will repay them for the cares and sorrows of today. They wish simple laws which protect them and their families and their possessions and are afraid of anything which harms their jobs and makes their lives more difficult. . . .

The dissatisfied classes are chiefly wealthy men who are looking out for their own advantage at the expense of changing the way things are. This includes officials and writers and lawyers and teachers. . . .

I am convinced that our way of life can no longer be saved unless our governments act quickly and vigorously while they still are free to do this. . . .

There is a rule of behavior common to individuals and to states which has been proven correct because it has been practiced over the centuries and in everyday life. This rule declares that "man should not dream of changing things while emotionally excited about the matter; wisdom directs that at such moments we should limit ourselves to maintaining the status quo."

If all kings will only accept this rule and prove by word and action their determination not to change things without careful thought, they will find people everywhere who support them. If the governments establish the principle of stability, this will not exclude future improvement of conditions. Firmness does not mean that nothing can change. But, it is these individuals who bear the heavy responsibility of government who should help their fellow-men to prosper. It is the duty of governments to govern as the needs of the times require. Wise changes cannot be carried out if dissatisfied groups of men, who have neither the right to ask for such changes nor the ability to keep the changes from going too far, force them from the legal governmental authorities.

Respect for all is what we should have. That means there should be freedom for every government to watch over the well-being of its own people. There should exist a union between all governments to prevent the dissatisfied self-seekers from stirring up trouble in the various countries. Good citizens should have proper contempt for the meaningless words which these men use to stir up discontent. And, finally, there should be respect for change and new development along slow, peaceful paths. These ought to be the ideas of all great kings, and the world will be saved if they do something about them. It will be lost if they do not.

II

THE POLITICAL COLLAPSE OF EUROPE / by Hajo Holborn

Reprinted by permission of Alfred A. Knopf, Inc. Copyright 1951 by Hajo Holborn. Pp. 27-32.

The peace settlement of Vienna has more often been condemned than praised. The accusation most frequently levelled against the Congress of Vienna has been that it lacked foresight in appraising the forces of modern nationalism and liberalism. Foresight is, indeed, one of the main qualities that distinguishes the statesman from the mere political professional. But even a statesman can only build with the bricks at hand and cannot hope to construct the second floor before he has modelled the first by which to shelter his own generation. His foresight of future developments can often express itself only by cautious attempts at keeping the way open for an evolution of the new forces.

It is questionable how successful the Congress of Vienna was in this respect. None of the Congress representatives was a statesman or political thinker of the first historic rank. All of them were strong partisans of conservatism or outright reaction, and they found the rectitude of their convictions confirmed by the victory of the old powers over the revolutionary usurper. Still, they did not make a reactionary peace. They recognized that France could not live without a constitutional charter, and they knew, too, that the Holy Roman Empire was beyond resurrection. The new German Confederation represented a great improvement of the political conditions of Germany if one remembers that in Germany as well as in Italy the national movements were not strong enough to serve as pillars of a new order. In eastern Europe, furthermore, the modern ideas of nationality had hardly found more than a small academic and literary audience. A peace treaty cannot create new historical forces; it can only place the existing ones in a relationship most conducive to the maintenance of mutual confidence and least likely to lead to future conflict. The rest must be left to the ever continuing and never finished daily work of statesmen.

In this light the Vienna settlement was a constructive peace treaty. Its chief authors, Castlereagh, Metternich, Alexander I, and Hardenberg, had a very inadequate vision of the ideas and forces that were to dominate the nineteenth century, but they had clear notions about the vital necessity of establishing an equilibrium among the powers that determined the political life of Europe. They had carefully directed the war efforts of their countries with this necessity in mind and were able to create such an equilibrium in the Peace of Vienna.

The statesmen of Vienna, however, believed that it was not enough merely to revive the eighteenth century balance of power. The experience of common danger, shared by all the European states in the years between 1792 and 1815, would, it was thought, persuade the states to look at the balance of power less as a means for the advancement of their selfish interests than as the foundation of concerted action for the general welfare of the European community. These expectations were only partly fulfilled, but they were no idle and quickly forgotten dreams. During the early part of the nineteenth century the sharp conflicts of power were mitigated by a sense of European responsibility. And even when wars and national revolutions had put this to a hard test after the middle of the century, a common European consciousness survived.

But the victorious powers failed in 1814-15 and in the years thereafter to create international institutions that embodied these principles. The Congress of Aachen of 1818 codified the diplomatic

rules among states, which had been vague before. This code, however, was helpful only in a technical sense and did not solve problems
of political substance. The sovereignty of states remained unimpaired.
An attempt was made to transform the balance-of-power system into
some sort of federation of the four or, after the readmission of France,
five big powers. The Concert of Europe, through regular meetings of
the monarchs or their leading ministers, was to settle the controversial political issues. Four such conferences were held between 1818
and 1822 at Aachen, Troppau, Laibach, and Verona, but the nascent
confederation of Europe broke down, since the social and political
objectives of the five powers could not be unified.

The breach occurred over the question of whether or not the
guarantee of the Vienna settlement by the five powers should extend
to the preservation of the monarchical governments that had been
restored in 1815. Metternich and Alexander I were afraid of revolution. The rise of Napoleon, in their opinion, had been the result of
the French Revolution and the demonic forces that it had set loose.
The European equilibrium was dependent on the stability of the
social and political order of Europe. They urged, therefore, that the
powers that formed the five-power system . . . should intervene wherever internal revolution threatened the "legitimate" order. Britain,
on the other hand, even before the reform of 1832, felt differently.
Social and political change did not frighten British statesmen, who
knew already that the new forces could not be submerged, but could
only be guided and channelled. . . .

Metternich's conception of a European political system resting
upon the balance of power among the five major states, who would act
in concert to maintain both international "tranquillity" and internal
"stability," could not be realized. Metternich has gained in historical
stature, since modern historians have refused to view him through the
glasses of his nineteenth century liberal foes. He showed great
strength in the heroic years of his career, 1812-15, in his inflexible
determination to achieve a revival of the balance of power. But his
confidence that the new Concert of Europe could make the social and
political processes of western Europe and possibly the whole world
stand still or even retrogress showed the limits of his political realism.
He had no understanding of the dynamic forces that the industrial
revolution in England had produced in his own lifetime. . . . Even in
terms of Austrian self-interest his policy of international and internal
conservatism was a temporary, not a constructive, solution.

English Liberalism
in the 19th Century

John Stuart Mill was one of the most distinguished thinkers of Victorian England. He grew up with the Industrial Revolution, a believer in progress and laissez-faire economics. He held that everyone would benefit if each man could follow his own interests without undue interference. However, as Mill saw the rise of new industries crowding more and more people into England's already packed cities, he began to worry that liberty might be driven out of existence by the conformist pressures of democracy itself. Thus he came to believe in the need for some governmental regulation to protect the rights of citizens. In his famous work, *On Liberty,* he set out to defend individual freedom and to define its limitations.

This reading raises the problem of a historical definition of the word *liberty.* The introduction to Problem 3 discussed a historical definition of democracy, particularly as related to ancient Athens. It was held that a meaningful interpretation of a word like *democracy* or *liberty* must involve two parts: a general definition which would apply to any use of the word under any circumstances, and a specific definition which would apply to the word at a particular time and in a particular place. To our American Founding Fathers, liberty meant freedom from British control and the right to pass one's own laws. The excerpt below will give an idea of Mill's different attitude toward this concept.

Some of the language in the selection is difficult and may require re-reading. Pay particular attention to the second long paragraph and to the four short concluding paragraphs. Keep the following questions in mind as you read:

1   What did Mill mean by the word *liberty?* See particularly his second paragraph.

2   According to Mill, why should citizens be entitled to express all opinions which do not interfere with the liberty of thought of others? Do you agree with the four reasons he gives for this position at the end of this excerpt?

3   What conditions in Victorian England might account for Mill's ideas about liberty?

4   How would Rousseau have felt about Mill's concern over the possible tyranny of the majority in a democratic society?

ON LIBERTY / by John Stuart Mill

London: John W. Parker & Son, 1859.

The object of this Essay is to assert one very simple principle, as entitled to govern absolutely the dealings of society with the individual in the way of compulsion and control, whether the means used be physical force in the form of legal penalties, or the moral coercion of public opinion. That principle is, that the sole end for which mankind are warranted, individually or collectively, in interfering with the liberty of action of any of their number, is self-protection. That the only purpose for which power can be rightfully exercised over any member of a civilized community, against his will, is to prevent harm to others. His own good, either physical or moral, is not a sufficient warrant. He cannot rightfully be compelled to do or forbear because it will be better for him to do so, because it will make him happier, because, in the opinions of others, to do so would be wise, or even right. These are good reasons for remonstrating with him, or reasoning with him, or persuading him, or entreating him, but not for compelling him, or visiting him with any evil in case he do otherwise. To justify that, the conduct from which it is desired to deter him, must be calculated to produce evil to some one else. The only part of the conduct of any one, for which he is amenable to society, is that which concerns others. In the part which merely concerns himself, his independence is, of right, absolute. Over himself, over his own body and mind, the individual is sovereign.

[*In the following paragraphs Mill modifies the preceding by stating that these ideas cannot apply to what he calls "backward" states, societies not yet civilized. These peoples must be vigorously directed until they advance to a point where they can mutually decide what is for their own good, a point which England in 1859 had long since reached. He then mentions conditions under which society can control an individual—for example, if he commits a crime.*]

But there is a sphere of action in which society, as distinguished from the individual, has, if any, only an indirect interest; comprehending all that portion of a person's life and conduct which affects only himself, or if it also affects others, only with their free, voluntary, and undeceived consent and participation. . . . This, then, is the appropriate region of human liberty. It comprises, first, the inward domain of consciousness; demanding liberty of conscience, in the most comprehensive sense; liberty of thought and feeling; absolute freedom of opinion and sentiment on all subjects, practical or speculative, scientific, moral, or theological. The liberty of expressing and publishing opinions may seem to fall under a different principle, since it belongs to that part of the conduct of an individual which concerns other people; but, being almost of as much importance as the liberty of thought itself, and resting in great part on the same reasons, is practically inseparable from it. Secondly, the principle requires liberty of tastes and pursuits; of framing the plan of our life to suit our own character; of doing as we like, subject to such consequences as may follow: without impediment from our fellow-creatures, so long as what we do does not harm them, even though they should think our conduct foolish, perverse, or wrong. Thirdly, from this liberty of each individual, follows the liberty, within the same limits, of combination among individuals; freedom to unite, for any purpose not involving harm to others: the persons combining being supposed to be of full age and not forced or deceived.

No society in which these liberties are not, on the whole, respected, is free, whatever may be its form of government; and none is completely free in which they do not exist absolute and unqualified. The only freedom which deserves the name, is that of pursuing our own good in our own way, so long as we do not attempt to deprive others of theirs, or impede their efforts to obtain it. Each is the proper guardian of his own health, whether bodily, or mental and spiritual. Mankind are greater gainers by suffering each other to live as seems good to themselves, than by compelling each to live as seems good to the rest.

Though this doctrine is anything but new, and, to some persons, may have the air of a truism, there is no doctrine which stands more directly opposed to the general tendency of existing opinion and practice. Society has expended fully as much effort in the attempt (according to its lights) to compel people to conform to its notion of personal, as of social excellence. The ancient commonwealths thought themselves entitled to practise, and the ancient philosophers countenanced, the regulation of every part of private conduct by public authority, on the ground that the State had a deep interest in the whole bodily and mental discipline of every one of its citizens; a mode of thinking which may have been admissible in small republics surrounded by powerful enemies, in constant peril of being subverted by foreign attack or internal commotion, and to which even a short interval of relaxed energy and self-command might so easily be fatal, that they could not afford to wait for the salutary permanent effects of freedom.

[*In the modern world, continues Mill, the great size of political communities has prevented so great an interference* by law *in the details of private life.* "But the engines of moral repression have been wielded more strenuously against divergence from reigning public

*opinion . . . ." Among these "engines" he specifically includes
organized religious and popular morality.*]

Apart from the peculiar tenets of individual thinkers, there is
also in the world at large an increasing inclination to stretch unduly
the powers of society over the individual, both by the force of opinion
and even by that of legislation: and as the tendency of all the changes
taking place in the world is to strengthen society, and diminish the
power of the individual, this encroachment is not one of the evils
which tend spontaneously to disappear, but, on the contrary, to grow
more and more formidable. The disposition of mankind, whether as
rulers or as fellow citizens, to impose their own opinions and inclina-
tions as a rule of conduct on others, is so energetically supported by
some of the best and by some of the worst feelings incident to human
nature, that it is hardly ever kept under restraint by anything but want
of power; and as the power is not declining, but growing, unless a
strong barrier of moral conviction can be raised against the mischief,
we must expect, in the present circumstances of the world, to see it
increase.

It will be convenient for the argument, if, instead of at once
entering upon the general thesis, we confine ourselves in the first
instance to a single branch of it, on which the principle here stated
is, if not fully, yet to a certain point, recognised by the current opinions. This one branch is the Liberty of Thought: from which it is
impossible to separate the cognate liberty of speaking and of writing.
Although these liberties, to some considerable amount, form part of
the political morality of all countries which profess religious tolera-
tion and free institutions, the grounds, both philosophical and practical, on which they rest, are perhaps not so familiar to the general
mind, nor so thoroughly appreciated by many even of the leaders of
opinion, as might have been expected.

[*With a wealth of examples, Mill carefully elaborates his ideas on
freedom of the press, of opinion, and of discussion, and then summa-
rizes as follows:*]

We have now recognised the necessity to the mental well-being
of mankind (on which all other well-being depends) of freedom of
opinion, and freedom of the expression of opinion, on four distinct
grounds; which we will now briefly recapitulate.

First, if any opinion is compelled to silence, that opinion may,
for aught we can certainly know, be true. To deny this is to assume
our own infallibility.

Secondly, though the silenced opinion be an error, it may, and very commonly does, contain a portion of truth; and since the general or prevailing opinion on any subject is rarely or never the whole truth, it is only by the collision of adverse opinions that the remainder of the truth has any chance of being supplied.

Thirdly, even if the received opinion be not only true, but the whole truth; unless it is suffered to be, and actually is, vigorously and earnestly contested, it will, by most of those who receive it, be held in the manner of a prejudice, with little comprehension or feeling of its rational grounds. And not only this, but, fourthly, the meaning of the doctrine itself will be in danger of being lost, or enfeebled, and deprived of its vital effect on the character and conduct: the dogma becoming a mere formal profession, inefficacious for good, but cumbering the ground, and preventing the growth of any real and heartfelt conviction, from reason or personal experience.

Exploding Some Myths About the Industrial Revolution

The term *Industrial Revolution* was coined in 1880 by Arnold Toynbee, the uncle of the famous present-day historian, Arnold J. Toynbee. These two words are still in wide use, particularly in reference to economic developments in England in the 18th and 19th centuries. Contemporary economic historians, however, prefer to use the term *economic growth* to describe an economy in which both total productivity and productivity per man are increasing.

The vital significance of rapid economic growth for the history of the entire world can hardly be overemphasized. Like the Neolithic Revolution, the industrialism which triggered this growth changed the face of civilization. It crowded men into cities. It increased per capita wealth and the standard of living. It had a profound effect on education, on government, even on the family. Much of the non-Western world is today experiencing the same traumatic effects of industrialism that once beset England.

Some scholars argue that advanced industrial societies have passed through five stages of economic development:

1) *The Traditional Society*, a period often many centuries long in which methods of production are based upon the technological skills, social attitudes, and scientific thought typical of the era before Newton.

2) *The Preconditions for Take-Off*, a stage of slow changes often lasting a century or more in which the society establishes the institutions and attitudes toward work that make industrialization possible.

3) *The Take-Off*, a stage lasting twenty or thirty years, during which the rate of industrialization quickens measurably.

4) *The Drive to Maturity*, a stage of steady progress for many years during which all industry embraces modern technological methods.

5) *The Age of High Mass Consumption*, a stage during which the emphasis in production shifts from manufacturing capital goods to making consumer goods and services available in larger amounts to more people.

Not all economic historians agree that these five stages accurately describe the process of economic growth in all societies. Indeed, some scholars think that the entire hypothesis should be discarded. In any case, however, a hypothesis like this one — sometimes called a *model* — is useful as an analytical device; that is, it can serve as a source of fruitful questions to put to the evidence. Although the material in the reading for today bears on only the first three of these five stages, you will still have an opportunity to use the model for analysis.

As you read, consider the following questions:

1 According to Heaton, what are the common myths about the Industrial Revolution? How does he attack them?

2 Does the evidence cited by Heaton support the idea of the stages outlined in the introduction?

3 To what degree did the development of industry depend upon developments in other areas of life, such as politics or the class system? What effects did the new world of industry have in turn upon political life and the class system? Should you always expect a change in one area of a culture to have effects in other areas?

THE INDUSTRIAL REVOLUTION / by Herbert Heaton

Reprinted from *Social Education*, Vol. II, 1938, by permission of the National Council for the Social Studies. Pp. 159-165.

That old picture [*of the Industrial Revolution*], painted about 1880 by Arnold Toynbee, is a triptych, or a melodrama in three acts. First there is "The Eve," still, placid, quiet, at the end of a long day that reaches back to the Normans, Nero, or even Noah. The methods of agriculture, industry, and transportation have changed little in a thousand years. Production is carried on by small manufacturers or farmers. The former, like the latter, live in the country, combine industry and agriculture, and supplement the family labor supply by training an apprentice and perhaps employing a journeyman or two. The wage earner usually works, aided by his family, in his own home on materials put out to him by his employer; but he may work under his master's roof. Between master and man is a "warm attachment"; they call each other by their Christian nicknames. The class of capitalist employers is still "in its infancy"; some merchant-employers put out material to be processed in the homes of their employees or of small masters, and a few factories or central workshops exist. But in general the family firm and the family farm prevail. Division of class and of labor is slight. The worker can express his personality in his work, though what happens if it is crooked is not clear. Production is for local markets or for the producer's larder and wardrobe, since defective means of transportation and mercantilistic policies shut off distant consumers. No one earns great rewards, but the domestic system insures on the whole a sound and healthy life under conditions favorable to the development of mind, body, and personal dignity. Contentment spins at the cottage door; there is plenty of honeysuckle, ivy, and good ale in this "quiet world" of "scarcely perceptible movement." A comprehensive code of state regulation of production and trade combines with technical inertia to prevent anything from changing.

Then, with a rapidity known in the tropics, "The Night" falls, a night full of noise and action. Seven men—four Lancashire men (Kay, Hargreaves, Arkwright, and Crompton), two Scots (Adam Smith and James Watt), and one Episcopalian parson (Cartwright)—invent some textile machines, improve the steam engine, or write *The Wealth of Nations*. Meanwhile other men revolutionize agriculture and redraw the village map, while others improve roads and rivers or cut canals. But it is the seven men who get their names on the record, for their actions or thoughts "destroyed the old world and built a new one." And what they did was crowded into a brief night that lasted from about 1760 to 1780.

Act Three is "The Murky Dawn," in which the effects become visible. It is a period of "economic revolution and anarchy," as machinery and steam overrun industry, and Smith's plea for laissez faire sweeps the statute book clear of the mercantilistic devil. Population is "torn up by the roots" and dragged "from cottages in distant valleys into factories and cities"; independent farmers, expelled from their lands and impoverished by the extension of sheep raising and the inclosure movement, join the small manufacturing master or journeymen in this rural exodus. In the towns a landless propertyless proletariat is the victim of the seven deadly sins of unrestrained inhuman industrial capitalists. The sins are the factory system, long hours, child labor, the exploitation of women, low wages, periodical or chronic unemployment, and slums. If the victims dislike the contrast between their deplorable lot and the fortunes made by fat factory owners; if they object, riot, join labor unions, or become chartists or socialists, they are shot down, put in jail, or sent to Botany Bay. The economic masters become their political lords by displacing the landowners in the seats of government, and then legislate—or refuse to do so—with one eye on the cashbox and the other on some page of Smith, Ricardo, or Malthus. A dreary, tragic, selfish, sort of dawn! But by lunch time the weather is improving. The exploited grow class-conscious and organized, some employers grow softhearted, laws are passed to permit unions, to regulate child labor, or to provide a better water supply. Mass production makes goods cheaper, the corn laws are repealed, Victoria becomes queen, Albert the Good builds the Crystal Palace, and by the time it is opened in 1851 the grim tragedy is promising to turn into whatever the urban counterpart of a pastoral should be called.

This story has got into the general books, and the title for it has become so widely accepted that some wit has said all college courses now begin with the amoeba, Aristotle, or the industrial revolution. That is—all courses except those given by the economic historian, for he is getting more and more suspicious of the name and of the crisp dramatic conception. In the great university schools of economic history, Manchester admits that the name was useful when first adopted but thinks it has now served its turn and can scarcely be applied aptly to a movement which was in preparation for two centuries and then occupied at least one more. Oxford finds there is "no hiatus in economic development, but always a constant tide of progress and change, in which the old is blended almost imperceptibly with the new." Edinburgh chimes in with the remark that "sudden catastrophic change is inconsistent with the slow gradual process of human evolution." Harvard insists that the technological changes of the eighteenth century were "only the completion of tendencies which had been significantly evident since Leonardo da Vinci." Birmingham reinforces this by asserting that the developments between 1760 and 1830 "did but carry further, though on a far greater scale and with far greater rapidity, changes which had been proceeding long before." Cambridge finds the period presents a study in slow motion, and in London they tell the pass students there was an industrial revolution, but tell the honors students there never was any such thing.

These quotations give a composite picture of the revised view of the industrial revolution. Let me put it in three generalizations. (1) Steam and the textile machines did not break in on an almost unchanging world of smallscale slightly capitalistic enterprise. (2) The rate of technical change was *lento* rather than *allegro* for a long time; it took decades or even generations to transform old industries and build up new ones. (3) The social and economic "evils" were not new; they were not as black or as widespread as is usually asserted; their causes were often due to special or noneconomic factors; and they were in no small measure offset by a substantial improvement in the real wages and living standards of a large part of the wage-earning population. Sentimental unhistorical hysteria is not a good approach to a problem, whether present or past, but it dominated much of the discussion a hundred years ago and the description of a hundred years ago.

Let me elaborate these three contentions. In Toynbee's day little was known of sixteenth-century economic life, and little of any eighteenth-century industry except textiles. Now we know that during this period there were important changes in methods of production, and a quickening spirit of scientific inquiry and of inventive curiosity. New methods of extracting and refining metals were discovered; the preparation of silk yarn, the knitting of hose, the weaving of ribbons, the making of clocks, the finishing of cloth, all obtained new or improved equipment, as did shipbuilding, brewing, mining, sugar refining, and the manufacture of chemicals. The harnessing of wind, water, and animal power was made more efficient, and coal was used in increasing quantities by industries which needed heat. Professor Nef has shown that England had an industrial revolution between 1540 and 1640, and that the rate of technical change was possibly as striking during the age of Shakespeare as during that of Wordsworth or Byron. Holland, Sweden, France, and England alike contributed to technical progress, and by 1700 scientists, especially physicists, had learned enough to be able to answer some questions asked by industrialists. True, some industries or processes stood still, and spinning and weaving did not change much; but many were on the march.

At the same time the organization of production was changing. Small craftsmen did not have the capital necessary for some of the new equipment, or for bridging the long gap between buying raw material and getting paid for the finished article by a dilatory or distant customer. Hence where materials were costly or came from afar, where equipment was expensive, where the market was large or distant, the initiative had to be taken by merchants or large producers. Some of them bought the raw materials and put them out to be processed by small masters or by wage earners. Sometimes they supplied the equipment as well and paid the master only for his labor, just as he in turn might pay wages to his journeymen. Some of them gathered workers in, because the material could not be put out. You could not put out coal mining, smelting, sugar refining, building, cloth finishing, shipbuilding, calico printing, or the making of glass, bricks, paper, leather, or gunpowder. As these industries grew, so did the number of persons working for wages in their employer's plant; and the combined expansion of putting out and gathering in had created a large propertyless proletariat long before 1760. It may be true that in 1640 the great majority of industrial workers "laboured in their homes, in town cellars or garrets, or in village cottages. But that majority was by no means so overwhelming as has been supposed" (Nef) and was declining rapidly before a flying shuttle flew

or a spinning jenny was devised, even in Lancashire cotton production. Wherever men worked, many of them were wage earners.

If they were, their wages tended to be low; but so were all returns in an age of low productivity. Their hours were long—twelve
or more a day—but so were those of their employers and of independent workers, since the rate of production was so slow. Their
children and their wives had to work, for every scrap of labor was
needed; but so did all children and wives, except those of the rich.
Unemployment was frequent and severe, industrial diseases and
accidents were common, living and working conditions were often
dank, unhealthy, and malodorous, whether in town or village. Labor
unions were formed, class conflicts occurred, and the state usually
took the employers' side.

This sketch of the period before 1760 takes much of the melodrama out of the next seventy years. Some of the remainder disap-
pears, when we examine the pace at which the textile machines and
the improved steam engines were adopted. The cotton industry,
which was the scene of the famous inventions, has been used as a
sample case. But it was not typical; various factors, such as the
newness of the industry, the suitability of the cotton fiber for mechanical treatment, and the great market existing for cheap cotton cloth,
prevent the story of cotton from being typical of the changes in industry at large. The transfer from domestic hand spinning of cotton to
factory machine spinning was rapid—a matter of about twenty years.
By 1815 "the power loom was entering into effective rivalry with
the hand loom in the cotton industry, though another generation was
to elapse before the battle was finally decided." But cotton was a
lonely hare in an industrial world of tortoises. It loomed far less
large in that world than it has done in the textbooks, for even in the
1830's the number of its employees was only two-thirds that of the
number of female domestic servants.

When we get our eyes off this exception, we find the pace of
change in the rest of industry much more sedate. Wool spinning, on
hand jennies instead of on wheels, was still being done in Yorkshire
homes in 1850. Power looms had not seriously threatened the woolen
hand weaver at that date; the transfer from hand to power weaving
came quietly during the next twenty-five years, but even in 1877 I
find one manufacturer contending that the old method was as cheap
as the new. As for steam power, Watt had only 320 of his engines at
work in England in 1800, and in 1830 a quarter of the power used by

cotton mills was still drawn from waterwheels. Mining had no great technical change, but a series of little ones. Building remained a manual industry until the concrete mixer came. The pottery industry relied less on machinery than on other factors. Clothes making, glass blowing, and printing were late in getting mechanical equipment, while mechanical engineering only slowly developed the tools it needed for shaping metal parts cheaply and accurately. In 1850 everything was not over except the shouting. Cheap steel, cheap lubricants, industrial chemistry, and cheap electricity were still to come. The railroad had won its battle, but the steamship was still fighting its sailing rival, even on the North Atlantic. Away from Lancashire and the railroad tracks, technical change between 1760 and 1850 had been gradual, slow, and unspectacular.

What then of the social and economic consequences and of the seven deadly sins? In the first place, if we leave out one or two exceptional industries or areas, people were not torn loose from a rural life of pleasant and virtually independent enterprise and plunged almost overnight into the horrible existence of an urban factory slum-dwelling proletariat. Many of them were already proletarian; many of them already lived in industrial towns which now grew large or in villages which grew into towns; and some of them already worked under the employer's roof. For them there was not much shift of habitat or of economic class. There was little mass migration, and little long distance movement, except by the Irish, who swarmed into England before they swarmed into North America, and who made many labor and urban problems much more acute than they would otherwise have been.

In the second place, before we beat our anger to white heat in describing the slums, the foul streets, the smoke-laden atmosphere, the lack of water or sanitation, the ravages of disease, etc., let us remember three controlling considerations. (a) Technical. Cheap bricks, cheap sewer or water pipes, and cheap house fixtures were not available till at least 1840, and knowledge concerning public health was still scanty. Compare conditions in the industrial towns with those of non-industrial communities or with rural housing facilities; then it is evident that the housing and sanitary shortcomings of the manufacturing districts were not wholly due to the new machinery and the factory system. (b) Constitutional. Until 1835 no town government had adequate powers to cope with the new urban problems. (c) Economic. The provision of houses was never, until recent years, regarded as a public duty. It was left to private enterprise and the stimulus of investment or speculation. The potential builder considered whether his capital would yield a better return in houses than in the many other fields that were thirsty for capital; and the amount he put into a dwelling was limited by what the tenant could afford to pay. In one English town 76 per cent of the houses were rented at a dollar a week or less in 1839; the total capital outlay for one house could not be more than six hundred dollars. In view of the western world's housing impasse since 1914, we must speak more kindly of the builder who a century ago put a roof over the head of the poor, without the aid of mass-produced materials, machinery, or government subsidies.

In the third place, few of the factory working conditions were new. Not even the discipline of fixed hours of work was new to industries which had been conducted in central workshops. Night work may have been new, but long and late hours were not. The cruel treatment of some children by foremen was a personal matter; parents had not been free from it in the domestic workshop, and it was part of that streak of cruelty common in prisons, the army and navy, schools, and homes. The thing that was new and revolutionary was not the "evils," but the discovery that they were evils. For that we have to thank those employers who were heartless. We have to thank the factory for making noticeable in the mass what had been ignored in scattered small instances. We can thank onlookers, whether lay or ecclesiastic, and even Tory politicians who saw in factory conditions a new whip with which to flog their Whig industrial opponents. Finally, much credit must go to those employers—and they were many—who treated their workers decently. These men belonged to that growing army of humanitarians who cleaned up slavery, made the penal code less fierce, welcomed the attack on excessive drinking, pushed the cause of education, built hospitals, dispensaries, and charitable institutions, organized the relief of the unemployed in depressed days, established good working conditions, and fought for better factory laws and better town government.

One final comment may help us to understand better the years between 1760 and 1830. Twenty-six of those years (1789-1815) were dominated by the emotions and strain of the French Revolution and the Napoleonic war, and sixteen of them (1815-1830) were filled with the task of readjustment after a generation of war. The first period was torn by the fear of Jacobinism and the stress of war and famine.

There could be little tolerance of mutterings of social discontent or of organized protest during those years; and there was little time to think of domestic problems. The second period we understand better because we have lived through a similar one. The legacies of war were high prices which collapsed, high interest rates and taxes which did not, a scarcity of houses, wide agrarian distress, a disarranged currency, a chaotic credit system, economic nationalism, choked trade channels, prohibitive tariffs, demobilized soldiers without jobs, and so forth. Much that has been blamed on the economic transition was not new, and much of the rest has to be put on the shoulders of the war. The remarkable thing is that by 1830 British opinion had got rid of most of its war phobias and was tackling its problems realistically and constructively by a combination of voluntary organization and state action. If anything was rapid and revolutionary in this whole period it was the change in outlook that between 1824 and 1835 removed the ban on labor organization, passed an effective factory act, reformed the poor law, lowered the tariff wall, made a hole in the navigation laws, remodelled urban government, reformed the House of Commons, liberated the slaves, emancipated Roman Catholics, fashioned a good banking system, and sowed the seeds of national education, trade unionism, and the cooperative movement.

Behind all this was the intense energy of manufacturers and merchants who, either with old equipment or new, enterprised and adventured. This energy is denounced by some as "an orgy of soulless cupidity," and praised by others as "a triumph of the spirit of enterprise." In general it was a bit of both. Cupidity, yes, as in all ages and occupations. Enterprise, yes, but not always triumphant, for the field was strewn with the wreckage of men who failed. When the classical economists said profit was the reward of risk and interest the reward of abstinence, they meant it. Not the abstinence that today would lead a man to pick a Buick for his twelfth car instead of a Rolls Royce, but one which meant meager living and the ploughing back of every spare penny into the business. As for risk, some day somebody will study the industrial revolution through the bankruptcy records; but we know enough to realize on what a treacherous sea the entrepreneur launched his tiny bark.

The Communist Manifesto
as a Product of its Time

Early in 1847, a tiny group of radicals, the Communist League, commissioned Karl Marx and Friedrich Engels to draw up a program setting forth the principles of the organization. Marx, a newspaperman and professional radical, had been banished from his native Germany because of socialist activities. Engels, a German living in England, had also spent many years abroad as the agent of his father, who owned a textile mill in Manchester. The Manifesto was published early in 1848 but it had no influence on the revolutions of that year. Not until several years later did it come to have real importance among European revolutionaries.

The Communist Manifesto was a product of historical forces operating in Europe in the mid-19th century, and should be studied as such. To the contemporary American high-school student, some of the statements in the Manifesto may seem absurd. One example is the prediction that the middle classes would inevitably disappear in industrial societies. However, in 1848 in much of Europe, signs did point to the possibility that giant industry would drive the small entrepreneur to the wall. Thus only in the context of 1848 can the Manifesto make real sense; three aspects of that period deserve particular attention.

One vital factor was the faith of many Europeans in the effectiveness of revolution. The lesson of the French Revolution of 1789 shone clear: men could remake their society, throwing off many remnants of past eras, through a violent revolution. The many revolts that took place in 1820, 1830, and in 1848 illustrate how widely revolutionary ideas were accepted. Marx and Engels agreed with the doctrine of violent revolution and applied it to the overthrow of capitalism.

Another important consideration was industrialism, which by 1848 was transforming Great Britain into one vast workshop and had begun to make an impact on Germany, France, Belgium, and Scandinavia. With industrialism, a number of new problems brought intense hardship to factory workers, particularly those who lacked skills. Engels had spent many years among Manchester's cotton textile workers, where he tasted the bitterness of their lives. In 1848 these workers had no vote, and the new laws for their protection which Parliament was beginning to pass had not yet had a noticeable effect. Engels therefore believed that only violent revolt could win a better life for these people.

Finally, both Marx and Engels were steeped in German philosophy, particularly the ideas of Georg Wilhelm Friedrich Hegel. From Hegel, Marx borrowed the idea that history was an evolutionary process produced by a conflict of opposite ideas. Marx substituted classes for ideas and emerged with the fundamental notion of the class struggle as the determining force in history.

As you read, consider the following questions:

1 Do you find specific evidence that the authors of the Communist Manifesto were influenced by the times in which they wrote?

2   Does Marx's conception of class agree with what you know about classes in modern American society? Why is this issue important?

3   Was Marx a good historian? Think about his exclusive emphasis on class struggle. Is this emphasis consistent with your understanding of causation in history? What would Gustavson think about Marx's analysis of causation?

4   Do you think that Marx's belief in the necessity of revolution contradicts his prediction at the end of the Manifesto that many reforms will take place before a revolution breaks out?

MANIFESTO OF THE COMMUNIST PARTY
by Karl Marx and Friedrich Engels

Authorized English translation, edited by Friedrich Engels. New York: New York Labor News Co., 1888.

A specter is haunting Europe—the specter of Communism. All the powers of old Europe have entered into a holy alliance to exorcise this specter; Pope and Czar, Metternich and Guizot, French radicals and German police-spies.

Where is the party in opposition that has not been decried as communistic by its opponents in power? Where the opposition that has not hurled back the branding reproach of Communism, against the more advanced opposition parties as well as against its reactionary adversaries?

Two things result from this fact.

I.   Communism is already acknowledged by all European powers to be itself a power.

II.   It is high time that Communists should openly, in the face of the whole world, publish their views, their aims, their tendencies, and meet this nursery tale of the Specter of Communism with a Manifesto of the party itself.

To this end Communists of various nationalities have assembled in London, and sketched the following manifesto to be published in the English, French, German, Italian, Flemish and Danish languages.

I   BOURGEOIS AND PROLETARIANS

The history of all hitherto existing society is the history of class struggles.

Freeman and slave, patrician and plebeian, lord and serf, guild-master and journeyman, in a word, oppressor and oppressed, stood in constant opposition to one another, carried on an uninterrupted, now hidden, now open fight, that each time ended, either in revolutionary re-constitution of society at large, or in the common ruin of the contending classes.

In the earlier epochs of history, we find almost everywhere a complicated arrangement of society into various orders, a manifold gradation of social rank. In ancient Rome we have patricians, knights, plebeians, slaves; in the middle ages, feudal lords, vassals, guild-masters, journeymen, apprentices, serfs; in almost all of these classes, again, subordinate gradations.

The modern bourgeois society that has sprouted from the ruins of feudal society, has not done away with class antagonisms. It has but established new classes, new conditions of oppression, new forms of struggle in place of the old ones.

Our epoch, the epoch of the bourgeoisie, possesses, however, this distinctive feature; it has simplified the class antagonisms. Society as a whole is more and more splitting up into two great hostile camps, into two great classes directly facing each other: Bourgeoisie and Proletariat.

[*After tracing briefly the evolution of the modern bourgeoisie from the Middle Ages to the present, the authors continue.*]

We see, therefore, how the modern bourgeoisie is itself the product of a long course of development, of a series of revolutions in the modes of production and of exchange.

Each step in the development of the bourgeoisie was accompanied by a corresponding political advance of that class. An oppressed class under the sway of the feudal nobility, an armed and self-governing association in the medieval commune, here independent urban republic (as in Italy and Germany), there taxable "third estate" of the monarchy (as in France), afterwards, in the period of manufacture proper, serving either the semi-feudal or the absolute monarchy as a counterpoise against the nobility, and, in fact, corner-stone of the great monarchies in general, the bourgeoisie has at last, since the establishment of Modern Industry and of the world's market, conquered for itself, in the modern representative State, exclusive political sway. The executive of the modern State is but a committee for managing the common affairs of the whole bourgeoisie.

The bourgeoisie, historically, has played a most revolutionary part.

The bourgeoisie, wherever it has got the upper hand, has put an end to all feudal, patriarchal, idyllic relations. It has pitilessly torn asunder the motley feudal ties that bound man to his "natural superiors," and has left remaining no other nexus between man and man than naked self-interest, than callous "cash payment." . . .

The bourgeoisie has stripped of its halo every occupation hitherto honored and looked up to with reverent awe. It has converted the physician, the lawyer, the priest, the poet, the man of science, into its paid wage-laborers.

The bourgeoisie has torn away from the family its sentimental veil, and has reduced the family relation to a mere money relation.

[*In succeeding paragraphs, Marx and Engels describe the accomplishments of the bourgeoisie in creating an industrial society, but predict that the vast forces it has unleashed are beyond its control.*]

But not only has the bourgeoisie forged the weapons that bring death to itself; it has also called into existence the men who are to wield those weapons — the modern working class — the proletarians.

In proportion as the bourgeoisie, *i.e.*, capital, is developed, in the same proportion is the proletariat developed, the modern working class developed; a class of laborers, who live only so long as they find work, and who find work only so long as their labor increases capital. These laborers, who must sell themselves piecemeal, are a commodity, like every other article of commerce, and are consequently exposed to all the vicissitudes of competition, to all the fluctuations of the market.

Owing to the extensive use of machinery and to division of labor, the work of the proletarians has lost all individual character, and, consequently, all charm for the workman. He becomes a mere appendage of the machine, and it is only the most simple, most monotonous, and most easily acquired knack, that is required of him. Hence, the cost of production of a workman is restricted almost entirely to the means of subsistence that he requires for his maintenance, and for the propagation of his race. But the price of a commodity, and therefore also of labor, is equal to its cost of production. In proportion, therefore, as the repulsiveness of the work increases, the wage decreases. . . .

Modern industry has converted the little workshop of the patriarchal master into the great factory of the industrial capitalist. Masses of laborers, crowded into the factory, are organized like soldiers. As privates of the industrial army they are placed under the command of a perfect hierarchy of officers and sergeants. Not only are they slaves of the bourgeois class, and of the bourgeois State, they are daily and hourly enslaved by the machine, by the over-looker, and, above all, by the individual bourgeois manufacturer himself. . . .

The less the skill and exertion of strength implied in manual labor, in other words, the more modern industry becomes developed, the more is the labor of men superseded by that of women. Differences of age and sex have no longer any distinctive social validity for the working class. All are instruments of labor, more or less expensive to use, according to age and sex. . . .

The lower strata of the middle class—the small tradespeople, shopkeepers, and retired tradesmen generally, the handicraftsmen and peasants—all these sink gradually into the proletariat, partly because their diminutive capital does not suffice for the scale on which modern industry is carried on, and is swamped in the competition with the large capitalists, partly because their specialized skill is rendered worthless by new methods of production. Thus the proletariat is recruited from all classes of the population.

The proletariat goes through various stages of development. With its birth begins its struggle with the bourgeoisie. At first the contest is carried on by individual laborers, then by the workpeople of a factory, then by the operatives of one trade, in one locality, against the individual bourgeois who directly exploits them. They direct their attacks not against the bourgeois conditions of production, but against the instruments of production themselves; they destroy imported wares that compete with their labor, they smash to pieces machinery, they set factories ablaze, they seek to restore by force the vanished status of the workman of the Middle Ages. . . .

. . .with the development of industry the proletariat not only increases in number; it becomes concentrated in greater masses, its strength grows and it feels that strength more. The various interests and conditions of life within the ranks of the proletariat are more and more equalized, in proportion as machinery obliterates all distinctions of labor, and nearly everywhere reduces wages to the same low level. The growing competition among the bourgeois, and the resulting commercial crises, make the wages of the workers ever more fluctuating. The unceasing improvement of machinery, ever more rapidly developing, makes their livelihood more and more precarious; the collisions between individual workmen and individual bourgeois take more and more the character of collisions between two classes. Thereupon the workers begin to form combinations (Trades' Unions) against the bourgeois; they club together in order to keep up the rate of wages; they found permanent associations in order to make provision before-hand for these occasional revolts. Here and there the contest breaks out into riots.

Now and then the workers are victorious, but only for a time. The real fruit of their battles lies not in the immediate result but in the ever improved means of communication that are created in modern industry and that place the workers of different localities in contact with one another. It was just this contact that was needed to centralize the numerous local struggles, all of the same character, into one national struggle between classes. But every class struggle is a political struggle. And that union, to attain which the burghers of the Middle Ages, with their miserable highways, required cen-turies, the modern proletarians, thanks to railways, achieve in a few years. . . .

Altogether collisions between the classes of the old society further, in many ways, the course of development of the proletariat. The bourgeoisie finds itself involved in a constant battle. At first with the aristocracy; later on, with those portions of the bourgeoisie itself, whose interests have become antagonistic to the progress of industry; at all times with the bourgeoisie of foreign countries. In all these countries it sees itself compelled to appeal to the proletariat, to ask for its help, and thus to drag it into the political arena. The bourgeoisie itself, therefore, supplies the proletariat with weapons for fighting the bourgeoisie.

Further, as we have already seen, entire sections of the ruling classes are, by the advance of industry, precipitated into the prole-tariat, or are at least threatened in their conditions of existence. These also supply the proletariat with fresh elements of enlightenment and progress.

Finally, in times when the class struggle nears the decisive hour, the process of dissolution going on within the ruling class, in fact within the whole range of old society, assumes such a violent, glaring character, that a small section of the ruling class cuts itself adrift, and joins the revolutionary class, the class that holds the future in its hands. Just as, therefore, at an earlier period, a section of the nobility went over to the bourgeoisie, so now a portion of the bourgeoisie goes over to the proletariat, and in particular, a portion of the bourgeois ideologists, who have raised themselves to the level of comprehend-ing theoretically the historical movement as a whole.

Of all the classes that stand face to face with the bourgeoisie to-day, the proletariat alone is a really revolutionary class. The other classes decay and finally disappear in the face of modern industry; the proletariat is its special and essential product.

The lower middle class, the small manufacturer, the shopkeeper, the artisan, the peasant, all these fight against the bourgeoisie to save from extinction their existence as fractions of the middle class. They are therefore not revolutionary, but conservative. Nay, more, they are reactionary, for they try to roll back the wheel of history. If by chance they are revolutionary, they are so only in view of their impending transfer into the proletariat; they thus defend not their present, but their future interests, they desert their own standpoint to place themselves at that of the proletariat. . . .

II   PROLETARIANS AND COMMUNISTS

In what relation do the Communists stand to the proletarians as a whole? . . .

The Communists are distinguished from the other working-class parties by this only: 1. In the national struggles of the proletarians of the different countries, they point out and bring to the front the common interests of the entire proletariat, independently of all nationality. 2. In the various stages of development which the struggle of the working class against the bourgeoisie has to pass through, they always . . . represent the interests of the movement as a whole. . . .

The immediate aim of the Communists is the same as that of all other proletarian parties: Formation of the proletariat into a class, overthrow of bourgeois supremacy, conquest of political power by the proletariat. . . .

The distinguishing feature of Communism is not the abolition of property generally, but the abolition of bourgeois property. But modern bourgeois private property is the final and most complete expression of the system of producing and appropriating products that is based on class antagonisms, on the exploitation of the many by the few.

In this sense, the theory of the Communists may be summed up in a single sentence: Abolition of private property. . . .

You are horrified at our intending to do away with private property. But in your existing society, private property is already done away with for nine-tenths of the population; its existence for the few is solely due to its non-existence in the hands of those nine-tenths. . . .

Communism deprives no man of the power to appropriate the products of society; all that it does is to deprive him of the power to subjugate the labor of others by means of such appropriation. . . .

The Communists are further reproached with desiring to abolish countries and nationality.

The workingmen have no country. We cannot take from them what they have not got. Since the proletariat must first of all acquire political supremacy, must rise to be the leading class of the nation, must constitute itself *the* nation, it is, so far, itself national, though not in the bourgeois sense of the word. . . .

The proletariat will use its political supremacy to wrest, by degrees, all capital from the bourgeoisie, to centralize all instruments of production in the hands of the state, *i.e.*, of the proletariat organized as a ruling class; and to increase the total of productive forces as rapidly as possible. . . .

When, in the course of development, class distinctions have disappeared and all production has been concentrated in the hands of a vast association of the whole nation, the public power will lose its political character. Political power, properly so called, is merely the organized power of one class for oppressing another. If the proletariat during its contest with the bourgeoisie is compelled, by the force of circumstances, to organize itself as a class, if, by means of a revolution, it makes itself the ruling class, and, as such, sweeps away by force the old conditions of production, then it will, along with these conditions, have swept away the conditions for the existence of class antagonisms, and of classes generally, and will thereby have abolished its own supremacy as a class.

In place of the old bourgeois society with its classes and class antagonisms we shall have an association in which the free development of each is the condition for the free development of all.

[*After a discussion of socialist and communist literature, and of other political parties, the Manifesto ends with the following famous passage.*]

The Communists disdain to conceal their views and aims. They openly declare that their ends can be attained only by the forcible overthrow of all existing social conditions. Let the ruling classes tremble at a Communistic revolution. The proletarians have nothing to lose but their chains. They have a world to win.

Workingmen of all countries unite!

A Study of Changing
Latin America

Many nations of Central and South America were born in the democratic revolutions of the early 19th century. The changes that followed these up-heavals, however, did not necessarily create democratic regimes. Nor was the social and economic life of the average Latin American significantly altered. For a century thereafter, Latin-American peasants followed their ancient ways, poorly educated and almost completely unexposed to modern technology.

In the 20th century, the pace of social change all over Latin America was greatly accelerated. The coming of industrialism touched the lives of Latin Americans as political movements of the past had failed to do. The rise of cities and the growth of a new urban working class changed the old social order. As former peasants received more education and learned new skills, their dissatisfaction increased. Many joined organized labor movements and made greater demands on their employers.

The shift from farm to factory and from country to city also brought grave social problems. Uprooted from their villages and families, workers discovered that increased physical comforts often could not compensate for the security of the familiar. The new life and the new loyalties were confusing and frus-trating. The reading for today personalizes this revolution. It explores the life of a Guatemalan carpenter, Esteban Pazuj, who left his native mountains for a better job in the lowlands.

In the process of analyzing historical phenomena, writers make use of evidence from any number of possible sources. As we saw in Problems 1 and 11, historians profit from the work of archaeologists and anthropologists. In today's Problem, where the reading consists of a sociological study, our insight into social change — one aspect of history in the making — is broadened through the discipline of another social science. Sociologists, by systematically studying human groups both as societies and through their individual mem-bers, contribute vital information about changes in the minds and hearts of men. Looking at changing conditions in Latin America through the eyes of one transplanted Indian peasant, Pazuj, should help you understand more clearly the problems which our neighbors to the south face today.

As you read this selection, consider the following questions:

1   Do you think that the way in which Europeans established themselves in Latin America explains the traditional type of society described in this article?

2   Compare the social and economic changes that affected the workers of Guatemala with those affecting English laborers, as described in Problem 21.

3   What types of problems do emerging nations such as Guatemala face as they try to adjust to urban, industrial life?

4   What are the advantages of a personalized account to a historian? What are the dangers in using such evidence?

THE UPROOTED: A GUATEMALA SKETCH / by Richard F. Behrendt

From *New Mexico Quarterly Review*, Vol. XIX, No. 1
(Spring 1949). Copyright 1949 by the University of New
Mexico. Pp. 25-31.

Esteban Pazuj was an Indian carpenter in Guatemala. He made
chairs and tables from a poor type of pine, fitted together without
nails. In order to find customers, he had to take them from Totonicapán to Guatemala City, one hundred and twenty miles of mountain
road at altitudes ranging down from eight thousand to four thousand
feet. He carried on his shoulders and back the table and six chairs
suspended from a tump-strap pressed against his forehead. He had to
take his food along and would spend the nights in caves or under
trees near the road. It took him eight days to reach the capital, several
days to sell his goods on a special market, and another week to return
home. He used to get three dollars for the table and the chairs or
forty cents for each chair if sold separately. He charged for the lumber
and his work only, not for the time spent en route. When he returned
home, he had usually just enough left to buy more lumber and sustain
himself and his family until his next sale.

During a few weeks every year, Esteban and his family used to
go down to the western slopes of the volcanic mountain range, at
about 3000 feet altitude, to pick coffee beans on a large plantation
owned by Germans. He received twenty cents a day and his children,
who were working with him in the field, ten cents a day. They lived
in a large shack together with dozens of other families of seasonal
workers. Each family prepared its meals, consisting mostly of corn
and beans, over open fires inside the building. They slept on home-
made woolen blankets spread on the dirt floors. There was no furni-
ture of any kind. The women got their water from a brook half a mile
away. Nature served as an open-air toilet. The Indian workers greeted
the German administrators or their families, when these happened to
cross their path, with bare heads and folded arms. If the workers
broke any of the rules they were denied payment or put in the stocks.

Four years ago, an agent of the United Fruit Company came to
Esteban's home town near Totonicapán to hire workers for the
banana plantations around Tiquisate, in the lowlands of the west
coast. He offered seventy cents a day, free housing, food at lower
prices than it could be had in the stores, and the use of a plot of land
for any worker who wanted to grow food of his own. It sounded
fantastic to Esteban, but he accepted.

Now he loads banana stems on railway lorries from six o'clock in the morning to two o'clock in the afternoon. Sometimes he works overtime and is paid fifty per cent extra. In the afternoon he works for a few hours on his lot, if he feels like it. He and his family occupy a medium-sized room in a low, long wooden building housing several families. They have a kitchen of their own and share a toilet with their neighbors. They have electric light. They can buy rations of staple foods in the company commissary, at prices lower than those in regular stores. Their children go to a near-by school provided by the company, as required by the law of the country. The company fights the malaria-carrying mosquitoes and provides safe water supply. The company hospital, the second largest in the country, gives free service to the workers and their families.

But Esteban is not happy. For one thing, he and his family have never liked the hot, humid climate of the lowlands. He knows that he, his wife, and his children have more things to eat and a better place to live than before. However, to get these things he had to leave his village where generations of his family had spent their lives. His neighbors are comparative strangers, not related to him by blood, custom or even language. Esteban does not speak Spanish very well and his neighbors, having come from other parts of the country, do not speak his language, which is Quiché. He had to discard his aboriginal dress, with its patterns and colors distinctive of his native village. He now lives on an outlying *finca,* very different from his old, tight little home town whose people had been organized for centuries in kinships, *cofradías* (civic hereditary fraternities), and parishes. There everybody knew—although not necessarily spoke to—everybody else, and there everyone's position in the community was strictly defined by tradition.

Tiquisate is very different indeed from those parts of Guatemala where Esteban spent his earlier life. There are no old buildings; everything seems to him too new. In fact, the entire town and the outlying plantations were established only fifteen years ago when the fruit company shifted part of its operations from the Atlantic to the Pacific coast, because of plant diseases and soil exhaustion. There was then very little population and very little of anything—except climate and soil. Workers like Esteban had to be hired in the highlands where too many people try to eke out a living from thin soil on steep hillsides. Housing, transportation, communications, sanitation, irrigation, schools, hospital, entertainment had to be provided by the company. People from various countries, speaking different languages, professing even different religions, having different traditions and customs – and very different living standards – came to live here.

Esteban, and some ten thousand workers like him, with their families, changed from a form of life which had remained essentially fixed for centuries, almost unaffected by outside influences, in which people had obeyed traditional institutions and leaders, to a new, planned form of life which was organized by a foreign corporation for the one purpose of producing and marketing a profitable commodity. . . . they know nothing [of the company] except that it is controlled by an indefinite number of foreigners, somewhere in the United States, nobody knows exactly how. They have never seen those people and never will. Some foreigners they do see: the North Americans who manage and supervise local operations. The Guatemalan workers do not bow with folded arms to them. Nor are they put in the stocks for infractions. Still they are not closer to them than they were to their German bosses. The *americanos* live in a small town of their own, divided from the "native" town by a barbed wire fence. They have their own school, commissary, club house, swimming pool, and pleasant one-family bungalows on well-kept grounds. Esteban and most of his fellow workers do not see much of the *americanos*, because the time keepers and foremen are Guatemalans; but they know that those *americanos* are the bosses. Or, rather, that they represent the real bosses who live in a faraway country where everything seems to be plentiful, and whence they send orders which may mean great changes for every one of the thirty thousand or more people of Tiquisate, even the loss of their jobs. Formerly, Esteban had lived in his own house, poor as it was, and most of the time he had been his own boss, engaged in a fairly steady trade, even if it paid him only a barest living.

Thus, Esteban is torn between gratification and dissatisfaction. He is bewildered. He is not sure that the advantages of his new life outweigh its disadvantages. In spite of the fact that he earns more than he ever did before, he sometimes feels that he is not paid enough. He knows of neighbors who earn as much as one quetzal (equal to a dollar) or one quetzal and forty cents a day. They were skilled workers: sprayers, or banana pickers, or mechanics, or drivers. They have mastered certain techniques and know how to handle some of the innumerable tools and machines which were unknown to them and most of their fellows until they came to work for the North Americans. These better paid skilled workers have gone to school and can read, write, and use elementary arithmetic. Their number is increasing steadily, as more efficient, more highly mechanized methods of production and transportation are being introduced and elementary school instruction is becoming more common. Esteban's children will probably belong to them.

Strangely enough, the skilled workers are more dissatisfied than Esteban. It is they who are most active in the labor unions which were founded during the last few years, taking advantage of the liberal laws adopted after the overthrow of the dictatorship in 1944. It is they who demand higher wages, better working conditions, free transportation on vacation trips, more school facilities, and many other things of which Esteban would never have dreamed a few years ago in his highland village. Some of these people have even learned English so that they can read the company's reports on its earnings. They now claim that the foreign owners of the company are taking too much money out of the country and they should be forced to leave greater benefits to the nationals, by paying higher wages and offering more social services of all kinds. They are not impressed with the arguments that the company already pays the best wages in the country, and that Esteban and his fellows would still be living the miserable, unhealthy, undernourished, and illiterate life of the past if it had not been for the many millions of dollars of North American capital invested by the company's stockholders. Some of the leaders of the union of which Esteban is a member, though not a very active one, even say that they, the Guatemalans, can take over the banana industry if the North Americans want to pull out of the country—just as the Guatemalans have taken charge of the German coffee and sugar plantations since the last war.

Esteban and his fellow workers have moved from a stationary way of life to a way of life where change—technological, economic, social, geographic—is the rule. They are not yet adjusted to it, but they are becoming accustomed to change. In fact, they may want to operate changes of their own, against the powerful corporation which has exposed them to this new way of life. Up to now, change has been planned and administered by the businessmen and engineers from the United States. New techniques, machinery, and skills were taught by these people to the natives of an economically backward country. Material inducements were offered to them for working in new places and unaccustomed enterprises. Now the principle of change is going farther than its original sponsors had intended. Social status and income are no longer determined by tradition and the accident of birth and, therefore, no longer accepted without criticism or ambition for improvement, as they were for centuries. On the other hand, the new factors on which one's place in life now depends are uncertain and not clearly understood.

If ambition and change are good and should take the place of conformity and tradition, for the sake of progress and a better life, why not push change until Esteban and *all* Guatemalans will enjoy the good things which are now reserved to the gringos and a few Guatemalans? If children of illiterate Guatemalan peasants can learn how to operate a railway engine, repair a truck, service an airplane, and do double-entry bookkeeping, things which only foreigners did thirty years ago, why can't they also learn to run *all* of Tiquisate—for their own benefit? And if the ability to operate machines and to plan and administer the work of many men is not limited to the members of certain master races or superior nations or ruling classes—why not change the traditional division of property under which a few families have owned most of the good lands and exploited the majority of the landless people who have had to work for them? Why put up any longer with the rule of privileged cliques in politics and public administration? If Esteban's children can learn things he never learned, as they do right now in school and shops, things which until recently were considered the prerogative of the overlords, what will stop them, or their children, from taking the place of those overlords?

Esteban Pazuj is representative not only of some thousands of fellow workers on the banana plantations of Guatemala but of millions of people working in many parts of the world. They are all going through essentially the same experience. Soon there will be even more Estebans.

Someone in a discussion of the evils of cultural displacement uttered this baroque epigram which sums up aptly the risks of the situation: "The uprooted and the roots of the uprooted are roots of revolution."

The Meaning of Imperialism

As we have previously noted, many historical terms are used very loosely. Such words as *democracy* and *socialism,* for instance, have been handled so carelessly that they are often more confusing than explanatory. Imperialism, which is the subject of today's reading, is another such term. Some people refer to the territorial expansion of the 16th and 17th centuries (discussed in Problem 15) as imperialism when they should be using a more appropriate label—colonialism. Generally speaking, 19th-century expansionism was more organized and more aggressive than that of the earlier period, and grew out of more complex motives.

In the 20th century, the use of the term *imperialism* has become even more confused. Some use it to characterize the foreign policy of the Soviet Union, others to describe the foreign policy of the United States. The English and the French, who have been practically stripped of their empires, are accused of being imperialists by the Chinese communists, who seem intent on adding to their own vast territory.

As we have seen in Problems 3 and 20, historians like to define terms according to the time and place in which they were used. The word *imperialism* belongs to the last half of the 19th century. Although it first came into use in France to describe certain aspects of society under Napoleon III, it was being applied by the end of the century to the process of European expansion abroad. Until about 1870 European nations had not tried to win political control of underdeveloped areas. Then in a rush Germany, England, France, Italy, Russia, and Belgium (as well as Japan and the United States) began to compete for this kind of colony. The term *imperialism* can be properly used to describe this development.

What were the motives of the imperialists? Marxists, such as Lenin, have argued that imperialism is merely the last stage of capitalism. According to their argument, capitalist nations extended their power overseas in order to postpone their inevitable downfall. They hoped to revive their internal economies—suffering from dwindling resources and profits—by exploiting lands and peoples abroad. On the other hand, some persons have argued that "advanced" nations felt they had a moral duty to spread their institutions and cultures to so-called "backward" peoples. Still others have held that one of the strongest factors was the desire of Western countries to control naval bases and coaling stations in case of war.

The four documents below will help you to work out a historical definition of the word *imperialism* as it was used in Great Britain and the United States about 1900. The first reading is from a book written by F. D. Lugard of the British East Africa Company, an enterprise which was instrumental in developing Kenya. Next you will read Rudyard Kipling's famous poem "The White Man's Burden," written in February 1899, shortly after the Spanish-American War. Senator Albert J. Beveridge's speech to the Senate, given on January 9, 1900, in support of a resolution to retain control of the Philippine Islands, illustrates the viewpoint of a particularly important American imperialist. Finally, the short passage from a book by Admiral Alfred T. Mahan indicates the attitude of a prominent naval officer who was a close friend of Theodore Roosevelt.

Consider the following questions as you read:

1 What were the stated or implied motives of the authors represented in these readings? Do you see selfish and selfless motives combined? Do the four writers share the same point of view?

2 How do you think educated Africans and Asians would react to the attitudes expressed in these four documents? What bearing does this issue have on international politics in the mid-20th century?

3 If you used the word *imperialist* to describe a man living about 1900, what would you want the word to mean? Would you use the same word to describe present-day Russian expansion into Europe? Why or why not?

I

THE RISE OF OUR EAST AFRICAN EMPIRE / by F. D. Lugard

Edinburgh: Wm. Blackwood & Sons, 1893.

The value of the Industrial mission . . . depends, of course, largely on the nature of the tribes among whom it is located. Its value can hardly be over-estimated among such people as the Waganda, both on account of their natural aptitude and their eager desire to learn. But even the less advanced and more primitive tribes may be equally benefited, if not only mechanical and artisan work, such as the carpenter's and blacksmith's craft, but also the simpler expedients of agriculture are taught. The sinking of wells, the system of irrigation, the introduction and planting of useful trees, the use of manure, and of domestic animals for agricultural purposes, the improvement of his implements by the introduction of the primitive Indian plough, etc. — all of these, while improving the status of the native, will render his land more productive, and hence, by increasing his surplus products, will enable him to purchase from the trader the cloth which shall add to his decency, and the implements and household utensils which shall produce greater results for his labour and greater comforts in his social life. . . .

In my view . . . instruction (religious or secular) is largely wasted upon adults, who are wedded to custom and prejudice. It is the rising generation who should be educated to a higher plane, by the establishment of schools for children. They, in turn, will send their children for instruction; and so a progressive advancement is instituted, which may produce really great results. I see, in a recent letter, that Dr. Laws supports this view, and appositely quotes the parallel of the Israelites after their exodus from Egypt, who were detained for forty years in the desert, until the generation who had been slaves in Egypt had passed away. The extensive schools at his mission at Bandawi were evidence of the practical application of his views. These schools were literally thronged with thousands of children, and chiefs of neighbouring tribes were eagerly offering to erect schools in their own villages at their own cost. . . .

An administrative mission can, of course, only be founded in a country not under the aegis of any European Power. Under such circumstances, a mission may be justified in undertaking to some extent administrative functions, pending the absorption of the country under European protection, especially where no central native authority exists, and there is no cohesion to repel the attacks of slave-traders, or the tyranny of the dominant tribe. This, of course, is more especially the case when the community has grown up in a previously unpopulated country. . . . But when a secular administration is established, it appears to me that the missions should resign entirely into the hands of the authorized executive Government all functions pertaining to administration. . . .

One word as regards missionaries themselves. The essential point in dealing with Africans is to establish a respect for the European. Upon this—the prestige of the white man—depends his influence, often his very existence, in Africa. If he shows by his surroundings, and by his assumption of superiority, that he is far above the native, he will be respected, and his influence will be proportionate to the superiority he assumes and bears out by his higher accomplishments and mode of life. In my opinion—at any rate with reference to Africa—it is the greatest possible mistake to suppose that a European can acquire a greater influence by adopting the mode of life of the natives. In effect, it is to lower himself to their plane, instead of elevating them to his. The sacrifice involved is wholly unappreciated, and the motive would be held by the savage to be poverty and lack of social status in his own country. The whole influence of the European in Africa is gained by his assertion of a superiority which commands the respect and excites the emulation of the savage. To forego this vantage-ground is to lose influence for good. I may add, that the loss of prestige consequent on what I should term the humiliation of the European affects not merely the missionary himself, but is subversive of all efforts for secular administration, and may even invite insult, which may lead to disaster and bloodshed. To maintain it a missionary must, above all things, be a gentleman; for no one is more quick to recognize a real gentleman than the African savage. He must at all times assert himself, and repel an insolent familiarity, which is a thing entirely apart from friendship born of respect and affection. His dwelling-house should be as superior to those of the natives as he is himself superior to them. And this, while adding to his prestige and influence, will simultaneously promote his own health and energy, and so save money spent on invalidings to England, and replacements due to sickness or death. . . .

It is sufficient to reiterate here, that as long as our policy is one of free trade, we are compelled to seek new markets; for old ones are being closed to us by hostile tariffs, and our great dependencies, which formerly were the consumers of our goods, are now becoming our commercial rivals. It is inherent in a great colonial and commercial empire like ours that we go forward or go backward. To allow other nations to develop new fields, and to refuse to do so ourselves, is to go backward; and this is the more deplorable, seeing that we have proved ourselves notably capable of dealing with native races, and of developing new countries at less expense than other nations. We owe to the instincts of colonial expansion of our ancestors, those vast and noble dependencies which are our pride and the outlets of our trade to-day; and we are accountable to posterity that opportunities which now present themselves of extending the sphere of our industrial enterprise are not neglected, for the opportunities now offered will never recur again. . . .

If some initial expense is incurred, is it not justified by the ultimate gain? I have already pointed out what other nations are doing in the way of railway extension. The Government is not asked to provide the capital of the railway, but only a guarantee on the subscribed capital. . . . Independently of money spent on railways, the conquest of Algeria alone cost France £150,000,000, and it is estimated that her West Coast colonies cost her half a million yearly. Italy spends on her Abyssinian protectorate a sum variously estimated at £400,000 or £600,000 per annum. Belgium, besides her heavy expenses for the Congo railway, the capital of which she has advanced without interest, guarantees £80,000 per annum to the Congo State, and is altering her constitution in order to allow her to take over that State as a colonial possession. Germany has spent over a million sterling in East Africa, besides her expenditure on the west and south-west colonies. The parallel is here complete, for the German Company failed, and Government stepped in to carry out the pledges and obligations incurred. Even Portugal is content to support a yearly deficit on each of her African possessions, gives heavy subsidies to the mail-steamers, and £10,000 per annum to the Cable. All these nations are content to incur this yearly cost in the present, confident that in the future these possessions will repay the outlay. . . .

II

THE WHITE MAN'S BURDEN / by Rudyard Kipling

From *Rudyard Kipling's Verse*, inclusive edition, and *The Five Nations* by Rudyard Kipling. Reprinted by permission of Mrs. George Bambridge, The Macmillan Company of Canada, Ltd., A. P. Watt & Son, Methuen & Co. Ltd., and Doubleday & Company, Inc.

Take up the White Man's burden —
Send forth the best ye breed —
Go bind your sons to exile
To serve your captives' need;
To wait in heavy harness,
On fluttered folk and wild —
Your new-caught, sullen peoples,
Half-devil and half-child.

Take up the White Man's burden —
In patience to abide,
To veil the threat of terror
And check the show of pride;
By open speech and simple,
An hundred times made plain,
To seek another's profit,
And work another's gain.

Take up the White Man's burden —
The savage wars of peace —
Fill full the mouth of Famine
And bid the sickness cease;

And when your goal is nearest
The end for others sought
Watch Sloth and heathen Folly
Bring all your hopes to nought.

Take up the White Man's burden—
No tawdry rule of kings,
But toil of serf and sweeper—
The tale of common things.
The ports ye shall not enter,
The roads ye shall not tread,
Go make them with your living,
And mark them with your dead.

Take up the White Man's burden—
And reap his old reward:
The blame of those ye better,
The hate of those ye guard—
The cry of hosts ye humour
(Ah, slowly!) toward the light:—
"Why brought ye us from bondage,
Our loved Egyptian night?"

Take up the White Man's burden—
Ye dare not stoop to less—
Nor call too loud on Freedom
To cloak your weariness;
By all ye cry or whisper,
By all ye leave or do,
The silent, sullen peoples
Shall weigh your Gods and you.

Take up the White Man's burden—
Have done with childish days—
The lightly proffered laurel,
The easy, ungrudged praise.
Comes now, to search your manhood
Through all the thankless years,
Cold, edged with dear-bought wisdom,
The judgment of your peers!

III

ADDRESS TO THE SENATE / by Albert J. Beveridge

Congressional Record, 56th Cong., 1st Sess., pp. 704, 708, 711.

The Philippines are ours forever, "territory belonging to the United States," as the Constitution calls them. And just beyond the Philippines are China's illimitable markets. We will not retreat from either. We will not repudiate our duty in the archipelago. We will not abandon our opportunity in the Orient. We will not renounce our part in the mission of our race, trustee, under God, of the civilization of the world. And we will move forward to our work, not howling out regrets like slaves whipped to their burdens, but with gratitude for a task worthy of our strength, and thanksgiving to Almighty God that He has marked us as His chosen people, henceforth to lead in the regeneration of the world. . . .

. . . The power that rules the Pacific . . . is the power that rules the world. And, with the Philippines, that power is and will forever be the American Republic. . . .

. . . it would be better to abandon this combined garden and Gibraltar of the Pacific, and count our blood and treasure already spent a profitable loss, than to apply any academic arrangement of self-government to these children. They are not capable of self-government. How could they be? They are not of a self-governing race. They are Orientals, Malays, instructed by Spaniards in the latter's worst estate.

They know nothing of practical government except as they have witnessed the weak, corrupt, cruel, and capricious rule of Spain. What magic will anyone employ to dissolve in their minds and characters those impressions of governors and governed which three centuries of misrule has created? What alchemy will change the oriental quality of their blood and set the self-governing currents of the American pouring through their Malay veins? How shall they, in the twinkling of an eye, be exalted to the heights of self-governing peoples which required a thousand years for us to reach, Anglo-Saxon though we are? . . .

Mr. President, this question is deeper than any question of party politics: deeper than any question of the isolated policy of our country even; deeper even than any question of constitutional power.

It is elemental. It is racial. God has not been preparing the English-speaking and Teutonic peoples for a thousand years for nothing but vain and idle self-contemplation and self-admiration. No! He has made us the master organizers of the world to establish system where chaos reigns. He has given us the spirit of progress to overwhelm the forces of reaction throughout the earth. He has made us adept in government that we may administer government among savage and senile peoples. Were it not for such a force as this the world would relapse into barbarism and night. And of all our race He has marked the American people as His chosen nation to finally lead in the regeneration of the world. This is the divine mission of America, and it holds for us all the profit, all the glory, all the happiness possible to man. We are trustees of the world's progress, guardians of its righteous peace. The judgment of the Master is upon us: "Ye have been faithful over a few things; I will make you ruler over many things."

IV

THE INTEREST OF AMERICA IN SEA POWER / by Alfred T. Mahan

Boston: Little, Brown & Company, 1897.

The interesting and significant feature of this changing attitude [*an increasing interest in overseas markets*] is the turning of the eyes outward, instead of inward only, to seek the welfare of the country. To affirm the importance of distant markets, and the relation to them of our own immense powers of production, implies logically the recognition of the link that joins the products and the markets, — that is, the carrying trade; the three together constituting that chain of maritime power to which Great Britain owes her wealth and greatness. Further, is it too much to say that, as two of these links, the shipping and the markets, are exterior to our own borders, the acknowledgment of them carries with it a view of the relations of the United States to the world radically distinct from the simple idea of self-sufficingness? We shall not follow far this line of thought before there will dawn the realization of America's unique position, facing the older worlds of the East and West, her shores washed by the oceans which touch the one or the other, but which are common to her alone. . . .

There is no sound reason for believing that the world has passed into a period of assured peace outside the limits of Europe. Unsettled political conditions, such as exist in Haiti, Central America, and many of the Pacific islands, especially the Hawaiian group, when combined with great military or commercial importance as is the case with most of these positions, involve, now as always, dangerous germs of quarrel, against which it is prudent at least to be prepared. Undoubtedly, the general temper of nations is more averse from war than it was of old. If no less selfish and grasping than our predecessors, we feel more dislike to the discomforts and sufferings attendant upon a breach of peace; but to retain that highly valued repose and the undisturbed enjoyment of the returns of commerce, it is necessary to argue upon somewhat equal terms of strength with an adversary. It is the preparedness of the enemy, and not the acquiescence in the existing state of things, that now holds back the armies of Europe. . . .

When the Isthmus [*of Panama*] is pierced, this isolation will pass away, and with it the indifference of foreign nations. From wheresoever they come and whithersoever they afterward go, all ships that use the canal will pass through the Caribbean. Whatever the effect produced upon the prosperity of the adjacent continent and islands by the thousand wants attendant upon maritime activity, around such a focus of trade will centre large commercial and political interests. To protect and develop its own, each nation will seek points of support and means of influence in a quarter where the United States always has been jealously sensitive to the intrusion of European powers. The precise value of the Monroe Doctrine is understood very loosely by most Americans, but the effect of the familiar phrase has been to develop a national sensitiveness, which is a more frequent cause of war than material interests; and over disputes caused by such feelings there will preside none of the calming influence due to the moral authority of international law, with its recognized principles, for the points in dispute will be of policy, of interest, not of conceded right. Already France and Great Britain are giving to ports held by them a degree of artificial strength uncalled for by their present importance. They look to the near future. Among the islands and on the mainland there are many positions of great importance, held now by weak or unstable states. Is the United States willing to see them sold to a powerful rival? But what right will she invoke against the transfer? She can allege but one,—that of her reasonable policy supported by her might.

Causes of World War I

Several readings in this volume have investigated the causes of major developments in European history. Problem 14 brought together a number of ideas
about causation itself. In that reading, Carl Gustavson distinguished between
the immediate cause of a major historical change and long-range causes, and
suggested a method of investigating the significance of these events. His
approach illustrated clearly the complexity of the entire problem of causation
in history.

The following excerpt is from a book by the American historian Sidney
Bradshaw Fay, entitled *Origins of the World War*. It focuses on the problem,
long debated by historians, of fixing responsibility for the outbreak of World
War I. This issue is complicated. Everyone agrees that the murder of the Austrian
Archduke Francis Ferdinand by a Bosnian patriot at Sarajevo was the incident
that touched off the war, but there is little agreement about the underlying
causes of the war or the ultimate responsibility for the outbreak of hostilities.
As you read this excerpt, consider it in the light of the method of analysis
proposed by Gustavson.

Fay's two-volume work on the causes of the war, first published in 1928,
has stood the test of time and critical scholarship. To Professor Fay's credit is
the fact that he waited until official records of events were available. In his
first volume he explored the long-range causes of the war, extending his study
far back into the 19th century. He devoted his entire second volume to the
immediate causes of the war and examined in detail the responsibilities of
each major party. The section here is a summary of his conclusions.

As you read, consider the following questions:

1   In what way was each of the nations involved partly responsible for
the outbreak of hostilities? Do you agree with Fay's analysis of individual
responsibility?

2   Why, according to Fay, is the argument that Germany was solely
responsible for the outbreak of World War I no longer tenable? Why do you
think this interpretation developed in the first place?

3   What do you think of Fay's analysis of the British position, which you
will find near the end of the article? Can he bring evidence to support his
position, or is his argument merely speculation?

ORIGINS OF THE WORLD WAR / by Sidney Bradshaw Fay

Reprinted with permission of the publisher. Copyright
1930, The Macmillan Company. Volume II, pp. 547-558.

None of the powers wanted a European War. Their governing rulers
and ministers, with very few exceptions, all foresaw that it must be
a frightful struggle, in which the political results were not absolutely certain, but in which the loss of life, suffering, and economic
consequences were bound to be terrible. . . .

Nevertheless, a European War broke out. Why? Because in each country political and military leaders did certain things which led to mobilizations and declarations of war, or failed to do certain things which might have prevented them. In this sense, all the European countries, in a greater or less degree, were responsible. One must abandon the dictum of the Versailles Treaty that Germany and her allies were solely responsible. It was a dictum exacted by victors from vanquished, under the influence of the blindness, ignorance, hatred, and the propagandist misconceptions to which war had given rise. It was based on evidence which was incomplete and not always sound. It is generally recognized by the best historical scholars in all countries to be no longer tenable or defensible. They are agreed that the responsibility for the War is a divided responsibility. But they still disagree very much as to the relative part of this responsibility that falls on each country and on each individual political or military leader.

Some writers like to fix positively in some precise mathematical fashion the exact responsibility for the war. This was done in one way by the framers of Article 231 of the Treaty of Versailles. It has been done in other ways by those who would fix the responsibility in some relative fashion, as, for instance, Austria first, then Russia, France and Germany and England. But the present writer deprecates such efforts to assess by a precise formula a very complicated question, which is after all more a matter of delicate shading than of definite white and black. . . . Moreover, even supposing that a general consensus of opinion might be reached as to the relative responsibility of any individual country or man for immediate causes connected with the July crisis of 1914, it is by no means necessarily true that the same relative responsibility would hold for the underlying causes, which for years had been tending toward the creation of a dangerous situation.

One may, however, sum up very briefly the most salient facts in regard to each country.

Serbia felt a natural and justifiable impulse to do what so many other countries had done in the nineteenth century—to bring under one national Government all the discontented Serb people. She had liberated those under Turkish rule; the next step was to liberate those under Hapsburg rule. She looked to Russia for assistance, and had been encouraged to expect that she would receive it. After the assassination [*of the Archduke Ferdinand*], Mr. Pashitch [*Nicholas*

Pashitch, premier of Serbia] took no steps to discover and bring to justice Serbians in Belgrade who had been implicated in the plot. One of them, Ciganovitch, was even assisted to disappear. Mr. Pashitch waited to see what evidence the Austrian authorities could find. When Austria demanded cooperation of Serbian officials in discovering, though not in trying, implicated Serbians, the Serbian Government made a very conciliatory but negative reply. They expected that the reply would not be regarded as satisfactory, and, even before it was given, ordered the mobilization of the Serbian army. Serbia did not want war, but believed it would be forced upon her. That Mr. Pashitch was aware of the plot three weeks before it was executed, failed to take effective steps to prevent the assassins from crossing over from Serbia to Bosnia, and then failed to give Austria any warning or information which might have averted the fatal crime, were facts unknown to Austria in July, 1914; they cannot therefore be regarded as in any way justifying Austria's conduct; but they are part of Serbia's responsibility, and a very serious part.

Austria was more responsible for the immediate origin of the war than any other Power. Yet from her own point of view she was acting in self-defence — not against an immediate military attack, but against the corroding Greater Serbia and Jugoslav agitation which her leaders believed threatened her very existence. No State can be expected to sit with folded arms and await dismemberment at the hands of its neighbors. Russia was believed to be intriguing with Serbia and Rumania against the Dual Monarchy. The assassination of the heir to the throne, as a result of a plot prepared in Belgrade, demanded severe retribution; otherwise Austria would be regarded as incapable of action, "wormeaten" as the Serbian Press expressed it, would sink in prestige, and hasten her own downfall. To avert this Berchtold [*Count Leopold von Berchtold, Austrian foreign minister*] determined to crush Serbia with war. He deliberately framed the ultimatum with the expectation and hope that it would be rejected. He hurriedly declared war against Serbia in order to forestall all efforts at mediation. He refused even to answer his own ally's urgent requests to come to an understanding with Russia, on the basis of a military occupation of Belgrade as a pledge that Serbia would carry out the promises in her reply to the ultimatum. Berchtold gambled on a "local" war with Serbia only, believing that he could rattle the German sword; but rather than abandon his war with Serbia, he was ready to drag the rest of Europe into war. . . .

Germany did not plot a European War, did not want one, and made genuine, though too belated efforts, to avert one. She was the victim of her alliance with Austria and of her own folly. Austria was her only dependable ally, Italy and Rumania having become nothing but allies in name. She could not throw her over, as otherwise she would stand isolated between Russia, where Panslavism and armaments were growing stronger every year, and France, where Alsace-Lorraine, Delcassé's fall, and Agadir were not forgotten. Therefore, Bethmann [*German Chancellor Theobald von Bethmann-Hollweg*] felt bound to accede to Berchtold's request for support and gave him a free hand to deal with Serbia; he also hoped and expected to "localize" the Austro-Serbian conflict. Germany then gave grounds to the Entente for suspecting the sincerity of her peaceful intentions by her denial of any foreknowledge of the ultimatum, by her support and justification of it when it was published, and by her refusal of Sir Edward Grey's conference proposal. However, Germany by no means had Austria so completely under her thumb as the Entente Powers and many writers have assumed. It is true that Berchtold would hardly have embarked on his gambler's policy unless he had been assured that Germany would fulfil the obligations of the alliance, and to this extent Germany must share the great responsibility of Austria. But when Bethmann realized that Russia was likely to intervene, that England might not remain neutral, and that there was danger of a world war of which Germany and Austria would appear to be the instigators, he tried to call a halt on Austria, but it was too late. He pressed mediation proposals on Vienna, but Berchtold was insensible to the pressure, and the Entente Powers did not believe in the sincerity of his pressure, especially as they produced no results.

Germany's geographical position between France and Russia, and her inferiority in number of troops, had made necessary the plan of crushing the French army quickly at first and then turning against Russia. This was only possible, in the opinion of her strategists, by marching through Belgium, as it was generally anticipated by military men that she would do in case of a European War. On July 29, after Austria had declared war on Serbia, and after the Tsar had assented to general mobilization in Russia (though this was not known in Berlin and was later postponed for a day owing to the Kaiser's telegram to the Tsar), Bethmann took the precaution of sending to the German Minister in Brussels a sealed envelope. The Minister was not to open it except on further instructions. It contained the later demand for the passage of the German army through Belgium. This does not mean, however, that Germany had decided for war. In fact, Bethmann was one of the last of the statesmen to abandon hope of peace and to consent to the mobilization of his country's army. General mobilization of the continental armies took place in the following order: Serbia, Russia, Austria, France and Germany. General mobilization by a Great Power was commonly interpreted by military men in every country, though perhaps not by Sir Edward Grey, the Tsar, and some civilian officials, as meaning that the country was on the point of making war, – that the military machine had begun to move and would not be stopped. Hence, when Germany learned of the Russian general mobilization, she sent ultimatums to St. Petersburg and Paris, warning that German mobilization would follow unless Russia suspended hers within twelve hours, and asking what would be the attitude of France. The answers being unsatisfactory, Germany then mobilized and declared war. It was the hasty Russian general mobilization, assented to on July 29 and ordered on July 30, while Germany was still trying to bring Austria to accept mediation proposals, which finally rendered the European War inevitable.

Russia was partly responsible for the Austro-Serbian conflict because of the frequent encouragement which she had given at Belgrade – that Serbian national unity would be ultimately achieved with Russian assistance at Austrian expense. This had led the Belgrade Cabinet to hope for Russian support in case of a war with Austria, and the hope did not prove vain in July, 1914. Before this, to be sure, in the Bosnian Crisis and during the Balkan Wars, Russia had put restraint upon Serbia, because Russia, exhausted by the effects of the Russo-Japanese War, was not yet ready for a European struggle with the Teutonic Powers. But in 1914 her armaments, though not yet completed, had made such progress that the militarists were confident of success, if they had French and British support. In the spring of 1914, the Minister of War, Sukhomlinov, had published an article in a Russian newspaper, though without signing his name, to the effect, "Russia is ready, France must be ready also." Austria was convinced that Russia would ultimately aid Serbia, unless the Serbian danger were dealt with energetically after the Archduke's murder; she knew that Russia was growing stronger every year; but she doubted whether the Tsar's armaments had yet reached the point at which Russia would dare to intervene; she would therefore run less risk of Russian intervention and a European War if she used the

Archduke's assassination as an excuse for weakening Serbia, than if she should postpone action until the future.

Russia's responsibility lay also in the secret preparatory military measures which she was making at the same time that she was carrying on diplomatic negotiations. These alarmed Germany and Austria. But it was primarily Russia's general mobilization, made when Germany was trying to bring Austria to a settlement, which precipitated the final catastrophe, causing Germany to mobilize and declare war.

The part of France is less clear than that of the other Great Powers, because she has not yet made a full publication of her documents. To be sure, M. Poincaré [*president of France, Raymond Poincaré*], in the fourth volume of his memoirs, has made a skilful and elaborate plea, to prove *La France innocente*. But he is not convincing. It is quite clear that on his visit to Russia he assured the Tsar's Government that France would support her as an ally in preventing Austria from humiliating or crushing Serbia. Paléologue [*Maurice Paléologue, French ambassador to Russia*] renewed these assurances in a way to encourage Russia to take a strong hand. He did not attempt to restrain Russia from military measures which he knew would call forth German counter-measures and cause war. Nor did he keep his Government promptly and fully informed of the military steps which were being taken at St. Petersburg. President Poincaré, upon his return to France, made efforts for peace, but his great preoccupation was to minimize French and Russian preparatory measures and emphasize those of Germany, in order to secure the certainty of British support in a struggle which he now regarded as inevitable.

Sir Edward Grey made many sincere proposals for preserving peace; they all failed owing partly, but not exclusively, to Germany's attitude. Sir Edward could probably have prevented war if he had done either of two things. If, early in the crisis, he had acceded to the urging of France and Russia and given a strong warning to Germany that, in a European War, England would take the side of the Franco-Russian Alliance, this would probably have led Bethmann to exert an earlier and more effective pressure on Austria; and it would perhaps thereby have prevented the Austrian declaration of war on Serbia, and brought to a successful issue the "direct conversations" between Vienna and St. Petersburg. Or, if Sir Edward Grey had listened to German urging, and warned France and Russia early in the crisis, that if they became involved in war, England would remain neutral, probably Russia would have hesitated with her mobilizations, and France would probably have exerted a restraining influence at St. Petersburg. But Sir Edward Grey could not say that England would take the side of France and Russia, because he had a Cabinet nearly evenly divided, and he was not sure, early in the crisis, that public opinion in England would back him up in war against Germany. He could resign, and he says in his memoirs that he would have resigned, but that would have been no comfort or aid to France, who had come confidently to count upon British support. He was determined to say and do nothing which might encourage her with a hope which he could not fulfil. Therefore, in spite of the pleadings of the French, he refused to give them definite assurances until the probable German determination to go through Belgium made it clear that the Cabinet, and Parliament, and British public opinion would follow his lead in war on Germany. On the other hand, he was unwilling to heed the German pleadings that he exercise restraint at Paris and St. Petersburg, because he did not wish to endanger the Anglo-Russian Entente and the solidarity of the Triple Entente, because he felt a moral obligation to France, growing out of the Anglo-French military and naval conversations of the past years, and because he suspected that Germany was backing Austria up in an unjustifiable course and that Prussian militarists had taken the direction of affairs at Berlin out of the hands of Herr von Bethmann-Hollweg and the civilian authorities. . . .

In the forty years following the Franco-Prussian War, as we have seen, there developed a system of alliances which divided Europe into two hostile groups. This hostility was accentuated by the increase of armaments, economic rivalry, nationalist ambitions and antagonisms, and newspaper incitement. But it is very doubtful whether all these dangerous tendencies would have actually led to war, had it not been for the assassination of Franz Ferdinand. That was the factor which consolidated the elements of hostility and started the rapid and complicated succession of events which culminated in a World War, and for that factor Serbian nationalism was primarily responsible.

But the verdict of the Versailles Treaty that Germany and her allies were responsible for the War, in view of the evidence now available, is historically unsound. It should therefore be revised. However, because of the popular feeling widespread in some of the Entente countries, it is doubtful whether a formal and legal revision is as yet practicable. There must first come a further revision by historical scholars, and through them of public opinion.

The Treaty of Versailles
and the German Position

The Treaty of Versailles, signed at Paris on June 28, 1919, is one of the most controversial documents of the 20th century. The brilliant assemblage of statesmen who attended the Paris Peace Conference included representatives of all the important nations of the world, with the exception of Russia and the Central Powers. The drafting of the agreement, however, was mainly the work of the so-called Big Three—Woodrow Wilson, President of the United States; David Lloyd George, prime minister of Great Britain; and Georges Clemenceau, premier of France.

Wilson, the idealist, represented the historical forces growing out of the Enlightenment of the 18th century. He viewed peace treaties of the past as essentially evil and foredoomed to failure. To him they were products of cynical diplomats, and fell far short of representing the legitimate aspirations of mankind for peace and security. Wilson's ideas on a just settlement of World War I problems were set forth in a speech to Congress on January 8, 1918; his principles became known as the Fourteen Points.

Although the other Allied powers had apparently accepted the Fourteen Points as a basis for negotiating with the Germans, many of their aims were actually embodied in secret agreements concluded among themselves. Both Lloyd George and Clemenceau were interested above all in destroying Germany as a serious rival; neither shared Wilson's idealism. The Germans, however, proceeded on the assumption that the settlement would be based on Wilsonian principles of "peace without victory."

Today's readings shed light on three aspects of the World War I peace settlement: the hopes of Wilson, as embodied in his Fourteen Points; the reality of the settlement itself, as represented by selected articles of the Treaty of Versailles; and the disappointment of the German delegation, as revealed in excerpts from a formal criticism they submitted in October 1919.

To help you in making judgments about the Versailles settlement, it may be useful to consider each of these documents in the light of specific issues.

As you read, try to answer the following questions:

1   What position is taken in the Fourteen Points, the Treaty of Versailles, and the Comments by the German Delegation on the following questions:

    a. colonies

    b. Alsace-Lorraine

    c. the Polish Corridor

2   How did the Fourteen Points and the Treaty of Versailles approach the question of disarmament and demilitarization?

3   What does the Treaty of Versailles say about war guilt and reparations? What is the position of the German delegation on these two important points?

I

WILSON'S FOURTEEN POINTS

Congressional Record, 65th Cong., 2nd Sess., pp. 680-681.

We entered this war because violations of right had occurred which touched us to the quick and made the life of our own people impossible unless they were corrected and the world secure once for all against their recurrence. What we demand in this war, therefore, is nothing peculiar to ourselves. It is that the world be made fit and safe to live in; and particularly that it be made safe for every peace-loving nation which, like our own, wishes to live its own life, determine its own institutions, be assured of justice and fair dealing by the other peoples of the world as against force and selfish aggression. All the peoples of the world are in effect partners in this interest, and for our own part we see very clearly that unless justice be done to others it will not be done to us. The programme of the world's peace, therefore, is our programme: and as we see it, is this:

I.   Open covenants of peace, openly arrived at, after which there shall be no private international understandings of any kind, but diplomacy shall proceed always frankly and in the public view.

II.   Absolute freedom of navigation upon the seas, outside territorial waters, alike in peace and in war, except as the seas may be closed in whole or in part by international action for the enforcement of international covenants.

III.   The removal, so far as possible, of all economic barriers and the establishment of an equality of trade conditions among all the nations consenting to the peace and associating themselves for its maintenance.

IV.   Adequate guarantees given and taken that national armaments will be reduced to the lowest point consistent with domestic safety.

V.   A free, open-minded, and absolutely impartial adjustment of all colonial claims, based upon a strict observance of the principle that in determining all such questions of sovereignty the interests of the populations concerned must have equal weight with the equitable claims of the government whose title is to be determined.

VI.   The evacuation of all Russian territory and such a settlement of all questions affecting Russia as will secure the best and freest cooperation of the other nations of the world in obtaining

for her an unhampered and unembarrassed opportunity for the independent determination of her own political development and national
policy, and assure her of a sincere welcome into the society of free
nations under institutions of her own choosing; and, more than a
welcome, assistance also of every kind that she may need and may
herself desire. The treatment accorded Russia by her sister nations in
the months to come will be the acid test of their good will, of their
comprehension of her needs as distinguished from their own interests, and of their intelligent and unselfish sympathy.

VII.   Belgium, the whole world will agree, must be evacuated
and restored, without any attempt to limit the sovereignty which she
enjoys in common with all other free nations. No other single act
will serve to restore confidence among the nations in the laws which
they have themselves set and determined for the government of their
relations with one another. Without this healing act, the whole structure and validity of international law is forever impaired.

VIII.   All French territory should be freed and the invaded portions restored, and the wrong done to France by Prussia in 1871 in
the matter of Alsace-Lorraine, which has unsettled the peace of the
world for nearly fifty years, should be righted, in order that peace
may once more be made secure in the interest of all.

IX.   A readjustment of the frontiers of Italy should be effected
along clearly recognizable lines of nationality.

X.   The peoples of Austria-Hungary, whose place among the
nations we wish to see safeguarded and assured, should be accorded
the freest opportunity of autonomous development.

XI.   Rumania, Serbia, and Montenegro should be evacuated;
occupied territories restored; Serbia accorded free access to the sea;
and the relations of the several Balkan states to one another determined by friendly counsel along historically established lines of
allegiance and nationality; and international guarantees of the political and economic independence and territorial integrity of the several
Balkan states should be entered into.

XII.   The Turkish portions of the present Ottoman Empire
should be assured a secure sovereignty, but the other nationalities
which are now under Turkish rule should be assured an undoubted
security of life and an absolutely unmolested opportunity of autonomous development, and the Dardanelles should be permanently
opened as a free passage to the ships and commerce of all nations
under international guarantees.

XIII.   An independent Polish state should be erected which
should include the territories inhabited by indisputably Polish
populations, which should be assured a free and secure access to the
sea, and whose political and economic independence and territorial
integrity should be guaranteed by international covenant.

XIV.   A general association of nations must be formed under
specific covenants for the purpose of affording mutual guarantees
of political independence and territorial integrity to great and small
states alike. . . .

We have spoken now, surely, in terms too concrete to admit of
any further doubt or question. An evident principle runs through the
whole programme I have outlined. It is the principle of justice to
all peoples and nationalities, and their right to live on equal terms
of liberty and safety with one another, whether they be strong or
weak. Unless this principle be made its foundation, no part of the
structure of international justice can stand.

·II

THE TREATY OF VERSAILLES

The Treaty of Versailles and After. Washington: United
States Government Printing Office, 1947.

Article 42.   Germany is forbidden to maintain or construct any forti-
fications either on the left bank of the Rhine or on the right bank to the
west of a line drawn 50 kilometers to the East of the Rhine. . . .

Article 45.   As compensation for the destruction of the coal-
mines in the north of France and as part payment towards the total
reparation due from Germany for the damage resulting from the war,
Germany cedes to France in full and absolute possession, with exclusive rights of exploitation, unencumbered and free from all debts
and charges of any kind, the coal-mines situated in the Saar
Basin. . . .

Article 49.   Germany renounces in favour of the League of Nations, in the capacity of trustee, the government of the territory defined above.

At the end of fifteen years from the coming into force of the
present Treaty the inhabitants of said territory shall be called upon
to indicate the sovereignty under which they desire to be placed. . . .

[*Article 51, preface.*]   The High Contracting Parties, recognizing

the moral obligation to redress the wrong done by Germany in 1871
both to the rights of France and to the wishes of the population of
Alsace and Lorraine, which were separated from their country in
spite of the solemn protest of their representatives at the Assembly
of Bordeaux, agree upon the following Articles:

Article 51.   The territories which were ceded to Germany in
accordance with the Preliminaries of Peace signed at Versailles on
February 26, 1871, and the Treaty of Frankfort of May 10, 1871, are
restored to French sovereignty as from the date of the Armistice of
November 11, 1918.

The provisions of the Treaties establishing the delimitation of
the frontiers before 1871 shall be restored. . . .

Article 80.   Germany acknowledges and will respect strictly the
independence of Austria, within the frontiers which may be fixed in
a Treaty between that State and the Principal Allied and Associated
Powers; she agrees that this independence shall be inalienable, except with the consent of the Council of the League of Nations.

Article 81.   Germany, in conformity with the action already taken
by the Allied and Associated Powers, recognizes the complete independence of the Czecho-Slovak State which will include the autonomous territory of the Ruthenians to the south of the Carpathians.
Germany hereby recognizes the frontiers of this State as determined
by the Principal Allied and Associated Powers and the other interested states. . . .

Article 87.   Germany, in conformity with the action already taken
by the Allied and Associated Powers, recognizes the complete
independence of Poland. . . .

Article 89.   Poland undertakes to accord freedom of transit to
persons, goods, vessels, carriages, wagons and mails in transit between East Prussia and the rest of Germany over Polish territory,
including territorial waters, and to treat them at least as favourably
as the persons, goods, vessels, carriages, wagons and mails respec-
tively of Polish or of any other more favoured nationality, origin,
importation, starting point, or ownership as regards facilities, restrictions and all other matters. . . .

Article 102.   The Principal Allied and Associated Powers undertake to establish the town of Danzig, together with the rest of the
territory described in Article 100, as a Free City. It will be placed
under the protection of the League of Nations. . . .

Article 116.   Germany acknowledges and agrees to respect as permanent and inalienable the independence of all the territories which were part of the former Russian Empire on August 1, 1914.

. . . Germany accepts definitely the abrogation of the Brest-Litovsk Treaties and of all other treaties, conventions and agreements entered into by her with the Maximalist [*Bolshevik*] Government in Russia.

The Allied and Associated Powers formally reserve the rights of Russia to obtain from Germany restitution and reparation based on the principles of the present Treaty. . . .

Article 119.   Germany renounces in favour of the Principal Allied and Associated Powers all her rights and titles over her oversea possessions. . . .

Article 159.   The German military forces shall be demobilized and reduced as prescribed hereinafter.

Article 160.   By a date which must not be later than March 31, 1920, the German Army must not comprise more than seven divisions of infantry and three divisions of cavalry.

After that date the total number of effectives in the Army of the States constituting Germany must not exceed one hundred thousand men, including officers and establishments of depots. The Army shall be devoted exclusively to the maintenance of order within the territory and to the control of the frontiers.

The total effective strength of officers, including the personnel of staffs, whatever their composition, must not exceed four thousand. . . .

Article 198.   The armed forces of Germany must not include any military or naval air forces. . . .

Article 231.   The Allied and Associated Governments affirm and Germany accepts the responsibility of Germany and her Allies for causing all the loss and damage to which the Allied and Associated Governments and their nationals have been subjected as a consequence of the war imposed upon them by the aggression of Germany and her allies.

Article 232.   The Allied and Associated Governments recognize that the resources of Germany are not adequate, after taking into account permanent diminutions of such resources which will result from other provisions of the present Treaty, to make complete reparation for all such loss and damage.

The Allied and Associated Governments, however, require, and Germany undertakes, that she will make compensation for all damage done to the civilian population of the Allied and Associated Powers and to their property during the period of the belligerency of each as an Allied or Associated Power against Germany. . . .

Article 233.   The amount of the above damage for which compensation is to be made by Germany shall be determined by an Inter-Allied Commission. . . .

This Commission shall consider the claims and give to the German Government a just opportunity to be heard.

The findings of the Commission as to the amount of damage defined as above shall be concluded and notified to the German Government on or before May 1, 1921, as representing the extent of that Government's obligations. . . .

Article 234.   The Reparation Commission shall after May 1, 1921, from time to time, consider the resources and capacity of Germany, and, after giving her representatives a just opportunity to be heard, shall have discretion to extend the date, and to modify the form of payments, such as are to be provided for in accordance with Article 233; but not to cancel any part, except with the specific authority of the several Governments represented upon the Commission. . . .

Article 428.   As a guarantee for the execution of the present Treaty by Germany, the German territory situated to the west of the Rhine, together with the bridgeheads, will be occupied by Allied and Associated troops for a period of fifteen years from the coming into force of the present Treaty. . . .

Article 431.   If before the expiration of the period of fifteen years Germany complies with all the undertakings resulting from the present Treaty, the occupying forces will be withdrawn immediately.

III

COMMENTS BY THE GERMAN DELEGATION ON THE CONDITIONS OF PEACE

From *International Conciliation*, October 1919, No. 143.

The peace to be concluded with Germany was to be a peace of right, not a peace of might. . . .

The peace document shows that none of [the] repeated solemn assurances has been kept.

To begin with the territorial questions:

In the West, a purely German territory on the Saar with a population of at least 650,000 inhabitants is to be separated from the German Empire for at least fifteen years merely for the reason that claims are asserted to the coal abounding there.

[*Several other examples follow.*]

The settlement of the colonial question is equally contradictory to a peace of justice. For the essence of activity in colonial work does not consist in capitalistic exploitation of a less developed human race, but in raising backward peoples to a higher civilization. This gives the Powers which are advanced in culture a natural claim to take part in colonial work. Germany, whose colonial accomplishments cannot be denied, has also this natural claim, which is not recognized by a treaty of peace that deprives Germany of all her colonies. . . .

Although President Wilson, in his speech of October 20th, 1916, has acknowledged that "no single fact caused the war, but that in the last analysis the whole European system is in a deeper sense responsible for the war, with its combination of alliances and understandings, a complicated texture of intrigues and espionage that unfailingly caught the whole family of nations in its meshes," "that the present war is not so simply to be explained and that its roots reach deep into the dark soil of history," Germany is to acknowledge that Germany and her allies are responsible for all damages which the enemy Governments or their subjects have incurred by her and her allies' aggression. This appears all the less tolerable as it is an indisputable historical fact that several of the hostile Powers, such as Italy and Roumania, on their part entered the war for the purpose of territorial conquests. Apart from the consideration that there is no incontestable legal foundation for the obligation for reparation imposed upon Germany, the amount of such compensation is to be determined by a commission nominated solely by Germany's enemies, Germany taking no part. . . .

As there are innate rights of man, so there are innate rights of nations. The inalienable fundamental right of every state is the right of self-preservation and self-determination. With this fundamental right the demand here made upon Germany is incompatible. . . .

The same is also true with regard to Alsace-Lorraine. If Germany has pledged herself "to right the wrong of 1871," this does not mean any renunciation of the right of self-determination of the inhabitants of Alsace-Lorraine. A cession of the country without consulting the population would be a new wrong, if for no other reason, because it would be inconsistent with a recognized principle of peace.

On the other hand, it is incompatible with the idea of national self-determination for two and one-half million Germans to be torn away from their native land against their own will. By the proposed demarcation of the boundary, unmistakably German territories are disposed of in favor of their Polish neighbors. . . . This disrespect of the right of self-determination is shown most grossly in the fact that Danzig is to be separated from the German Empire and made a free state. Neither historical rights nor the present ethnographical conditions of ownership of the Polish people can have any weight as compared with the German past and the German character of that city. Free access to the sea, satisfying the economic wants of Poland, can be secured by guarantees founded on international law, by the creating of free ports. Likewise the cession of the commercial town of Memel, which is to be exacted from Germany, is in no way consistent with the right of self-determination. The same may be said with reference to the fact that millions of Germans in German-Austria are to be denied the union with Germany which they desire and that, further, millions of Germans dwelling along our frontiers are to be forced to remain part of the newly created Czecho-Slovakian State. . . .

. . . . The German Government agrees with the Governments of the Allied and Associated Powers in the conviction that the horrible devastation caused by this war requires the establishment of a new world order, an order which shall insure the "effective authority of the principles of international law," and "just and honorable relations between the nations." The restoration and perfection of international order in the world can only be assured if the existing authorities, in a new spirit, succeed in realizing the great idea of democracy; if, as President Wilson declared on the 4th of July, 1918, "the settlement of every question is brought about . . . upon the basis of the free acceptance of that settlement by the people immediately concerned . . . ." Only the nations that enjoy freedom and independence, based upon law, may give each other the guarantee of just and honorable relations. But their fairness and honor also require that they warrant each other freedom and life as the most sacred and inalienable fundamental rights.

There is no evidence of these principles in the peace document which has been laid before us. Expiring world theories, emanating from imperialistic and capitalistic tendencies, celebrate in it their last horrible triumph. As opposed to these views, which have brought unspeakable disaster upon the world, we appeal to the innate sense of right of men and nations, under whose token the English State developed, the Dutch People freed itself, the North American nation established its independence, France shook off absolutism. The bearers of such hallowed traditions cannot deny this right to the German people, that now for the first time has acquired in its internal politics the possibility of living in harmony with its free will based on law. A treaty such as has been proposed to Germany is incompatible with the respect for this innate right.

The Failure
of the League of Nations

Men have tried a number of ways to maintain peace among nations. Despotic rulers have tried to prevent war by brute force, keeping subject peoples too weak to rise up against them. During the Middle Ages the Church enacted religious sanctions against war in the Truce of God. The principle of the balance of power has sometimes been used to make the costs of victory seem so high that potential aggressors would hesitate to break the peace. The Concert of Europe, created after the Congress of Vienna, attempted to organize the most powerful nations of Europe in an armed alliance designed to nip war in the bud. In the 20th century, we have seen two attempts to prevent war through international organizations, the League of Nations and the United Nations. Although successful on occasion, none of these systems has lived up to expectations.

Woodrow Wilson helped to develop the idea of a League of Nations as an international instrument that would make World War I the "war to end war." He hoped that several provisions in the covenant would prevent war from breaking out, and that if one did break out, sanctions, or penalties, imposed by peace-loving nations would soon bring the aggressor to heel. His hopes were vain. The League's machinery was too weak to cope with the fascist aggressors of the 1930's. Yet the League did prevent several smaller wars and also made conspicuous contributions to international welfare.

Some authorities have attributed the failure of the League to the fact that the United States failed to join. Without the power and prestige of American participation, this argument goes, the League was doomed from the start. The selection below questions this simplified view and raises additional possible explanations for the failure of the League.

As you read, consider the following questions:

1 What were the major characteristics of each of the first three periods into which the authors divide the history of the League?

2 What could have been done in the period 1932-1939 to prevent war from breaking out?

3 In what basic assumption did the drafters of the League Covenant resemble the statesmen of the Congress of Vienna?

4 How can you establish criteria for judging whether the League "failed" or "succeeded"?

TOWARD WORLD ORDER / by Amry Vandenbosch and Willard N. Hogan

Copyright 1963. McGraw-Hill Book Company, Inc. Used by permission. Pp. 41-47.

. . . the history of the [*League of Nations*] may be divided into periods as follows: 1920-1927, growth; 1927-1932, uncertainty; 1932-

1939, decline; 1939-1946, suspension, termination, and rebirth in a new organization.

1920-1927, Growth

During the first period the foundations had to be laid and the superstructure erected. Because of the failure of the United States to become a member, the League could not become what the framers of the Covenant had designed. The British, who had not been very happy about guaranteeing the territorial integrity and political independence of all members of the League, now lost all enthusiasm for it. They had hoped that the League might be the means of bringing the British and American peoples into close association and cooperation in world politics, but with the United States out of the League and the American people reverting to their former isolationist ideas, the League threatened to serve as a wedge to drive the two countries apart and even into increasing hostility. If the British Navy should be called upon to apply sanctions against an aggressor and if the United States government should assert the same neutral rights that it did before it became a belligerent in the late war, the possibility of an open clash between the two countries was not a remote one. This no sane Britisher cared to contemplate. British policy in the League of Nations, therefore, was to dilute the guarantee function.

The absence of the United States from the League also tended to drive Britain and France apart. What France desired most of all in the peace settlement was a guarantee against future attack and invasion by Germany. Clemenceau had at first demanded the detachment of the left bank of the Rhine from Germany, either by annexation to France or by the creation of a demilitarized buffer state. President Wilson would not yield to this demand. As a substitute, France accepted a tripartite alliance which pledged Britain and the United States to go to the aid of France in case of attack by Germany. Great Britain and France ratified the treaty, but the United States Senate refused to give its consent to the President for ratification, and since the treaty specifically stipulated that it would be binding only if ratified by all three parties, the alliance did not become a fact. France now felt itself aggrieved. It had surrendered what it regarded as vital national interests without receiving anything in exchange. France, therefore, became very insistent that the security provisions of the Covenant be faithfully and fully enforced. Because the British would not concur in its League policy, France adopted a policy toward Germany which the British thought unreasonable and which provoked considerable British sympathy for Germany. . . .

The absence of the United States from the new organization was also largely responsible for the failure of the plan to place all international bureaus, those already established as well as those which might be created in the future, under the direction of the League. Existing bureaus could be placed under the League only with the consent of all parties to the treaties under which they were established, but since some important countries were not members of the League, this was not possible in every case. Prewar international bureaus, such as the Telegraphic Union and the Universal Postal Union, were not brought under the League. The League established a Health Organization in 1920, but the old International Office of Public Health was not abolished, because some of its members who were not members of the League were unwilling to give their consent. The result was the parallel operation of two organizations with very similar functions and, in large part, with overlapping memberships.

During the early years, the League did develop a system of international administrative cooperation. Three so-called "technical organizations" were formed, namely, the Economic and Financial Organization, the Communications and Transit Organization, and the Health Organization. There were also created a number of permanent advisory commissions, whose functions did not differ greatly from the technical organizations. These commissions dealt with such problems as intellectual cooperation, protection of children and young people, and slavery.

During this period, the League also enjoyed a minor success in stopping a Greek invasion of Bulgaria, which occurred in the autumn of 1925. The Council, whose chairman at the time happened to be Briand of France, acted vigorously on the basis of Article 11 and was able to restore peaceful relations between the two small states.

Also during this period the Locarno treaties were signed, as a result of which Germany became a member of the League in 1926. The Locarno Pact was regarded as a long step forward in organizing the peace of Europe, and the admission of Germany to the League made the latter more of a universal organization and less of an alliance of victorious powers. However, the admission of Germany to the League, with a permanent seat on the Council, provoked a constitutional crisis, as three middle-class powers [*nations of middle rank*]

— Poland, Spain, and Brazil — likewise demanded permanent Council
seats. This was denied them . . . . Upon their failure to obtain
permanent seats, Brazil and Spain gave notice of their intention to
withdraw from the League; however, Spain withdrew its resignation
before the required two years' notice had expired. Brazil ceased to
be a member in June, 1928.

1927-1932, Uncertainty
     This period of the League's history began with a fairly hopeful
movement. During 1927 and 1928, the Kellogg-Briand Pact was nego-
tiated. It was signed August 27, 1928, by fifteen governments; it came
into force on July 24, 1929. Other states were invited to adhere, and
within a few years it had more adherents than the League had members. It was hoped that the Kellogg-Briand Pact, the adherents of
which renounced war as an instrument of national policy, might serve
as a bridge between the United States and the League. No state could
go to war in violation of the Covenant without also violating the Pact,
and although the latter contained no provisions for implementation,
it was hoped that, in case of application of sanctions against an aggressor by the League, the United States would do nothing to hinder such
action and possibly might give it some passive support. These hopes
do not seem to have been wholly unfounded when it is remembered
that the isolationist Senator William E. Borah, who was Chairman of
the important Senate Foreign Relations Committee during these
years, declared that it was inconceivable that the United States would
be indifferent to a violation of the Kellogg-Briand Pact.
     An important factor in the troubles and uncertainties of these
years was the world economic depression of 1929 and the years
following. Although the World Economic Conference, convened by
the League in 1927, issued what amounted to a Magna Charta for
international commercial cooperation, nothing came of it in practice.
With the deepening of the depression, economic nationalism became
more rampant than ever. The *rapprochement* between Germany
and France also came to an abrupt end in 1929, with the death of
Stresemann and the election of a considerable number of National
Socialists to the German parliament.
     In September of 1931 occurred the "incident" in Manchuria
[*the Japanese seized several provinces*], which soon developed into
a flagrant case of aggression. This clear violation of the Covenant, the
Nine Power Treaty, and the Kellogg-Briand Pact was met with little

coordination of action or policy between Washington and Geneva. None of the powers upon whom the enforcement of sanctions would fall was prepared to join in any form of collective action which might involve military action . . . .

1932-1939, Decline

On March 27, 1933, Japan gave notice of its intention to withdraw from the League, and Germany followed by a similar action on October 24 of the same year; in conformity with the requirement of two years' notice, these two countries ceased to be members in 1935. This loss of two Great Powers was somewhat offset by the admission of the Soviet Union in September, 1934, but it had entered the League only out of fear of Hitler's rise to power on a platform of bitter anti-communism. Encouraged by Japan's successful defiance of the League, Germany took one step after another to set aside provisions of the Treaty of Versailles and in March, 1936, denounced the treaty of Locarno. In 1935, Italy invaded Ethiopia and on May 9 of the following year declared that country annexed. League sanctions, half-heartedly applied and never extended to include military measures, failed to stop the aggression. There now began a flight from the Covenant and the League. Some members made interpretative declarations diluting their obligations under the Covenant. Others withdrew from the League altogether. Notice of withdrawal was given by Paraguay in February, 1935; by Nicaragua in June, 1935; by Guatemala in May, 1936; by Honduras in July, 1936; by El Salvador in July, 1937; by Italy in December, 1937; by Venezuela in July, 1938; by Hungary in April, 1939; and by Spain in May, 1939.

As a result of these events, there developed a movement for the reform of the League. On July 4, 1936, the Assembly of the League, in an extraordinary session, passed a resolution requesting the Council to invite governments to send in proposals to improve "the application of the principles of the Covenant," and three months later it set up a committee of inquiry to examine these proposals. The committee recommended that the Covenant should be amended to eliminate all expressions recalling the divisions of the Great War or, in other words, to separate the Covenant from the peace treaties. There was a widespread feeling that it had been a mistake to tie the Covenant to the peace treaties and that the League was breaking down under the burden of these treaties. The committee also recommended the coordination of the various peace pacts — the Kellogg-

Briand Pact and the Treaty of Rio de Janeiro of 1933—and the Covenant in order to facilitate cooperation between member and non-member states in the maintenance of peace. There was also a strong demand for universality of membership, but this demand ran into the difficulty that a general membership could be obtained only by watering down the obligations that membership would impose. However that may be, the movement for reform came to naught.

1939-1946, Suspension and Termination

It was evident long before World War II broke out that the League would be powerless to do anything about it. Such efforts as were made to prevent the war were made outside the League. Too weak to do anything to prevent or to suppress armed hostilities, the League performed a courageous but quixotic act in expelling the Soviet Union, on December 14, 1939, for attacking Finland. After this the League became dormant. The Assembly, which had not met in several years, convened for its last session on April 8, 1946, when it took the necessary steps legally to terminate its existence . . . .

Quite naturally, the question of why the League failed has been repeatedly raised. A multitude of answers have been given, but unfortunately there is no simple or easy explanation. It has been asserted frequently that the United States' failure to join was the primary reason for the League's weakness. Few will deny that the absence of the United States was a severe blow to the League's strength and prestige, but there is no guarantee that the United States government would have continued to give the League hearty support. With the first real difficulties, the American people might easily have become isolationist again. It may be that the bitter experience of a second world war was necessary to convince them that there is no security apart from collective security. By a lukewarm or reluctant participation in the League, the United States might have been a greater detriment to the successful development of the League inside than outside of it. The League certainly needed the membership of all the Great Powers, but this it would not have had even if the United States had joined. More was needed, however, than just the membership of all the Great Powers. What was also needed was the solidarity of the Great Powers, and that was sadly lacking, especially in the 1930's. There is little to justify the belief that the mere presence of the United States at the Council table would have profoundly altered this fundamental lack of agreement.

Some critics hold that the League suffered from a grave constitutional weakness in that it permitted states to resort to war under certain conditions. By permitting exceptions to the prohibition of war, the Covenant seemed to assume that war remained a normal solution of international conflicts. The rule requiring unanimity of all the members of the Council, other than parties to a dispute, in making decisions with respect to peaceful settlement has been widely criticized as unworkable. This criticism also applies, of course, to the general rule that decisions of the Assembly or of the Council required the agreement of all the members present.

From the point of view of organizing peace, the League of Nations rested upon three or four main pillars. These were the provision for the reduction of armaments (Article 8), the guarantees against aggression (Articles 10 and 16), the settlement of disputes (Articles 12 to 15 and 17), and the provision for peaceful change (Article 19). The last two dovetailed into each other somewhat, as the settlement of a dispute may involve a considerable revision of existing treaties. Because these pillars were not of equal strength, the League suffered from imbalance. The drafters of the Covenant attempted to make the guarantees against aggression very strong, while the provisions for the reduction of armaments and for peaceful change were made relatively weak. Not only was the provision for peaceful change weak, but it seems to have been tacked on as an afterthought. It is true that order is the first condition of all civilized society and that without it justice is hardly possible, but on the other hand no amount of force can maintain a *status quo* that a large number of peoples have come to regard as grossly unjust. Order and change must be linked together as Siamese twins; the one is impossible without the other. The League Covenant probably placed too much emphasis upon order and too little upon change.

However, the failure of the League was fundamentally due not to weaknesses of constitution or structure, serious as these may have been; the basic difficulty was the absence of the will to make it work. Good machinery for international cooperation can be very helpful if the will to cooperate exists, and it can make common action more effective, but without that will the best organization will be useless. Simply stated, the League of Nations failed because an international community to support it did not exist.

Because the League failed to provide security, which is the necessary condition for nearly everything else, the excellent work of the League and its agencies in many fields failed to receive the attention that it deserved. Both the International Labor Organization and the Permanent Court of International Justice were highly successful institutions, and both survived the League in fact if not in each case in name. The League demonstrated that the difficulties of creating an international secretariat can be overcome. The Secretariat apparently was an effective and loyal body of international civil servants; at least there was very little criticism of it. The mandates system may be judged moderately successful. The League was very successful in its activities in promoting human welfare, even while it was failing dismally in its security function. When the League of Nations is adjudged a failure, these achievements must not be forgotten.

Lenin as the Architect of the Russian Revolution

The Bolshevik Revolution of November 1917 was one of the most crucial events in modern history. Since those dramatic days, the communist movement has steadily grown to a position of critical importance in international affairs. It is impossible to understand world problems properly without knowing the nature of the Russian Revolution and the society it produced. Today's reading offers insights into the leadership and strategy of the communist party during the hectic days of 1917, and helps explain present-day Soviet authoritarianism.

The reading for today also deals with a recurring issue — the role of the individual in history — through a study of the part Lenin played in the Revolution. In Problem 16 we examined the way in which Peter the Great tried to remake Russia in the early 18th century. We saw that he usually succeeded in changing his nation when he worked in areas where there were clear precedents for change, and usually failed when he flew in the face of long-established customs.

Peter's career might lead us to conclude that the individual can do little to change the course of history. Sidney Hook, professor of philosophy at New York University, argues that this is not always so. He contends that at several strategic points in 1917, the presence of Lenin in Russia — and his presence alone — saved the Bolshevik Revolution from failure. In a sense, Lenin accomplished almost overnight what Peter the Great failed to do in more than twenty-five years: he gave a new direction to Russian life.

As you read, consider the following questions:

1   What evidence does Hook offer to support his thesis about Lenin? Is it convincing?

2   According to Hook, what conditions in Russia in 1917 made Lenin's role possible? What personal characteristics helped Lenin?

3   Do you think that circumstances and historical forces were of greater importance in creating the Revolution than Hook admits?

4   Why was Lenin more successful in changing Russia than Peter the Great had been?

THE HERO IN HISTORY / by Sidney Hook

New York: Humanities Press, Inc., 1950. Pp. 203-210, 220-223, 226-227.

The thesis of this chapter is that had it not been for the work of one man we should be living in a vastly different world today. . . .

. . . without Nicolai Lenin the work of the Bolshevik Party from April to October 1917 is unthinkable. Anyone who familiarizes himself with its internal history will discover that objectives, policy, slogans, controlling strategy, day-by-day tactics were laid down by

Lenin. Sometimes he counseled in the same painstaking way that a tutor coaches a spirited but bewildered pupil; sometimes he commanded like an impatient drill sergeant barking at a raw recruit. But from first to last it was Lenin. Without him there would have been no October Revolution. Here is the evidence.

    a.   Until Lenin's return to Russia on April 3, and his presentation of his thesis of April 4, the Bolshevik Party and its official organ were supporting the Provisional Government of Kerensky. Lenin's April Theses, which called for the overthrow of this government by armed insurrection and for all power to the Soviets, came as a bombshell in his own party.

    Speaking of the position of the Bolshevik Party in Russia before Lenin arrived, Joseph Stalin wrote on November 19, 1924:

"This position was utterly erroneous, for it begot pacifist illusions, poured water on the mill of defensism and hampered the revolutionary education of the masses. In those days I shared this erroneous position with other Party comrades, and completely renounced it only in the middle of April, when I endorsed Lenin's thesis."

At the beginning Lenin was absolutely alone in his stand. His intransigent demand for immediate cessation of the war against Germany, his call "to turn the imperialist war into a civil war," outraged all political parties. It played into the hands of his enemies who desperately sought to pin on him the false label of "German agent." Nonetheless, before the month was out Lenin had converted the executive committee and the most active spirits of his party. Before his arrival the local Bolsheviks were seriously considering organic fusion with the Mensheviks. Lenin changed all that. He drew a sharp line of division between his own party and all the other working-class parties that refused to accept his program.

    The significance of Lenin's work in arming his party with a new set of objectives may be gauged by the fact that this involved abandoning doctrines the Bolsheviks had firmly held for an entire decade. Until the February Revolution, all Bolsheviks, including Lenin, believed in what they called "the democratic dictatorship of the workers and peasants." The task of this regime would be to carry out in Russia the achievements of the democratic revolutions of the west. In 1917 Lenin changed his position and that of his party. The Russian Revolution was to be the first breach in the world economy of capitalism. It was to be a "dictatorship of the proletariat" that would stimulate similar dictatorships in the west which co-operatively would initiate the transition to world socialism.

His opponents predicted that Lenin's program would not appease the hunger of the Russian masses for peace, land, and bread; that world-wide socialist revolutions would not follow upon the dictatorship of the proletariat in Europe; that Russia would be devastated by civil war and chaos; that the autocracy of the Czarist bureaucrats and landlords would be replaced by an even more ruthless autocracy of Bolshevik bureaucrats. Despite all criticism from without as well as within his own party, Lenin won his way without yielding an inch.

b. Once Lenin had converted his party to the program of civil war and armed insurrection against the democratic Provisional Government, the main task was clear. It was to choose the proper moment to strike. Until that moment, Lenin was careful to exploit the status of legality in order to carry on his propaganda for overthrow, and to accumulate weapons. After the abrupt turn had been made from critical collaboration to outright opposition, it was not easy to restrain the Bolshevik rank and file, its periphery and sympathizers, from precipitating matters prematurely. If one shoots at a king, one must not miss. And if an insurrection is begun, it is death to fail. Lenin, therefore, was compelled to keep a very close check on the more exuberant of his followers as well as on the mass outbursts that rose periodically as a consequence of delay in meeting the urgent, immediate demands of workers and peasants. . . .

During the June days, and much more so during early July, extremist sentiment was rife in influential sections of the Petrograd working class and military garrison. Even some of the Bolshevik leaders were toying with the idea of giving the signal for an all-out attack against the Kerensky government. It was Lenin who held them back. He warned that they would be unable to finish what they started, that they would be crushed, and that the opportunity to strike for power would be lost, perhaps forever. Even so, a considerable number of workers got out of control and appeared on the streets with rifles in their hands. Although they had tried to call off this demonstration, which was largely the result of their previous agitation, the Bolshevik Party at Lenin's command placed itself at its head in order to prevent it from going over into open insurrection. The Bolsheviks were successful in this. But because the Party had taken public responsibility for the armed demonstration, their apparatus was

forced underground and they suffered a considerable loss of political
influence on the masses. They regained their influence and partially
emerged from illegality only after Kornilov attempted his *coup d'état*
from the right against the Kerensky government.

c.   The most decisive period in Lenin's career of mastery over
the Bolshevik Party was the very eve of the October Revolution.
Although in hiding, Lenin kept in close touch with the moods of the
discontented soldiery and peasants. He was well informed of the
disposition of military forces in and about the capital. The Central
Committee of the Bolshevik Party, having learned the lesson of the
July days, was inclined to go slow. The very furthest thing from their
minds was the desire to go over to an open offensive when they received word from Lenin that it was *now or never.*

At first Lenin was in the minority. He raged and stormed. He
threatened to go over their heads to the lower party functionaries and
to organize matters without them. He wrote letters to influential party
members to get them to bring pressure on the lagging executive
committee. After fierce and stubborn debate, he won them to his
position. How urgent Lenin considered the period they were in—as
the period in which to stake all on a bid for power—is apparent from
his letter of October 21, 1917, to the Central Executive Committee,
demanding the organization of an armed insurrection during the next
few days: "The success of both the Russian and world revolution
depends upon two or three days of struggle." When he finally won
his majority by a vote of ten to two, the die was cast. The Bolsheviks
took state power.

d.   That they kept state power during the subsequent year was
again due primarily to Lenin's guiding policy. One group of the
Central Committee desired to continue the war against Hohenzollern
Germany while appealing to the German workers to emulate the
Bolsheviks. Another group advocated the policy of "neither peace
nor war." Lenin stood firm for a signed treaty of peace which would
give the Bolsheviks respite from their foreign enemy for the moment
and sufficient time to consolidate themselves against their internal
foes. During these days, Lenin was again a hopeless minority at first
but hammered away until his colleagues yielded. The Treaty of Brest-
Litovsk was signed.

If Lenin had not returned to Russia or had died en route, there
is no evidence whatsoever to support the hypothesis that Kamenev,
Muranov, and Stalin, then in control of Bolshevik policy, would have

reversed helm and taken up war to the end against the democratic provisional Government. If during June and July Lenin had not been present to prevail upon the excited spirits among the Bolsheviks . . . and forestall an uprising, the whole organization would have been destroyed in blood. If, on the eve of October, the Bolsheviks had marked time despite Lenin's exhortations, Kerensky would have been able to garrison the capitol with reliable troops and easily cope with the Bolsheviks. If Lenin had not stopped the Germans by giving them all they wanted, their army would have taken both Petrograd and Moscow, since military resistance was no longer possible. . . .

Lenin, of course, was not the Bolshevik Party. But the Bolshevik Party became the instrument it did because of Lenin. It is doubtful whether any man before him ever wielded such power in a political party; certainly not in an organization that professed to be democratic or socialistic.

If Lenin had not been on the scene, not a single revolutionary leader could have substituted for him. Not Stalin, by his own confession. Not Zinoviev, Lenin's closest follower, who ran out on the October Revolution. Not Kamenev, whose mind Lenin changed at the same time he changed Stalin's, but who acted like Zinoviev. Not Trotsky. Although the record shows that Trotsky was the only outstanding Russian figure whose theoretical position and practical program were identical with those of Lenin *before* April 1917, he would have failed where Lenin succeeded. For one thing, he arrived in Russia a month after Lenin did. By that time Lenin had completed the reeducation of the Bolshevik Party. Trotsky would have had to do this, but he was not a member of the organization. His own party was numerically insignificant and relatively uninfluential. Finally, he owed whatever authority he enjoyed in the Bolshevik Party, which he joined in August, to Lenin's recognition of his capacities and Lenin's constant protection against the suspicion and opposition of the second-line Bolshevik leaders. Trotsky, alone, was doomed to failure because, despite his other great gifts, he lacked the organizational genius so necessary for political success. His imperious manner provoked people instead of reconciling them to his capacities. He could win an audience but, unlike Lenin, he could not win over party opponents. And he openly betrayed an impatience with mediocrity which no one forgives in a newcomer. . . .

What manner of man was Lenin who filled this event-making role in history? Under the circumstances, our curiosity is entirely legitimate, because it is the *character* of the individual which chiefly distinguishes the eventful man from the event-making man. What we are particularly interested in is discovering the combination of characteristics which gave Lenin political pre-eminence over a galaxy of individuals who as thinkers, writers, and mass orators displayed greater talents than he possessed. Analysis of this, as of any form of genius, is difficult to make. Particularly in politics, a medium in which virtues and vices, reason and stupidity, have an entirely different specific gravity than in the clear waters of personal relations and scientific activity, is it difficult to evaluate genius. No bare enumeration of character traits can do justice to the power of insight which flashes to the surface when these traits operate together in the context of problems, dangers, ideal goals.

One of the most conspicuous expressions of political insight is the sense of timing. Without it, great intelligence can be ineffective. Coupled with strong will, it can carry a mediocre mind to the heights. No one who knew, say, Plechanov and Stalin before February expected that one would fade out of the historical picture so soon and that the other would gradually emerge as the strong man of the strongest party. But it was Lenin's superb sense of political timing, nourished by an intelligence more practical than Plechanov's and a will more inflexible than Stalin's, that won an empire for the Bolsheviks.

Every adequate analysis of Lenin, the political man, must note his stubborn tenacity of purpose and unsurpassable confidence in himself. If he ever harbored a doubt about the ultimate success of his cause, the rightness of his tactical decisions, the high price of victory paid out in human suffering and injustice, he never expressed it to anyone. He was beyond the corruptions of pleasure and immune to the impractical delights of thought. His basic allegiance was to certain simple ideal socialist goals which were at the same time so vague that, given the consciousness of his own absolute integrity, he could always justify to himself what *he* did despite appearances.

Lenin could influence human beings only within the framework of organization. He had no power as an individual with the masses. Although unpretentious, he lacked the common touch which wins the masses by a radiant sympathy; and although he always had something to tell them, he could not strike the sparks of fire to inflame them into action.

Lenin was a party man. The life of the party was spiritual meat and substance to him. Just as some men's personalities are sustained by a church, and others are enriched by the passions and crises and problems of love, family, and knowledge, so Lenin's personality was sustained by, and developed within, the party. He was never far from the center of any organization of which he was a member. In his own mind, wherever he was, *there* was the party. His passions, his problems, his judgments all reflect this intense concentration on the party — a concentration which was all the more selfless because subconsciously he was the party. Whether he considered problems of state or art or philosophy, there was not a disinterested nerve in his body. In fact, all problems were for him problems of politics, even the listening to music and the playing of chess.

Lenin was not merely a party man. He raised the party to the level of a political principle. This is the source of all his deviations from the essentially democratic views of Marx. For Marx, a political party was conceived as a kind of cross between an international educational institution for the working class and a pressure group, as something that would come and go and be reconstituted in the forge of historical events. But for Lenin the political party was an army of professional revolutionists. The organization of professional revolutionists was of supreme importance in capturing state power. Iron clad control of organization was essential to victory. This ideal organization must, like Lenin himself, be acutely sensitive to the moods of the masses. It must have a perfect sense of timing. And above all, it must be imbued with the unshakeable conviction that it knew what the true interests of the masses were, better than they did themselves. In the light of this knowledge, it was justified in promising them anything to get them to move, and in manipulating them into actions which, even if they were foredoomed to failure, would educate them up to a level of Bolshevik understanding. The professional revolutionist by definition was one who wanted nothing for himself, and in fact cared so little for material goods that he could sincerely believe that he was free from the temptations and corruptions of absolute power.

Lenin was a Marxist who interchanged the "dictatorship of the proletariat" — which for Marx was a *broader* democracy of the working class counterposed to the narrower democracy of capitalist society — with the outright dictatorship of a minority Communist Party *over* the proletariat. Lenin believed that the hope of mankind lay in the struggle of the working class to abolish capitalism and therewith all economic classes. But he was even more convinced that this struggle could be successful *only* when led by his own party no matter what

its name. He did not flinch from the inexorable conclusion that, therefore, any individual or group who opposed *the* Party was objectively
"an enemy of mankind." . . .

The sense of his historic mission freed Lenin from any shame,
embarrassment, and regret in revising his course or in zigzagging from
one position to another. He accepted *practical* responsibility, but in
his own mind history absolved him from all *moral* responsibility.
What would have been utter hypocrisy in a man of little faith appeared
in him as flexible intelligence wrestling with the exigencies attendant
upon implementing high principle. It is characteristic that those who
struggled with him most bitterly in the arena of revolutionary struggle
— where no blows or holds are barred — acknowledge his absolute
sincerity and his moral force on others. They were fascinated by him
even when they most detested him. He wanted nothing for himself —
except to determine the destiny of mankind. His judgment could not
be swayed by women, friends, or comforts, or tempered by mercy or
pity. When Berkman and Goldman pleaded with him to release imprisoned anarchists who had criticized the Bolsheviks, he replied in
effect: "Genuine, thinking anarchists, agree with us: only bandits
posing as anarchists are in jail." This was monstrously false — but
undoubtedly Lenin believed it. When he advised foreign Communists, introducing Trojan horses into democratic organizations, to
lie about their beliefs and membership, he was firmly convinced that
this would be loyalty to a "higher" truth. . . . What is significant
here, as elsewhere, is the way Lenin takes it for granted that the rights
of opposition he claimed for himself when he was *out* of power are
completely without validity when claimed by others when he is *in*
power.

Organization and Program
of the Nazi Party

Despite the recent flood of books about Hitler and German fascism, the origins and character of Naziism have yet to be fully determined. Most Americans recoil instinctively when they read about the atrocities committed in Nazi concentration camps. They are shocked, too, by the violations of civil rights and the suppression of religious and political liberties that were integral parts of the Nazi movement. Historical understandings, however, come from analysis and not from revulsion. The readings for today, focusing on the organization and program of the Nazi party, should help to expose the true nature of the movement.

Hitler organized his followers into the National Socialist German Workers' Party (*National-Sozialistische Deutsche Arbeiter-Partei*, or NSDAP). After his rise to power, the NSDAP was the sole legal political party in Germany. Each word in the title theoretically expressed a fundamental characteristic of Naziism. Yet men in other nations would not use some of these words to mean what Hitler meant by them. Take the word *German*, for example. By this word Hitler did not mean all people who had been born in Germany or had become German citizens but only those with "Aryan" blood; no German-born Jew could belong to the party, even if he wanted to. Again, Hitler used the word *socialist* quite differently from the way Marx had used it, or the way it was used by moderate socialists in Western Europe and the United States. Likewise, Hitler had no intention of improving conditions for workers. Soon after he came to power, he seized the property of trade unions, sent many labor leaders to jail, and abolished collective bargaining. Hitler's use — or abuse — of language should remind us anew of the importance of defining a term historically, as we did in Problems 3, 20, and 24.

The Problem for today is in two parts. The first, an excerpt from William L. Shirer's *The Rise and Fall of the Third Reich*, describes the structure and organization of the NSDAP during its formative years in the 1920's. The second is the 1920 platform of the NSDAP, which sets forth many of the essential Nazi ideas.

As you read these two excerpts, consider the following questions:

1   How was the Nazi party organized? Why was each special group formed?

2   How did the organization of the Nazi party differ from the organization of other political parties in the West? What do these differences reveal about totalitarianism?

3   How are the major words in the title of the Nazi party (National, Socialist, German, Worker) reflected in planks of the platform? What did the party mean by each of these words?

4   To what groups in German society was the platform designed to appeal?

I

THE RISE AND FALL OF THE THIRD REICH / by William L. Shirer

. . . .Hitler was an organizer as well as a spellbinder. Curbing his
ire at being forbidden to speak in public, he set to work with furious
intent to rebuild the National Socialist German Workers' Party and to
make of it an organization such as Germany had never seen before.
He meant to make it like the Army—a state within a state. The first
job was to attract dues-paying members. By the end of 1925 they
numbered just 27,000. The going was slow, but each year some
progress was made: 49,000 members in 1926; 72,000 in 1927; 108,000
in 1928; 178,000 in 1929.

More important was the building up of an intricate party structure
which corresponded to the organization of the German government
and indeed of German society. The country was divided into districts,
or *Gaue*, which corresponded roughly with the thirty-four Reichstag
electoral districts and at the head of which was a gauleiter appointed
by Hitler. There were an additional seven *Gaue* for Austria, Danzig,
the Saar and the Sudetenland in Czechoslovakia. A *Gau* was divided
into *Kreise*—circles—and presided over by a *Kreisleiter*. The next
smallest party unit was an *Ortsgruppe*—a local group—and in the
cities these were further subdivided into street cells and blocks.

The political organization of the Nazi Party was divided into two
groups: P.O. I, as it was known, designed to attack and undermine
the government, and P.O. II to establish a state within a state. Thus
the second group had departments of agriculture, justice, national
economy, interior and labor—and, with an eye to the future, of race
and culture, and of engineering. P.O. I had departments of foreign
affairs and of labor unions and a Reich Press Office. The Propaganda
Division was a separate and elaborate office.

Though some of the party roughnecks, veterans of street fighting
and beerhouse brawls, opposed bringing women and children into
the Nazi Party, Hitler soon provided organizations for them too. The
Hitler Youth took in youngsters from fifteen to eighteen who had their
own departments of culture, schools, press, propaganda, "defense
sports," etc., and those from ten to fifteen were enrolled in the
Deutsches Jungvolk. For the girls there was the Bund Deutscher

Maedel and for the women the N. S. Frauenschaften. Students, teachers, civil servants, doctors, lawyers, jurists — all had their separate organizations, and there was a Nazi Kulturbund to attract the intellectuals and artists.

After considerable difficulties the S.A. [*Sturm-Abteilung, or Storm Troopers*] was reorganized into an armed band of several hundred thousand men to protect Nazi meetings, to break up the meetings of others and to generally terrorize those who opposed Hitler. Some of its leaders also hoped to see the S.A. supplant the Regular Army when Hitler came to power. To prepare for this a special office under General Franz Ritter von Epp was set up, called the Wehrpolitische Amt. Its five divisions concerned themselves with such problems as external and internal defense policy, defense forces, popular defense potential, and so on. But the brown-shirted S.A. never became much more than a motley mob of brawlers. . . .

To have at hand a more dependable band Hitler created the S.S. — Schutzstaffel — put their members in black uniforms similar to those worn by the Italian Fascisti and made them swear a special oath of loyalty to him personally. At first the S.S. was little more than a bodyguard for the Fuehrer. Its first leader was a newspaperman named Berchtold. As he preferred the relative quiet of the newsroom of the *Voelkischer Beobachter* to playing at cop and soldier, he was replaced by one Erhard Heiden, a former police stool pigeon of unsavory reputation. It was not until 1929 that Hitler found the man he was looking for as the ideal leader of the S.S., in the person of a chicken farmer in the village of Waldtrudering, near Munich, a mild-mannered fellow whom people mistook (as did this author when he first met him) for a small-town schoolmaster and whose name was Heinrich Himmler. When Himmler took over the S.S. it numbered some two hundred men. By the time he finished his job with it, the S.S. dominated Germany and was a name that struck terror throughout occupied Europe.

At the top of the pyramid of the intricate party organization stood Adolf Hitler with the highfalutin title of Partei-und-Oberster-S.A.-Fuehrer, Vorsitzender der N.S.D.A.P. — which may be translated as "Supreme Leader of the Party and the S.A., Chairman of the National Socialist German Labor Organization." Directly attached to his office was the Reich Directorate (Reichsleitung) which was made up of the top bosses of the party and such useful officials as the "Reich Treasurer" and the "Reich Business Manager." Visiting the palatial Brown

House in Munich, the national headquarters of the party, during the last years of the Republic, one got the impression that here indeed were the offices of a state within a state. That, no doubt, was the impression Hitler wished to convey, for it helped to undermine confidence, both domestic and foreign, in the actual German State, which he was trying to overthrow.

But Hitler was intent on something more important than making an impression. Three years after he came to power, in a speech to the "old fighters" at the Buergerbraü on the . . . evening of November 9, 1936, he explained one of the objectives he had had in building the party up into such a formidable and all-embracing organization. "We recognized," he said, in recalling the [early] days . . . "that it is not enough to overthrow the old State, but that the new State must previously have been built up and be practically ready to one's hand. . . . In 1933 it was no longer a question of overthrowing a state by an act of violence; meanwhile the new State had been built up and all that there remained to do was to destroy the last remnants of the old State — and that took but a few hours."

II

THE PROGRAM OF THE NSDAP

From *National Socialism*. Washington: United States Department of State, 1943.

The National Socialist German Workers' Party at a great mass meeting on February 25th, 1920, in the Hofbrauhaus-Festsaal in Munich announced their Programme to the world.

In section 2 of the Constitution of Our Party this Programme is declared to be inalterable.

The Programme of the German Workers' Party is limited as to period. The leaders have no intention, once the aims announced in it have been achieved, of setting up fresh ones, merely in order to increase the discontent of the masses artificially, and so ensure the continued existence of the Party.

1.   We demand the union of Germans to form a Great Germany on the basis of the right of the self-determination enjoyed by nations.

2.   We demand equality of rights for the German People in its dealings with other nations, and abolition of the Peace Treaties of Versailles and St. Germain.

3.   We demand land and territory [colonies] for the nourishment of our people and for settling our superfluous population.

4.   None but members of the nation may be citizens of the State. None but those of German blood, whatever their creed, may be members of the nation. No Jew, therefore, may be a member of the nation.

5.   Anyone who is not a citizen of the State may live in Germany only as a guest and must be regarded as being subject to foreign laws.

6.   The right of voting on the State's government and legislation is to be enjoyed by the citizen of the State alone. We demand therefore that all official appointments, of whatever kind, whether in the Reich, in the country, or in the smaller localities, shall be granted to citizens of the State alone.

We oppose the corrupting custom of Parliament of filling posts merely with a view to party considerations, and without reference to character or capability.

7.   We demand that the State shall make it its first duty to promote the industry and livelihood of citizens of the State. If it is not possible to nourish the entire population of the State, foreign nationals [non-citizens of the State] must be excluded from the Reich.

8.   All non-German immigration must be prevented. We demand that all non-Germans, who entered Germany subsequent to August 2nd, 1914, shall be required forthwith to depart from the Reich.

9.   All citizens of the State shall be equal as regards rights and duties.

10.   It must be the first duty of each citizen of the State to work with his mind or with his body. The activities of the individual may not clash with the interests of the whole, but must proceed within the frame of the community and be for the general good.

We demand therefore:

11.   Abolition of incomes unearned by work.

12.   In view of the enormous sacrifice of life and property demanded of a nation by every war, personal enrichment due to a war must be regarded as a crime against the nation. We demand therefore ruthless confiscation of all war gains.

13.   We demand nationalisation of all businesses which have been up to the present formed into companies [Trusts].

14.   We demand that the profits from wholesale trade shall be shared out.

15.   We demand extensive development of provision for old age.

16.   We demand creation and maintenance of a healthy middle class, immediate communalisation of wholesale business premises, and their lease at a cheap rate to small traders, and that extreme consideration shall be shown to all small purveyors to the State, district authorities and smaller localities.

17.   We demand land-reform suitable to our national requirements, passing of a law for confiscation without compensation of land for communal purposes; abolition of interest on land loans, and prevention of all speculation in land.

18.   We demand ruthless prosecution of those whose activities are injurious to the common interest. Sordid criminals against the nation, usurers, profiteers, etc. must be punished with death, whatever their creed or race.

19.   We demand that the Roman Law, which serves the materialistic world order, shall be replaced by a legal system for all Germany.

20.   With the aim of opening to every capable and industrious German the possibility of higher education and of thus obtaining advancement, the State must consider a thorough re-construction of our national system of education. The curriculum of all educational establishments must be brought into line with the requirements of practical life. Comprehension of the State idea [State sociology] must be the school objective, beginning with the first dawn of intelligence in the pupil. We demand development of the gifted children of poor parents, whatever their class or occupation, at the expense of the State.

21.   The State must see to raising the standard of health in the nation by protecting mothers and infants, prohibiting child labour, increasing bodily efficiency by obligatory gymnastics and sports laid down by law, and by extensive support of clubs engaged in the bodily development of the young.

22.   We demand abolition of a paid army and formation of a national army.

23.   We demand legal warfare against conscious political lying and its dissemination in the Press. In order to facilitate creation of a German national Press we demand:

(a)   that all editors of newspapers and their assistants, employing the German language, must be members of the nation;

(b)   that special permission from the State shall be necessary

before non-German newspapers may appear. These are not necessarily printed in the German language;

(c)   that non-Germans shall be prohibited by law from partici-
pating financially in or influencing German newspapers, and that the
penalty for contravention of the law shall be suppression of any such
newspaper, and immediate deportation of the non-German concerned
in it.

It must be forbidden to publish papers which do not conduce
to the national welfare. We demand legal prosecution of all tendencies
in art and literature of a kind likely to disintegrate our life as a nation,
and the suppression of institutions which militate against the requirements above-mentioned.

24.   We demand liberty for religious denominations in the State,
so far as they are not a danger to it and do not militate against the
moral feelings of the German race.

The Party, as such, stands for positive Christianity, but does not
bind itself in the matter of creed to any particular confession. It
combats the Jewish-materialist spirit within us and without us, and is
convinced that our nation can only achieve permanent health from
within on the principle: THE COMMON INTEREST BEFORE
SELF.

25.   That all the foregoing may be realized we demand the
creation of a strong central power of the State. Unquestioned authority of the politically centralised Parliament over the entire Reich
and its organisations; and formation of Chambers for classes and
occupations for the purpose of carrying out the general laws promul-
gated by the Reich in the various States of the confederation.

The leaders of the Party swear to go straight forward – if necessary
to sacrifice their lives – in securing fulfilment of the foregoing Points.

The Diplomatic Prelude
to World War II

Could World War II have been avoided? This is indeed a vital question, for the war, in addition to costing millions of lives and trillions of dollars, shaped the mid-20th century and catapulted both the United States and the Soviet Union into positions of world leadership. In the long run, World War II may prove to be the most influential war in all history. Certainly no other war involved so many people and resources or led to so much historical controversy.

The question of whether the war could have been prevented is the sort of inquiry historians try to avoid. Even posing the issues accurately is difficult. The German invasion of Poland touched off the war; the Japanese bombing of Pearl Harbor provoked the United States to join. If neither of these events had taken place, the war might never have broken out. Then what caused the German tanks to roll and the Japanese planes to take to the sky? Why were the tanks and planes built at all? And why did the people of Germany and Japan become saddled with governments more interested in armaments and territorial gains than in maintaining world peace? Could anyone have done anything about any of this in 1938? In 1935? In 1931? In 1919? Or before?

Clearly the question is an important one. How can a historian answer it to the satisfaction of his colleagues? He must employ logic and indulge in iffy answers. *If* the Treaty of Versailles had not set up issues which irritated the Germans, then . . . . *If* the democracies had called a halt to aggression in 1936, then . . . . When he does this, the historian assumes that all other factors in the historical situation would remain the same. Is he right? Obviously he is treading on dangerous ground.

The passage you will read for today is taken from a book by George F. Kennan, a former head of the Policy Planning Committee of the United States Department of State and a former American ambassador to the Soviet Union. A distinguished career diplomat, Kennan brings the experiences of a lifetime to his analysis of the events leading to World War II. As you read his words, think about the following questions:

1   By what criteria should we judge the success of a peace conference such as the one that ended World War I? By these criteria, was the Paris Peace Conference of 1919 as great a success as the Congress of Vienna? You may wish to review Problem 19 before you answer these questions.

2   What relationships did Kennan find between Versailles and the causes of World War II?

3   According to Kennan, what could statesmen have done to help prevent World War II once the Versailles treaty had been signed? Does he place greater stress upon long-range causes or upon the immediate events that touched off the war?

4   Does Kennan believe that wars should necessarily be fought until one side surrenders unconditionally? Upon what assumptions about the purpose of war and of peace treaties does he base his position?

AMERICAN DIPLOMACY: 1900-1950 / by George F. Kennan

Reprinted by permission of The University of Chicago Press. Copyright 1951 by the University of Chicago. Pp. 56-57, 67-69, 77-81, 83-84.

Eclipsed for many of us by the fresher and more vivid recollections of World War II, [the] first World War has become in many respects the forgotten factor. Yet all the lines of inquiry, it seems to me, lead back to it. World War II seemed really so extensively predetermined; it developed and rolled its course with the relentless logic of the last act of a classical tragedy. And the main elements of that tragic situation — the sickness and impatience of Germany, the weakness of eastern Europe, the phenomenon of bolshevism in Russia, and the weariness and debility in France and England — all these things took their origin so clearly in the period of 1914-20 that it seems to be here, if anywhere, that the real answers should be sought.

I do not mean to say that there were not still important things that could have been done in the twenties and the thirties, or perhaps even in the forties, to avert the worst dangers and to press the stream of events into more hopeful channels. Thirty years is a long time in the course of human events. The life of an international community can always be inclined to some extent, like a tree, by persistent pressure in a single direction over a long space of time.

But I would submit that a significant narrowing of the choices of the generations from 1920 to 1950 began with the outbreak of violence in 1914; that with the subsequent emergence of a military deadlock and the disappearance of hopes for a compromise peace this process was greatly advanced; and that by the time the fire of war had finally burned itself out, and the Treaty of Versailles had been signed, the area in which Western statesmen, and above all American statesmen, could act to restore genuine health and peace to Western civilization, and to give that civilization strength to withstand the growing challenge from the East, had been grievously and tragically narrowed.

So we come back to the fact that much of the cause for the decline in our security in the West lay with the course and outcome of the first World War. . . .

. . . a line of thought grew up, under Wilson's leadership, which provided both rationale and objective for our part in fighting the war to a bitter end. Germany was militaristic and antidemocratic. The Allies were fighting to make the world safe for democracy. Prussian militarism had to be destroyed to make way for the sort of peace we wanted. . . . Autocratic government would be done away with. Peoples would themselves choose the sovereignty under which they wished to reside. . . . Armaments would be reduced by mutual agreement. The peace would be just and secure.

In the name of such principles you could fight a war to the end. A future so brilliant would surely wash away the follies and brutalities of the war, redress its injuries, heal the wounds it had left. This theory gave us justification both for continuing the war to its bitter and terrible end . . . and at the same time for refusing to preoccupy ourselves with the practical problems and maladjustments to which the course of hostilities was leading. Under the protecting shadow of this theory, the guns continued their terrible work for a final year and a half after our entry. Under the shadow of this theory Wilson went to Versailles unprepared to face the sordid but all-important details of the day of reckoning. Under this theory he suffered his tragic and historic failure. Under this theory things advanced with a deadly logic and precision to a peace which was indeed [as Wilson had earlier feared] "forced upon the loser, a victor's terms imposed upon the vanquished, accepted in humiliation, under duress"—a peace that did indeed leave a sting, a resentment, a bitter memory, and upon which its own terms came later to rest "as upon quicksand."

And the tragedy of this outcome was not substantially mitigated by the fact that we were not signatories to the Treaty of Versailles and kept ourselves aloof from its punitive provisions. The damage had been done. The equilibrium of Europe had been shattered. Austria-Hungary was gone. There was nothing effective to take its place. Germany, smarting from the sting of defeat and plunged into profound social unrest by the breakup of her traditional institutions, was left nevertheless as the only great united state in Central Europe. Russia was no longer there, as a possible reliable ally, to help France contain German power. From the Russian plain there leered a single hostile eye, skeptical of Europe's values, rejoicing at all Europe's misfortunes, ready to collaborate solely for the final destruction of her spirit and her pride. Between Russia and Germany were only the pathetic new states of eastern and Central Europe, lacking in domestic stability and the traditions of statesmanship—their peoples bewildered, uncertain, vacillating between brashness and timidity in the exercise of the unaccustomed responsibilities of independence. And to the other side of Germany were France and England, reeling, themselves, from the vicissitudes of the war, wounded far more deeply than they themselves realized, the plume of their manhood gone, their world positions shaken.

Truly, this was a peace which had the tragedies of the future written into it as by the devil's own hand. . . .

The question as to what Western statesmen might have done to avoid World War II is not an easy one. It is a little disconcerting to find respectable scholars, such as the French historian Bainville, claiming as early as 1920 to see a peculiar logic in the situation flowing from World War I and predicting quite accurately, on the basis of this logic, the general course of events up to and including the outbreak of World War II. It is disconcerting because it leads you to ask whether World War II was not perhaps implicit in the outcome of World War I; in the fact that England and France had been injured and weakened far more deeply than they knew in that first encounter; in the fact that Austria-Hungary and Russia were both lost for the maintenance of European stability, Austria-Hungary because she had disappeared entirely, Russia because her energies and resources had been captured by people violently hostile to capitalist democracy in general; and in the fact that the Germans — frustrated, impoverished, stung with defeat, uncertain in the breakdown of their traditional institutions — were nevertheless left as the only great united people in Central Europe. Looking at these things, it is easy to conclude that World War II just could not help but develop, that it was nothing more than the inevitable aftermath of World War I. You then start poking back into the origins of the earlier war to discover the real sources of the instability of our time. And from this standpoint it is only a step to absolving the Western statesmen of the twenties and thirties of all responsibility for the second war and to regarding them exclusively as the actors in a tragedy beyond their making or repair.

This is of course an extremism. Statesmen, it is true, generally inherit from their predecessors predicaments and dilemmas to which they can see no complete solutions; their ability to improve situations by action over the short term is often quite genuinely limited; but over the long term (and two decades is a respectable length of time) there are always some choices at their disposal. I think it fair to say that World War I was a genuine tragedy which left the Western world much worse off afterward than it had been before and significantly narrowed the choices of Western statesmen in the postwar period; but it did not eliminate those choices entirely. There were, in other words,

still things that "could have been done" and which we may assume
would at least have been helpful and have had greater possibilities of
preventing further tragedy than the things that were done. In so far
as we are talking about Germany, there are two such things that strike
me as of obvious importance, and in both of them we Americans could,
had we wished, have taken a considerable part. First, we could have
tried to give greater understanding, support, and encouragement to
the moderate forces in the Weimar Republic. And if that did not
succeed in preventing the rise of naziism, then we could have taken
a stiffer and more resolute attitude against Hitler's earlier encroach-
ments and provocations.

It is the last of these two possibilities, that of a stronger stand
against Hitler at an earlier date, that has received most prominence in
Western thought and has constituted the source of most reproaches to
democratic statesmanship between the wars. Unquestionably, such a
policy might have enforced a greater circumspection on the Nazi
regime and caused it to proceed more slowly with the actualization of
its timetable. From this standpoint, firmness at the time of the re-
occupation of the Rhineland in 1936 would probably have yielded
even better results than firmness at the time of Munich. But I wonder
whether we do not tend to exaggerate the relative importance of this
question of stopping Hitler once he was in power, as compared with
the importance of seeing to it that a person of his ilk should not come
into power at all in a great Western country. It was a defeat for the
West, of course, that Hitler was able to consolidate his power and be
successful in the years 1933-39. But actually the West had suffered an
even greater defeat on the day when the German people found itself
in such a frame of mind that it could, without great resistance or
remonstrance, accept a Hitler as its leader and master.

A stiffer attitude on the part of the Western democracies might,
it is true, have resulted in Hitler's overthrow and his replacement by a
less obnoxious regime before war could come; in fact, there is evidence that a revolt might well have been attempted had the British
and French had the perceptiveness to stand firm at the time of
Munich. But great uncertainties lay along this path. The hypnotic
charm of naziism was already strong upon the German people. If anyone had overthrown Hitler, presumably it would have been the generals. Whether they would have been able to control the situation
subsequently, to lay the ghost not only of naziism but of German ag-
gressiveness in general, and to adjust peaceably their relations with

the West, is not certain. The great misfortune of the West, I suspect, was not Hitler but the weakness of German society which made possible his triumph. And it is this which takes us back to this question of the attitude of the Western democracies toward the Weimar Republic.

Events have moved so fast that we have almost lost sight of this intensely interesting period in German history—the period before 1933, with its amazing cultural and intellectual flowering, so full of hope and yet so close to despair. In the decade of the twenties Berlin was the most alive of the capitals of Europe, and things were taking place there from which the Western democracies might have derived profit and instruction. It is true that the peace treaty we Americans concluded with Weimar Germany was nonpunitive. Americans cannot be justly charged with any political offensiveness toward the new Germany. We even financed her lavishly, though foolishly. But what I am thinking of pertained not just to us but to the Western democracies in general, and it was something more than political or financial: it was a general attitude of distaste and suspicion, intermingled with a sort of social snobbery so grotesque that as late as 1927 a German could still be prohibited from using the golf links at Geneva, the seat of the League of Nations. We did nothing to harm Weimar Germany; but we left it very much to its own devices. There are times when that is a good policy toward another country. But I fear that this was not one of those times. Here, in any case, were lost opportunities; and it is significant that they lay as much in the cultural and intellectual as in the political field . . . .

. . . by the year 1939 affairs were really quite inauspicious for the Western democracies. The situation which they had allowed to arise was one for which there were no complete cures. Whether they realized it or not, the war could be for them, in the deeper sense, at best a war of defense: a war that might bring immediate survival but could scarcely bring an improvement in the stability of the world they lived in, and certainly not the advance of any of the more positive and constructive purposes of democracy. When this is borne in mind, the great decisions of the war years themselves appear for the most part in a more charitable light.

[One] of these great decisions which deserves mention seems to me to have been our own decision—if we may call it that—not to enter the European war until the Germans declared war upon us. This was of course comparable to our behavior in World War I, when we refrained from entering until an overt German action, namely, the declaration of unrestricted submarine warfare, brought us in. And what seems to me most interesting about our conduct in each of these cases is the marked change in our emotional attitude toward the struggle itself, once we had become formally involved in it. Theoretically, if the issues involved in the European struggle were really as vital to us as we persuaded ourselves they were in the years 1942-45, they were surely no less important from 1939 to 1941. Actually, in that earlier period, before the German attack on Russia, the cause of the British and French could really be called the cause of freedom and democracy, for very little else was involved on the Western side; whereas later, when we did discover that our vital stake in the anti-German cause warranted great military sacrifice on our part, it was at a time when that cause had been rendered ambiguous, as anything more than a defensive undertaking, by the participation of the U.S.S.R. on the side of the democracies.

Now I mention this, because, making all due allowance for the deliberateness of the opinion-forming process in a democracy, it does look as though the real source of the emotional fervor which we Americans are able to put into a war lies less in any objective under-standing of the wider issues involved than in a profound irritation over the fact that other people have finally provoked us to the point where we had no alternative but to take up arms. This lends to the democratic war effort a basically punitive note, rather than one of expediency. I mention this because, if there is anything in this thought, it goes far to explain the difficulty we have in employing force for rational and restricted purposes rather than for purposes which are emotional and to which it is hard to find a rational limit.

The Cold War

As is the case with most questions of historical causation, scholars disagree on what might be the causes of World War I and World War II. Historians and political analysts will continue to study and discuss the causes of these wars just as scholars continue to study the causes of the Peloponnesian War, the French Revolution, and the American Civil War.

Historians are normally reluctant to make serious judgments about contemporary events. They claim that no sound or reliable conclusions can be reached about such matters until a number of years have passed. How much time do historians require for these assessments? Fifty or a hundred years? More? Some revisions of historical data have come after thousands of years.

The difficulties and frustrations of historical research should not deter anyone from trying to understand current times. The eminent British scholar, E. H. Carr, thinks that history should "enable man to understand the society of the past and to increase his mastery over the society of the present." A conflict that grew out of World War II is intimately associated with all of present-day society. This conflict came to be known as the Cold War. Problem 31 presents several points of view about the Cold War and encourages thoughtful consideration of a crucial question facing mankind today — its survival in an atomic age.

The first selection of Problem 31 represents the ideas of John Foster Dulles, who, as Secretary of State in the Eisenhower administration, was closely identified with a firm policy toward the Soviet Union and communism. The second reading is from a Soviet magazine, published in many languages for world distribution. Although written several years after Dulles' 1954 speech it reflects the Soviet attitude toward Dulles' policy. Its author is M. Kapitsa a Moscow University professor. The final selection is by an American expert in the field of Soviet affairs and international relations, Professor Frederick L. Schuman of Williams College.

As you read, keep the following questions in mind:

1 In Problem 30, George F. Kennan speaks of the use of force for "rational and restricted purposes." How does this concept compare with Dulles' idea of "massive retaliation"? Is the threat of the Soviet Union comparable to the threat of Hitler in the 1930's?

2 Which analysis of the purposes of regional defense agreements appears most plausible to you — that of Dulles or that of the Soviet writer Kapitsa?

3 Do Kennan and Schuman agree on the significance of the Munich Pact of 1938?

4 Schuman claims the United States does not properly use the art of diplomacy. Is it possible to tell from the Dulles selection what importance he attaches to diplomacy? To what extent does Kapitsa discuss the benefits to be gained from the use of diplomacy?

I

POLICY FOR SECURITY AND PEACE / by John Foster Dulles

Quoted by special permission from *Foreign Affairs*, April 1954 issue. Copyright 1954 by the Council on Foreign Relations, Inc., New York. Pp. 355-359, 362-364.

The cornerstone of security for the free nations must be a collective system of defense. They clearly cannot achieve security separately. No single nation can develop for itself defensive power of adequate scope and flexibility. In seeking to do so, each would become a garrison state and none would achieve security.

This is true of the United States. Without the coöperation of allies, we would not even be in a position to retaliate massively against the war industries of an attacking nation. . . .

Security for the free world depends, therefore, upon the development of collective security and community power rather than upon purely national potentials. Each nation which shares the security should contribute in accordance with its capabilities and facilities. The Inter-American Treaty of Reciprocal Assistance (Rio Pact) of 1947 set a postwar example in establishing the principle that an armed attack against one would be considered as an attack against all. The North Atlantic Treaty is based on the same principle. Its members have gone much further in organizing joint forces and facilities as a part of the integrated security system. NATO provides essential air and naval bases, to which its various members can contribute — each according to its means and capabilities. . . .

The United Nations is striving to make collective security effective on a basis broader than regionalism. The central principle of the Charter is that any armed attack is of universal concern and calls for collective measures of resistance. The Soviet Union, by its veto power, has made it impractical, as yet, to make available to the Security Council the "armed forces, assistance, and facilities" contemplated by Article 43 of the Charter. . . .

The free world system of bases is an integral part of its collective security. At the recent Four-Power Conference in Berlin, Mr. Molotov repeatedly attacked these bases as evidence of aggressive purpose. Actually these bases on the territory of other sovereign countries are merely a physical expression of the collective security system. They were constructed only at the request of the host nation and their availability depends upon its consent, usually as a legal condition and always as a practical one. The requisite consent to the use of these bases would never be accorded unless it was clear that their use was in response to open aggression, and reasonably related to its scope and nature. This gives assurance of their community function.

Thus the free world has practical means for achieving collective security both through the United Nations and the various regional arrangements already referred to.

The question remains: How should collective defense be organized by the free world for maximum protection at minimum cost? The heart of the problem is how to deter attack. This, we believe, requires that a potential aggressor be left in no doubt that he would be certain to suffer damage outweighing any possible gains from aggression.

This result would not be assured, even by collective measures, if the free world sought to match the potential Communist forces, man for man and tank for tank, at every point where they might attack. . . .

The free world must devise a better strategy for its defense, based on its own special assets. Its assets include, especially, air and naval power and atomic weapons which are now available in a wide range, suitable not only for strategic bombing but also for extensive tactical use. The free world must make imaginative use of the deterrent capabilities of these new weapons and mobilities and exploit the full potential of collective security. Properly used, they can produce defensive power able to retaliate at once and effectively against any aggression.

To deter aggression, it is important to have the flexibility and the facilities which make various responses available. In many cases, any open assault by Communist forces could only result in starting a general war. But the free world must have the means for responding effectively on a selective basis when it chooses. It must not put itself in the position where the only response open to it is general war. . . .

Most areas within the reach of an aggressor offer less value to him than the loss he would suffer from well-conceived retaliatory measures. Even in such areas, however, local defense will always be important. In every endangered area there should be a sufficient military establishment to maintain order against subversion and to resist other forms of indirect aggression and minor satellite aggressions. . . .

A would-be aggressor will hesitate to commit aggression if he knows in advance that he thereby not only exposes those particular forces which he chooses to use for his aggression, but also deprives his other assets of "sanctuary" status. That does not mean turning every local war into a world war. It does not mean that if there is a Communist attack somewhere in Asia, atom or hydrogen bombs will necessarily be dropped on the great industrial centers of China or Russia. It does mean that the free world must maintain the collective means and be willing to use them in the way which most effectively makes aggression too risky and expensive to be tempting. . . .

The new [*Eisenhower*] Administration has sought to readjust, in an orderly way, the program for the military forces. Before this could be done, it was necessary to clarify the extent of our reliance on collective security; to define more clearly our basic strategy both in Europe and the Far East; to reassert our freedom of action in repelling future aggression; to assess the impact of newer types of weapons; and to relate the composition and size of our ready and potential forces to all these factors. . . .

. . . The potential of massive attack will always be kept in a state of instant readiness, but our program will retain a wide variety in the means and scope for responding to aggression. . . . Our policies are based squarely on a collective security system and depend for their success on its continuing vitality. . . .

The dictators face an impossible task when they set themselves to suppress, over a vast area and for a long time, the opportunities which flow from freedom.

We can be sure that there is going on, even within the Soviet empire, a silent test of strength between the powerful rulers and the multitudes of human beings. Each individual seems by himself to be helpless in this struggle. But their aspirations in the aggregate make up a mighty force. There are some signs that the Soviet rulers are, in terms of domestic policy, bending to some of the human desires of their people. There are promises of more food, more household goods, more economic freedom. This does not prove that the dictators have themselves been converted. It is rather that they may be dimly perceiving that there are limits to their power indefinitely to suppress the human spirit. That is a truth which should not be lost sight of as we determine our own policies. Our national purpose is not merely to survive in a world fraught with appalling danger. We want to end this era of danger.

II

NONALIGNMENT AND NATIONAL INTERESTS / by M. Kapitsa

Reprinted from *Soviet Union Illustrated Monthly*, No. 212, 1967, Moscow. P. 1

The system of aggressive military blocs that the United States has imposed on the countries dependent on its goodwill is an example of . . . [a] kind of political anachronism.

The credit, or rather discredit, for initiating the system of blocs and alignments on a global scale belongs to the late John Foster Dulles, US Secretary of State. Nearly twenty years have passed since this architect of the cold war started building the system. In 1949 came NATO into which Washington managed to cajole 14 countries. This was followed by an attempt to scrape together a bloc in the Middle East under a Pan-Islamic banner.

Progress in this area was slow, however, and in September 1954, soon after the Geneva conference on Indochina, the Manila Pact, giving birth to SEATO, was signed by eight countries, the United States, Britain, France, Australia, New Zealand, Thailand, the Philippines and Pakistan.

On February 24, 1955, Iraq and Turkey concluded the Baghdad Pact, which was joined by Britain in the March of the same year, and by Pakistan in September, thus initiating yet another bloc, which the United States also subsequently joined.

NATO, SENTO, SEATO, and ANZUS linking up the United States, Australia and New Zealand, along with the American-Japanese "security pact", and the military agreement between America and Chiang Kai-shek, formed a poisonous chain stretching from Europe to South-East Asia and the Far East.

The chain lacked several links, of course. It did not include a single country of Africa. With the exception of Iraq, which stayed in the Baghdad Pact until 1958, all the Arab countries refused to be aligned. India, Burma, Ceylon, Nepal and Cambodia also stand firm for nonalignment. Indonesia has been vigorously resisting pressure to join one of the aggressive blocs. Out of all the developing countries only six—Turkey, Iraq, Iran, Pakistan, Thailand and the Philippines—have been tied up in the various aggressive alignments.

These military-political alliances created by the imperialists have become sources of international tension and springboards of aggression and struggle against the national liberation movement.

In Europe, NATO has proved to be a means of bringing the West-European countries under the control of the American monopolies and a screen for the remilitarisation of Western Germany and war preparations. In 1956, Britain and France joined with Israel in launching aggression against Egypt. In 1958, NATO attempted to crush the revolution in Iran, while British and American forces landed in Libya and Jordan. Soon after this the United States and Turkey tried to put military pressure on Syria. In June 1967, the United States and Britain, both members of NATO, supported Israel's aggression against the Arab countries. . . .

In South-East Asia, which Alexei Kosygin has called an important sector of "struggle between the forces of imperialism and the forces of national independence", the SEATO countries have for a number of years been interfering in the internal affairs of independent states. In Burma, for example, they encourage the separatist tendencies of certain tribes. Moves by SEATO led to the collapse of the 1954 agreement on Laos, and that country again found itself on the brink of civil war. The new agreements on Laos of 1962 were also torpedoed. With the support of Thailand the United States is today betraying its pledge to observe Laotian neutrality, bombing parts of the country and violating its air space with bombers sent to attack Vietnam. Together with Thailand, the Philippines, Australia and New Zealand, its allies in SEATO, the United States is waging aggressive war against the people of South Vietnam, blatantly violating the Geneva agreements and international law, and American aircraft and warships are making barbaric bombing attacks on the Democratic Republic of Vietnam.

Experience shows that countries which enter these blocs inevitably become subject to American dictatorship in one form or another. They have to put up with American interference in their internal affairs, and alien political ideas and concepts of government are forced upon them from outside. They are compelled to adapt their policies to Washington's global strategy. They have to spend enormous sums on unproductive military expenditure. Their economic development is choked. For every financial or economic concession from the United States they have to stand cap in hand.

Ironically, not a single one of these countries feels any safer for being a member of a bloc, because America's reckless policies have more than once brought the world to the brink of war. America's allies are quite likely to be dragged into war by the Pentagon and may unwittingly and unwillingly become the target [of] . . . crushing retaliatory blows.

This fact, besides compromising the policy of building up blocs and aggressive alliances, has evoked a tendency to opt out of them. In an endeavour to free his country from American control and to ensure her safety General de Gaulle has withdrawn from NATO and sent its military institutions packing off French territory. On August 10, 1967, de Gaulle stated that, by leaving NATO, France had freed herself from subordination to the United States and no longer ran the risk of being drawn into conflicts that had nothing to do with her. He also said that by quitting the system of blocs France had perhaps given the signal for a general evolution towards an international detente, and that the great mass of people all over the world approved and applauded France's action.

France has also refused to associate herself with the aggressive actions of SEATO in Vietnam and Laos and has virtually ceased to participate in this bloc too.

In 1958, Iraq walked out of the military-political bloc into which she had been drawn. The Baghdad Pact found itself without Baghdad and had to be hurriedly renamed SENTO. Economically and politically Iraq has benefited considerably from this move. Her international ties have widened and she is now receiving assistance for defence purposes and the development of her economy from the socialist countries.

Then it was Pakistan's turn to have second thoughts. Field Marshal Ayub Khan, President of Pakistan, realised that his country's participation in SENTO and SEATO had isolated her internationally, endangered her security (the U-2 spy-plane's violation of Soviet air space) and had deepened her military and economic dependence on the United States. Gradually Pakistan began building up contacts with the countries of Asia and Africa, and with the socialist countries, refused to take part in the imperialist intervention in Laos, opposed the war in Vietnam, and condemned Israel's aggression against the Arab countries. Once the connecting link between SENTO and SEATO, Pakistan has now reduced her participation in these alliances to a purely nominal function. This has increased the prestige of Pakistan and her leader, as well as her opportunities of economic development.

It is understandable why Turkey and Iran are trying to shake off their dependence and maintain autonomy in matters of foreign policy. Both countries have started expanding relations and economic co-operation with the USSR and other socialist countries. . . .

The blocs become more and more anachronistic every day. The question of winding them up and replacing them with wider international co-operation is becoming more and more acute. Sensing this, Washington is straining to keep its grip on its partners and its ability to dictate policy to them. Everything is being done to breathe new life into this moribund system.

The Soviet Union and the other socialist countries have often proposed abolishing military blocs and have stressed that the Warsaw Treaty will cease to exist as soon as NATO is dismantled. In June 1967 the Head of the Soviet Government at a press conference in New York renewed the Soviet Union's proposal to dismantle the military blocs in Europe and thus bring about a real relaxation of tension. The NATO member-countries, however, turned their backs on the proposal.

The socialist countries are convinced that the road to peace, to international security lies through the abolition of military blocs, relaxation of tension, strengthening of trust between nations and strict observance of the principles of peaceful coexistence.

III

BEYOND THE COLD WAR / by Frederick L. Schuman

Abridged from "The Cold War: Retrospect and Prospect" from Beyond the Cold War by Frederick L. Schuman. Published 1967 by Louisiana State University Press. Reprinted by permission of the publisher. Pp. 70-74, 78-87.

The crucial question of our time, the question upon which depends the good fortune or the misfortune of the human race . . . is that of whether the global strife between America and Russia must take or will take the evil form of war and slaughter or may take the form . . . of a constructive, creative competition in the works of peace. . . .

Only a prophet with powers of prediction far beyond those which any of us here can claim would venture to forecast which form of strife will come utimately to prevail between Russia and America. . . . Therefore let us explore the problem without prejudice as to its most probable outcome.

We live in a time of crisis and thus of ever recurring crises in East-West relations and world affairs. . . .

. . . The danger is not Communism *per se*, although many among us quite honestly and sincerely believe that Communism is our greatest danger. Our greatest danger, as I see it, . . . is a continuation and extension of international anarchy, of power politics, of war—all of which are age-old habits of mankind—into the thermonuclear age when persistence in such habits may well spell the end of the human species.

More specifically, if we do not soon negotiate an end of the arms race as a step toward negotiating an end of the Cold War, we shall face the danger . . . where effective control of our destinies will pass out of our hands, and out of the hands of our political leaders, into the hands of professional military people and of the munitions industry. . . .

In the second place, if we do not soon negotiate an end of the arms race, we shall face the ever mounting danger of "accidental" war touched off by nervous bomber pilots, anxious technicians at missile bases, or neurotic scanners of radar screens. . . .

In the third place, if we do not soon negotiate an end to the arms race, we shall soon face the prospect of more and more nations joining the thermonuclear suicide club and of more and more stock-piles of infernal weapons bringing mankind ever closer to self-destruction. . . .

At all events, what we have long been calling the "Cold War" did not begin in 1945, in the aftermath of World War II and of the Yalta and Potsdam conferences. In a broader sense it began with the second Russian Revolution of 1917. The Communists were then convinced that the Russian Revolution would inevitably be followed by worldwide revolution and that it was their mission and duty to assist the inevitable to come to pass. The non-Communists and anti-Communists of the West were then convinced that the Communist regime in Russia would inevitably collapse and that it was their duty and mission to assist the inevitable to come to pass. Both sides, along with almost all other statesmen and peoples, shared what Norman Angell in 1910 called "The Great Illusion"—namely, the belief that national interests can be rationally served by war. Furthermore, Communists then believed Communism could be extended by war, and anti-Communists believed that Communism could be destroyed by war. Both were wrong.

Within ten months after Russia's October Revolution, Soviet
Russia and the West were at war. And the war was not a cold war
but a hot war, marked by many casualties and vast destruction. Be it
remembered, lest we forget what Russians never forget, that this war
was not begun by Communists sending armies against the West but
by the West sending armies against Soviet Russia. . . . The legacy of
mutual fear and suspicion and hatred which nourished the Cold War
of the 1940's and '50's originated in the hot war between East and
West in 1918-1921. The outcome of this war was a deadlock or
stalemate. . . .

. . . When war or preparation for war eventuates in a deadlock
or stalemate in which it is evident to all that neither side can impose
its will on the other or destroy the other, or that both will be destroyed
in the event of a resort to force, then only one other way is left for
dealing with problems of power among the Great Powers of our
world—i.e., the way of diplomacy, an ancient and honorable art
which, when wisely practiced, is the art of maintaining peace among
rival sovereignties in a State System lacking world government.
These are simple truisms and self-evident statements of the obvious.
But for forty years and more many Americans have been reluctant to
understand or act upon these eternal verities of international relations. And at times, although far less consistently, Russian policy-
makers, particularly in the last years of Stalin's autocracy, have been
equally obtuse.

Take note, if you will, of two simple and obvious corollaries of
the truisms just mentioned. The first is that in order to practice diplomacy, it is necessary to have diplomatic relations with those with
whom you expect to practice diplomacy. Otherwise, obviously, no
diplomacy is possible. Russians have always known this. Americans
have great difficulty in getting this through their heads, as shown by
American refusal for sixteen years to enter into diplomatic relations
with Soviet Russia and by American refusal in our time to enter into
diplomatic relations with Communist China or North Korea or North
Vietnam or East Germany. The second corollary is that in the practice
of diplomacy one cannot, if one hopes for agreement, always say "no"
or "nyet" to all the proposals and suggestions of the other side. One
must sometimes say "perhaps" and one must occasionally say
"yes." . . .

Suppose we proceed backward in time by way of establishing
causal relationships among crucial events and decisions in world

affairs. The Cold War in the narrower sense began in the late summer and fall of 1945, immediately after the surrender of Japan, with early, repeated, and emphatic American and British protests against the imposition of Soviet hegemony and Communist power on Eastern Europe north of Greece and east of the Elbe and the Adriatic. This vast and alarming extension of Russian power into Central Europe and the Balkans was alleged in London and Washington to constitute a Russian violation of the Yalta and Potsdam agreements of 1945 . . . . This expansion of Soviet power was also alleged to constitute a new totalitarian enslavement of the peoples of Eastern Europe, who must somehow be "liberated" and given the blessings of Western democracy, even though most of them had never known any of those blessings before.

And why were the Western Powers, until the last few months of a six-year war, unable to contribute more effectively to Hitler's defeat and to occupy more of Europe before the Russians occupied it? The answer surely lies in the "Peace" of Munich of September, 1938, whereby the Western Powers betrayed Czechoslovakia and in effect gave Hitler a free hand in Eastern Europe and the Balkans in the rather obvious hope that he would attack Russia and leave the Western Powers at peace. . . . The Western Powers did not surrender Eastern Europe at Potsdam or Yalta or on the bloody beachheads of Normandy in 1944. They surrendered Eastern Europe at Munich in 1938.

In international politics, as in our personal affairs, decisions have consequences. These consequences are often irrevocable. The consequences of Munich were irrevocable. They are with us today. They will be with us for a long time to come. The Cold War originated in Russian determination, thus far successful, to capitalize on the consequences and in Western determination, thus far unsuccessful, to undo or reverse these consequences. The matter is as simple as that. . . . The ultimate result was to bring Russian power to the Elbe and the Adriatic. The Cold War is a product of the fears and suspicions and mutual doubts and mistrusts generated among the major members of the United Nations coalition in the wake of the . . . "Peace" of Munich and of the ensuing global strategy of World War II.

Rich Country, Poor Country

A primary aim of *32 Problems* has been to help students become familiar with the nature of history as a scholarly discipline and to learn something of the techniques of history writing.

The historical problems presented in this book reflect the changing condition of man from the Neolithic Revolution to the Cold War. Problem 32 is concerned with contemporary society and the unequal conditions between the developed nations and the underdeveloped nations.

Sir Charles P. Snow, a British scientist and novelist, claims that too little understanding exists between the scientist and the humanist. Projected to the international scene, Snow argues, this cultural gap is reflected in the reluctance or inability of the West to address itself energetically to the needs of deprived peoples. He says that the failure of intellectuals to communicate properly with one another "is leading us to interpret the past wrongly, to misjudge the present, and to deny our hopes of the future." As a scholar who is both a scientist and a humanist, C. P. Snow discusses the problem of cultural gap.

As you read, consider the following questions:

1 Has the Cold War served to increase or decrease the amount of economic aid given to the poorer nations by the United States and the Soviet Union?

2 The Russians have an edge in the number of trained scientists and engineers available for aiding in the industrialization of the poorer nations. How can this situation be explained?

3 What force does Snow consider indispensable in the struggle to close the cultural gap? Do you agree?

4 Does Snow's versatility as a scientist and novelist necessarily equip him to make judgments on economic questions? Are the questions he raises economic in nature?

THE TWO CULTURES: AND A SECOND LOOK / by C. P. Snow

From *The Two Cultures: and a Second Look* by C. P. Snow. Copyright © 1959, 1963 by Cambridge University Press. Pp. 41-51.

The main issue [*of the scientific revolution*] is that the people in the industrialised countries are getting richer, and those in the non-industrialised countries are at best standing still: so that the gap between the industrialised countries and the rest is widening every day. . . .

. . . In the rich countries people are living longer, eating better, working less. In a poor country like India, the expectation of life is less than half what it is in England. There is some evidence that

Indians and other Asians are eating less, in absolute quantities, than they were a generation ago. . . . And they are working as people have always had to work, from Neolithic times until our own. Life for the overwhelming majority of mankind has always been nasty, brutish and short. It is so in the poor countries still.

This disparity between the rich and the poor has been noticed. It has been noticed, most acutely and not unnaturally, by the poor. Just because they have noticed it, it won't last for long. . . . Once the trick of getting rich is known, as it now is, the world can't survive half rich and half poor. . . .

The West has got to help in this transformation. The trouble is, the West with its divided culture finds it hard to grasp just how big, and above all just how fast, the transformation must be.

. . . During all human history until this century, the rate of social change has been very slow. So slow, that it would pass unnoticed in one person's lifetime. That is no longer so. The rate of change has increased so much that our imagination can't keep up. There is *bound* to be more social change, affecting more people, in the next decade than in any before. There is *bound* to be more change again, in the 1970's. In the poor countries, people have caught on to this simple concept. Men . . . are no longer prepared to wait for periods longer than one person's lifetime.

. . . Someone said, when the first atomic bomb went off, that the only important secret is now let out—the thing works. After that, any determined country could make the bomb, given a few years. In the same way, the only secret of the Russian and Chinese indus- trialisation is that they've brought it off. That is what Asians and Afri- cans have noticed. It took the Russians about forty years, starting with something of an industrial base . . . . The Chinese started with much less of an industrial base, but haven't been interrupted, and it looks like [*it is*] taking them not much over half the time. . . .

It is simply that technology is rather easy. Or more exactly, tech- nology is the branch of human experience that people can learn with predictable results. For a long time, the West misjudged this very badly. After all, a good many Englishmen have been skilled in me- chanical crafts for half-a-dozen generations. Somehow we've made ourselves believe that the whole of technology was a more or less incommunicable art. It's true enough, we start with a certain advan- tage. Not so much because of tradition, I think, as because all our children play with mechanical toys. They are picking up pieces of applied science before they can read. That is an advantage we haven't made the most of. Just as the Americans have the advantage that nine out of ten adults can drive a car and are to some extent mechanics. In the last war, which was a war of small machines, that was a real military asset. Russia is catching up with the U.S. in major industry—but it will be a long time before Russia is as convenient a country as the U.S. in which to have one's car break down.

The curious thing is, none of that seems to matter much. For the task of totally industrialising a major country, as in China today, it only takes will to train enough scientists and engineers and technicians. Will, and quite a small number of years. There is no evidence that any country or race is better than any other in scientific teachability: there is a good deal of evidence that all are much alike. Tradition and technical background seem to count for surprisingly little. . . .

. . . It is technically possible to carry out the scientific revolution in India, Africa, South-east Asia, Latin America, the Middle East, within fifty years. There is no excuse for western man not to know . . . that this is the one way out through . . . H-bomb war, over-population, the gap between the rich and the poor. This is . . . where the worst crime is innocence.

Since the gap between the rich countries and the poor can be removed, it will be. If we are shortsighted, inept, incapable either of good-will or enlightened self-interest, then it may be removed to the accompaniment of war and starvation: but removed it will be. The questions are, how, and by whom. To those questions, one can only give partial answers: but that may be enough to set us thinking. The scientific revolution on the world-scale needs, first and foremost, capital: capital in all forms, including capital machinery. The poor countries, until they have got beyond a certain point on the industrial curve cannot accumulate that capital. That is why the gap between rich and poor is widening. The capital must come from outside.

There are only two possible sources. One is the West, which means mainly the U.S., the other is the U.S.S.R. Even the United States hasn't infinite resources of such capital. If they or Russia tried to do it alone, it would mean an effort greater than either had to make industrially in the war. . . . The scale of the operation requires that it would have to be a national one. Private industry, even the biggest private industry, can't touch it, and in no sense is it a fair business risk. . . .

The second requirement, after capital, . . . is men. That is, trained scientists and engineers adaptable enough to devote themselves to a foreign country's industrialisation for at least ten years out of their lives. Here, unless and until the Americans and we [*the English*] educate ourselves both sensibly and imaginatively, the Russians have a clear edge. This is where their educational policy has already paid big dividends. They have such men to spare if they are needed. We just haven't, and the Americans aren't much better off. Imagine, for example, that the U.S. government and ours had agreed to help the Indians to carry out a major industrialisation, similar in scale to the Chinese. Imagine that the capital could be found. It would then require something like ten thousand to twenty thousand engineers from the U.S. and here to help get the thing going. At present, we couldn't find them.

These men, whom we don't yet possess, need to be trained not only in scientific but in human terms. They could not do their job if they did not shrug off every trace of paternalism. Plenty of Europeans, from St Francis Xavier to Schweitzer, have devoted their lives to Asians and Africans, nobly but paternally. These are not the Europeans whom Asians and Africans are going to welcome now. They want men who will muck in as colleagues, who will pass on what they know, do an honest technical job, and get out. Fortunately, this is an attitude which comes easily to scientists. . . .

That is why scientists would do us good all over Asia and Africa. And they would do their part too in the third essential of the scientific revolution . . . . That is, an educational programme as complete as the Chinese, who appear in ten years to have transformed their universities and built so many new ones that they are now nearly independent of scientists and engineers from outside. Ten years. With scientific teachers from this country and the U.S., and what is also necessary, with teachers of English, other poor countries could do the same in twenty.

That is the size of the problem. An immense capital outlay, an immense investment in men, both scientists and linguists . . . . With rewards negligible in the short term, apart from doing the job: and in the long term most uncertain.

People will ask me, in fact in private they have already asked me—' . . . Can you possibly believe that men will behave as you say they ought to? Can you imagine a political technique, in parliamentary societies like the U.S. or our own, by which any such plan could become real? Do you really believe that there is one chance in ten that any of this will happen?'

That is fair comment. I can only reply that I don't know. . . .

On the other hand, I confess . . . though I don't know how we can do what we need to do, or whether we shall do anything at all, I do know this: that, if we don't do it, the Communist countries will in time. They will do it at great cost to themselves and others, but they will do it. If that is how it turns out, we shall have failed, both practically and morally. At best, the West will have become an *enclave* in a different world—and this country [*England*] will be the *enclave* of an *enclave*. Are we resigning ourselves to that? History is merciless to failure. In any case, if that happens, we shall not be writing the history.

Meanwhile, there are steps to be taken which aren't outside the powers of reflective people. Education isn't the total solution to this problem: but without education the West can't even begin to cope. All the arrows point the same way. Closing the gap between our cultures is a necessity in the most abstract intellectual sense, as well as in the most practical. When those two senses have grown apart, then no society is going to be able to think with wisdom. For the sake of the intellectual life, for the sake of this country's special danger, for the sake of the western society living precariously rich among the poor, for the sake of the poor who needn't be poor if there is intelligence in the world, it is obligatory for us and the Americans and the whole West to look at our education with fresh eyes. This is one of the cases where we and the Americans have the most to learn from each other. We have each a good deal to learn from the Russians, if we are not too proud. Incidentally, the Russians have a good deal to learn from us, too.

Isn't it time we began? . . . We have very little time. So little that I dare not guess at it.

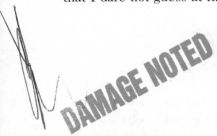

1 2 3 4 5 6 7 8 9 10 11 12 13 14 15 16 17 18 19 20 21 22 23 24 25 D 78 77 76 75 74 73 72 71 70 69 68